D1575167

By Dennis McDougal:

ANGEL OF DARKNESS
FATAL SUBTRACTION: How Hollywood Really Does
    Business (with Pierce O'Donnell)
IN THE BEST OF FAMILIES
MOTHER'S DAY*

Published by Fawcett Books

MOTHER'S DAY

Dennis McDougal

FAWCETT GOLD MEDAL • NEW YORK

Sale of this book without a front cover may be unauthorized. If this book is coverless, it may have been reported to the publisher as "unsold or destroyed" and neither the author nor the publisher may have received payment for it.

A Fawcett Gold Medal Book
Published by Ballantine Books
Copyright ©1995 by Dennis McDougal

All rights reserved under International and Pan-American Copyright Conventions. Published in the United States by Ballantine Books, a division of Random House, Inc., New York, and simultaneously in Canada by Random House of Canada Limited, Toronto.

Library of Congress Catalog Card Number: 95-90142

ISBN 0-449-14930-7

Manufactured in the United States of America

For Kate and Jennifer

Acknowledgments

Mother's Day belongs as much to Robert Knorr Jr. and his kid sister, Terry, as it does to my publisher or me. These two ravaged children, who were brought up in a nonstop atmosphere of hate, cruelty, sordidness, superstition, and murder, are living proof of the indomitable will and ever-evolving goodness of human beings. Along with Sergeant John Fitzgerald of the Placer County Sheriff's Department, Robert and Terry are the soul of this story. At the end of every human tragedy, there is always some glimmer of hope. If there weren't, none of us would have much reason to carry on. I don't think I give anything away here by revealing that these three people are that glimmer of hope at the end of *Mother's Day.*

Special thanks also to Don Dorfman, Carol Vogel, Ray Thielen, Robert Knorr Sr., Connie Sanders, Wayne Wilson of the *Sacramento Bee*, Janell Deter Bekauri of the *Galt Herald*, John Trumbo of the *Auburn Journal*, Jeff Cole of *Inside Edition*, Bill Steigerwald of the *Pittsburgh Post-Gazette*, the wonderful staff of Placer County Superior Court Judge J. Richard Couzens, and Inspector Johnnie Smith of the Placer County Sheriff's Department. My gratitude, too, to all those who shared their memories and mental notes with me about Theresa and her family, but asked to remain anonymous.

On the home front, I thank my support group, which seems to grow stronger and more dedicated with each of my published parables about California crime: my pal, partner, and first-line editor, Sharon McDougal; my wonderful parents, Carl and Lola McDougal; my sister, Colleen, and my brothers, Neal and Pat; my children, Jennifer, Amy, Kate, and Fitz; and a small army of friends and peers, including Pat and Jim Broeske, Julie Payne, David Cay Johnston of the *New York Times*, Dot Korber, Lee Gruenfeld, Vince Cosgrove, Randy Bean, Gary Abrams, Brian Zoccola, Richard Lewis, Bella Stumbo, Dave Farmer, David Levinson, Larry Lynch, Dominick Dunne, David and Margo Rosner, Kathy Cairns, Bob Sipchen, Michelle Winterstein, Steve Weinstein, Barbara Howar, John Horn, Leo Hetzel, Tim Fall, Laurie Pike, Wayne Rosso, Jim Bellows, Jill Stewart, Julie Castiglia, Lisa Sonne, Mark Gladstone, Pierce O'Donnell, Tom and Donna Szollosi, and Brian Taggert.

The men and women who keep the court and other public records in Sacramento, Las Vegas, Reno, Nevada City, and Auburn rarely hear a thank-you for their polite efficiency. With this acknowledgment, I hope to correct that. Same goes for the staffs at the Sacramento County Public Library, the library at California State University in Sacramento, and the morgues of the *Sacramento Bee*, *Las Vegas Review-Journal*, *Los Angeles Times*, and *Amarillo Globe News*.

Thanks to Susan Randol, my editor at Ballantine, who became a mother herself during the molding of *Mother's Day*; and to Alice Martell, another mom, who also happens to be the best agent in New York City; and to her aunt, Edna Harris, who became mother to *Mother's Day* when she had the audacity to send her niece a news clipping about an unbelievable crime that had been committed out in California, where all those crazy people live, along with the suggestion that it might make a good book.

Acknowledgments

And finally, thanks again to Irv Letofsky. He may not be a mother, but he remains the best editor on the planet, in addition to being an unswerving friend.

Foreword

When a beaming young mother and her helpless infant are wheeled out of the maternity ward together for the first time, any question that the mother might ever bring harm to her baby can only be viewed as sacrilege.

Even now, in the latter days of the twentieth century, mother love remains venerated and inviolate . . . always full of hope, never marked by despair. Mothers remain unassailable in our culture. In divorce, mothers are generally granted child custody over fathers. When domestic violence erupts, the mother is always the least likely suspect. Principals and teachers don't call fathers when children raise hell, need help, or get in trouble. They call mothers. When the most violent felon stands alone in court and no one else will stand by him, his mother can usually be counted upon to be there.

Mothers care. Period. End of argument.

That is the myth that we live by. A mother's love is unconditional. Maternal mystique is a fiber in every thread of the social fabric: government, courts, education, religion. We speak of Mother Nature, Mother Country, and Mother Earth. Roman Catholics tend to worship that ultimate mother, the Virgin Mary, as much or more than they do Jesus Christ. Joseph, the good man who stood by Mary and raised her son as if he were his own, is hardly worth a footnote in catechism classes.

But cracks have appeared in the motherhood myth over the centuries. From the ancient Greek tale of Medea, who killed her own children because her husband deserted her, to the sobering story of South Carolina's Susan Smith who confessed in 1994 to the drowning of her two tiny sons, the truth emerges that motherhood is no more consecrated than any other type of human bonding. Mothers may give birth, but that is all that nature requires of them. From the snipping of the umbilical cord onward, a mother's love for her child is a matter of choice, not some genetic requirement or divine mandate.

And many mothers choose in varying degrees not to love or care or do what is best for their children. Some abandon their progeny. Some beat them into submission. Some even kill them.

Theresa Cross was a toxic mother, but the maternity myth blinded, deafened, and silenced those that might have stopped her. When I set out to tell the story of how she destroyed her family, I wondered where the good people were who might have saved her children. Theresa's sins weren't the product of instant rage. She moved inexorably toward her hideous deeds over a period of years, leaving unmistakable signs as she lumbered toward her own and her children's awful destiny. She could have been stopped at any point along the way.

The fact is nobody tried to stop her. A legal system biased in favor of motherhood literally let Theresa Cross get away with murder, not once or twice, but three times.

Bad judges, lousy cops, greedy lawyers, lazy prosecutors, mediocre teachers, and incompetent bureaucrats are inevitable. When they happen, they should be weeded out and sent back to school to learn something about moral courage and the Golden Rule. The most egregious of their number usually are found out and bounced from their positions, but a residue of them always seems to remain in the system, and the harm that they do with their substandard civil service and self-serving abuse of authority is immeasurable.

The most insidious of these petty villains go utterly undetected. They are those who don't understand that looking the other way is a crime. They are the ones who refuse to intervene when they see a woman back-handing her baby in the supermarket or shrieking at a son or daughter for no apparent reason at all. These are the good people who go home every night and cluck their tongues in wonder over the latest atrocity they see on the nightly news, completely unaware that they are the ones who are responsible. They are your next-door neighbors, just doing their jobs—trying to get through another day. They are school nurses, police officers, social workers, doctors, baby-sitters, clerks, crossing guards, teachers, technicians, lawyers. . . .

Perhaps they are you.

In the story of Theresa Cross, many of them don't even have names. They aren't criminals. They seldom jaywalk and rarely run a red light. They pay their taxes, contribute to the United Way, and earn their paychecks through honest labor. They were among the Cross family's neighbors and friends and family. They were also the police officers who came on domestic disturbance calls and didn't want to get involved, or the school teachers who noticed a string of inexplicable absences, a bruise, or a burst of irrational anger in the classroom, but didn't ask the child any questions.

They might not even seem particularly germane to the tale of Theresa Cross and her children, let alone central to the story.

But they are central, these public servants and family members and acquaintances who did not want to get involved in someone else's problems. They were clearly and certainly as guilty of condemning Clifford Sanders and Suesan Knorr and Sheila Sanders to death as those who murdered them.

An oft-quoted African proverb tells us that it takes an entire village to raise a child. The corollary Theresa Cross teaches us is that a child's mother may not necessarily be a part of that nurturing village.

But the rest of us are.

Prologue

The Sierra side roads that feather off Interstate 80 into the high mountain forests near the top of the Donner Pass lead to the loveliest morgue in the world. Reno gamblers who pushed their credit too far, battered Sacramento housewives who pushed their volatile husbands too far, and drug-dealing hustlers who pushed the wrong pusher too far, have all wound up in a permanent prone position somewhere off of I-80 at one time or another. The reason is as simple as the geography: I-80 is the major thoroughfare between San Francisco and Reno, and yet it is bordered on both sides for nearly a hundred miles by millions of acres of sparsely populated, rarely explored wilderness.

Just before daybreak on Tuesday, July 17, 1984, Maybel Harrison saw a bright light in the woods near Squaw Creek. She made a U-turn and pulled off the two-lane blacktop that worms its way south of the Donner Pass toward Lake Tahoe, squinting through her windshield at a fire burning down near the waterline next to Squaw Creek. Despite the icy morning air, she climbed out of her Ford pickup to investigate further.

Maybel Harrison, forty-five, was not the first to see the blaze. Another motorist had reported it an hour earlier to the Squaw Valley Fire Department. Placer County Sheriff's Sergeant Stephen Ziegler had already been out to see what it might be. Ziegler could tell from his vantage point up on Highway 89 that it was probably just an isolated stump fire: the result of a lightning strike during a summer storm in the Sierras several days earlier. It had probably smoldered for a while and was just now bursting into flame. Even in the dark, Ziegler could see from the road that the flames were only about two feet high. Besides, the fire was burning next to the creek, far enough away from most of the trees to be any real threat even during summer fire season.

Ziegler had radioed in at 4:57 A.M. that the fire was isolated and would probably burn itself out. Even if it didn't, he told dispatch, it was a trivial enough blaze that it could certainly wait until daylight for someone from the Forest Service to put it out.

But Mrs. Harrison knew none of this during the first faint light of morning nearly an hour later, when she tripped down to the creek bed to take a closer look. What she saw and smelled burning was no tree stump.

Alarmed, she ran back up to the road and flagged down a diesel truck. It pulled off on the right shoulder and parked behind her pickup. Robert Eden, a transport driver from the Central Valley town of Tracy, climbed out of the cab. Mrs. Harrison pointed out the blaze, and Eden pulled a small fire extinguisher out of his truck, racing down to the fire. After spraying out most of the flames, he could make out a smoking figure laid out as on a funeral bier in the morning light. He ran back up to the truck for a three-gallon water can and brought Mrs. Harrison down to the creek with him, where he doused out the remaining embers of the charred figure.

"It looks like a mannequin," she said.

"No," Eden said grimly. "It's a body."

The body, as it turned out, of a young woman in her late teens, though it was difficult to tell at first whether it was male or female. The only part of the human remains that was not blackened was the left side of her face. The coroner would later record that she had blue eyes, but when Maybel Harrison and Robert Eden first saw that small patch of unburned flesh, the left eye was mercifully closed. In life, the young woman had pale skin and wavy light brown or blond hair and eyelashes. In death, her slender five-foot, three-inch body was reduced to a greasy mound of ashes and scorched flesh.

Mrs. Harrison returned to the highway and waited in the roadway until a car—a sheriff's patrol car, as it turned out—came along fifteen minutes later. The mountain temperatures had dropped into the thirties overnight and Mrs. Harrison was trembling when the two deputies asked her what had happened. Her trembling, however, was not only because of the cold.

"There's a burning body over there!" she hollered at the two deputies.

They told her to stay put and drove off the road, down by the creek, to within a hundred feet of the smoldering figure. Eden followed them down, but he stopped several feet behind when the two deputies saw what they had on their hands. They got out of their car and ordered Eden to stay back. The body was so badly burned that one of the legs had burned through at the knee and the singed thighbone protruded from the crisp flesh. A routine check for vital signs would have been ridiculous. Instead, the deputies opted to back away as carefully as possible in order to preserve whatever footprints or other clues might remain undisturbed around the makeshift funeral pyre. There might be something on the creek bank that could point to the cause of her death or her identity.

Soon she would become known only as Jane Doe #4858-84.

Two hours passed. It was nearly seven A.M. when homicide detectives Russell Potts and Larry Addoms showed up. Finding corpses along the highways of the Sierras was nothing new to Potts and Addoms.

It is no secret to lawmen on either side of the California–Nevada border that this—some of the most beautiful, rugged real estate in the country—is a dumping ground for corpses.

Here the headless body of nineteen-year-old Veronica Martinez was found off a highway embankment in March of 1992. Five months later, in August of 1992, sixty-seven-year-old Dale Cannon, a retired NBC-TV production employee and inveterate Las Vegas casino patron, was torched and left in the trunk of his 1981 Oldsmobile off a Pacific Gas and Electric access road. And the shallow grave of twenty-four-year-old Cesar Rodriguez, a gunshot victim, was found off a back road in December of 1992. Even when lawmen do find the bodies, the crimes often go unsolved because the tiny, impoverished cities and counties of the Sierras don't have the resources or detective power to solve or prosecute the murders.

In all, nearly two hundred murder victims have been dumped or buried beneath the pines over the past decade. Many of them, like the sad and horrifying case of the Squaw Creek girl, have gone for years without even being identified.

Armed with a Polaroid camera, an evidence kit, and a pair of arson investigators from the Tahoe City Fire Department, Potts and Addoms made their way down the brushy slope to the creek bank. The arson specialists carried a hydrocarbon detector to verify whether this latest body had, indeed, been doused with some sort of flammable liquid before it was set afire. Although the tests came up positive, they still took soil samples for further analysis in the lab. Once they finished, the two detectives took over the crime scene, spending the next four hours taking pictures, cataloging evidence, and scouting the forest floor for a hundred yards in all directions.

By eleven A.M. Potts and Addoms had been joined by investigators, criminalists, and photographers from the state department of justice in Sacramento as well as a small army of deputies from the main office of the Placer County Sheriff's Department nearly a hundred miles away in the county seat of Auburn. The new round of investigators used a Brownie Instamatic and thirty-five-millimeter cameras to shoot even more photos, supplementing Potts's Polaroids.

In all, the detectives found and cataloged thirty-one pieces of evidence, including a green Pepsodent toothbrush, an underwired size 32-C JCPenney bra, disposable diapers, a pair of Gloria Vanderbilt jeans, a yellow-and-black scarf, brown high heels, black flip-flop sandals, a pair of hoop earrings, a pair of sleigh-bell earrings, a heavy bracelet inlaid with black onyx, and the singed pages from a couple of books: *20,000 Leagues Under the Sea* and a Harlequin romance. There was more, but the two plastic trash bags that contained most of the remaining effects had been set afire along with Jane Doe. Most of the contents were destroyed.

As for Jane Doe herself, her mouth had been taped shut with silver duct tape and her wrists had been taped together. She wore an old-style white-gold wedding ring, studded with diamond chips. When she was torched, she had been wearing a yellow nylon windbreaker, white knit sweater, brown corduroy jacket, and a pair of corduroy pants. Her hair was worn in a ponytail, tied off with a bright yellow rubber band. It was all but impossible to determine much more about the victim at the scene, though. Jane Doe had suffered third-degree burns to 91 percent of her body.

At 1:59 P.M., Placer County Sheriff Donald Nunes put out the first of several teletypes to the missing persons divisions of police and sheriff's departments all over the state. *Request you check your records for any missing persons which may match this Jane Doe, or any similar homicides. Thanks in advance,* it read.

At two P.M., a driver from the county removal service arrived. He loaded the body in his truck and drove it down the mountain over Donner Pass to Auburn and the Placer County Morgue.

The autopsy began two hours later. Dr. A. V. Cunha, the pathologist assigned to the case, began dictating a dispassionate description of the charred body:

"The remains are those of a teenage-to-young-adult Caucasian female. . . ."

But as the survey of the body progressed it became increasingly difficult to remain clinical. The hands were curled into fists, thrust forward in a tortured "pugilistic" pose. The right ear was burned to ashes, but the left ear was still pliant and intact. Two small holes pierced in the earlobe marked spots where the girl had once worn her dangly earrings.

Dr. Cunha carefully removed the duct tape from Jane Doe's hands and mouth, using forceps on the outside chance that the killer or killers might have left fingerprints. Her lips were burned away on the right side, but still intact and slightly parted on the left.

Assisted by Dr. James Nordstrom, a dentist who contracted with the sheriff in orthodontic identification cases, Cunha would remove her maxilla and mandible in hopes that dental records might turn up giving Jane Doe a name. For the moment, however, all Nordstrom could tell from his examination was that the third molars at the back of her mouth had still been coming in when she died. Jane Doe was probably between fourteen and seventeen years of age, he concluded.

The only other grim bit of news Dr. Cunha was able to confirm after completing his autopsy was the cause of death. She hadn't been strangled or raped or shot or drowned or beaten to death. She did not die of a drug overdose or a knife wound or alcohol poisoning or an internal hemorrhage. The awful truth was that Jane Doe was not dead when she was doused with gasoline or kerosene or some other flammable liquid and set afire. She had been burned alive.

* * *

Jane Doe got more than the usual media attention devoted to I-80 body dumps during the first few days following her discovery in the Tahoe forest. Newspapers all over Northern California picked up the mystery and published perfunctory stories about the horrible murder that had apparently been committed within a few miles of the celebrated Squaw Valley Ski Resort. Television and radio reports echoed the newspaper articles. Who killed Jane Doe and why? And, even more important, who was she?

On July 26, Jane Doe's remains were X-rayed and frozen at the Sacramento County Coroner's Morgue. Under the law, her corpse had to remain under lock and key for ninety days in the event that investigators needed another look in their quest to identify her.

Thanks to newspaper reports of the grisly murder, there was no shortage of possible suspects or victims. Calls came in daily for the rest of the month. But by the end of August, Detectives Potts and Addoms had investigated about two hundred of those leads and were no closer to an identity of Jane Doe or her killer.

Fingerprint analysts at the state justice department's investigative services branch were able to pull a print from her right thumb before she was frozen, but a month after the body was found there was no match with any of the prints of missing persons submitted from police departments around the state. The analysts were also able to get some latent prints from several glass bottles recovered from the crime scene, and Potts tried matching the latent prints with several potential suspects. Again, there was no luck.

As September approached and a new school term began, Potts made up a flyer with the pertinent information about Jane Doe and an artist's rendering of what the young woman must have looked like when she was alive. Aside from a chipped front tooth, she had probably been rather pretty. Potts sent the flyer to districts all over the state, hoping a teacher might recognize a missing student or that a classmate might remember a friend who had disappeared over the summer. Once more, the response was negative.

As the weeks passed into months leads on the Jane Doe case dwindled. The investigation expanded beyond California with a set of the fingerprints and other pertinent information distributed throughout the West via the FBI.

At the end of ninety days, Jane Doe #4858-84 was still Jane Doe #4858-84. On October 25, she was laid to rest at the New Auburn District Cemetery.

Months passed.

By the following May, Potts had received an FBI printout with 235 possible matches on the fingerprints that he had submitted the previous autumn. He had his secretary call all 235 police agencies to follow up, but on June 18, 1985, he wrote the discouraging news in his official report:

All contacts have been negative at this time.

And there the case of Jane Doe #4858-84 remained for eight more years, until twenty-two-year-old Theresa Marie Groves made a call to the Placer County Sheriff's Office one October afternoon in 1993 and spent the next several hours trying to make detectives believe the improbable story of her life, her family, her survival, and her mother and namesake: Theresa Jimmie Francine Cross.

I

As the crow flies, Rio Linda is a hundred miles due west of the Donner Pass. But it might just as well be the distance from the earth to the moon.

Rio Linda means "beautiful river" in Spanish, but the central California town where Theresa Jimmie Francine Cross grew up and passed through her hard-edged adolescence in the 1950s and early sixties contradicts its own name. Rio Linda is flat, dusty, cold in the winter, and infernally hot in the summer. Then and now, Rio Linda was anything but beautiful and the closest river was the muddy Sacramento, more than a dozen miles to the west. The nearest thing Rio Linda has to a river is Dry Creek, which much of the year runs through the south side of town like a dusty scar.

The town where bright-eyed young Theresa Cross settled with her father, mother, and older sister, Rosemary, in 1953 was a hardscrabble matrix of weed lawns, chicken farms, beer bars, and pickup trucks loaded with restless teens who blared country tunes and early Elvis over the radio as they drove back and forth, from one side of the rawboned settlement to the other. It was the kind of town where the American Legion hall was the center of social life and extended families lived their whole lives in mobile homes that were going nowhere.

"It was a pretty dull place," said Mrs. Esther Davis,

whose own family, the Hafners, grew up next door to the Cross family. "There was not much going on and not much to go home to. I left forty years ago, and the only reason I'd ever go back after I left was to visit my mom."

Rio Linda has barely changed in the forty years since James and Swannie Gay Cross first moved in next door to Esther and her family at 820 Oak Lane. Today, despite a new layer of stucco dwellings and a general upgrade in lifestyle and literacy, Rio Linda has achieved a dubious notoriety as the butt of radio reactionary Rush Limbaugh's jokes about making his arguments simple enough for rednecks to understand in Rio Linda. To populist intellectuals and critics like Limbaugh, Rio Linda seems to represent a cross between Erskine Caldwell's Tobacco Road and the inbred backwoods of James Dickey's *Deliverance.*

That's how it was when eight-year-old Theresa Cross became a citizen of Rio Linda, too. Like her mother, father, and older sister, Rosemary, little Theresa found that people kept to themselves and tried not to mind other people's business . . . at least, not so that anyone would notice.

"Their mom was a very friendly person—a little on the heavy side, but neighborly," recalled Larry Hafner, Esther Davis's younger brother. The Cross home seemed tolerable enough, he remembered. Nobody was rude to visitors or behaved in an unfriendly manner. But the simple home and its four inhabitants rarely radiated much in the way of familial warmth either.

"It never seemed like a happy time at Rosemary's house," recalled Heike McGinnis, Rosemary's best friend throughout high school. "It was never really fun to go over to visit the way it was with my other friends."

In fact, Rosemary Cross always seemed eager to leave as soon as possible. She'd grab Heike by the arm and hustle her out the door rather than sit around the front room, making small talk with the Crosses.

Some remember the Cross family differently.

"I don't remember anything but pleasantness about the family," said Charlotte Harvey, a childhood playmate of both Cross girls.

The house itself was a little scary, however.

"One of the people that had owned it before Theresa moved in had hanged himself on the back porch," Harvey recalled. "So it was always kind of eerie, walking through that part of the house, like this ghost was still there."

Mrs. Cross could be a bit spooky, too. Theresa would later tell her own children about Swannie Gay's card readings and how she would predict the future. For Theresa, she predicted six children: three boys and three girls. She also predicted that one of the girls would bring Theresa grief.

Mr. Cross was three years older than his wife. Colder and more stern than Swannie Gay, he nevertheless seemed to defer to her when it came to running the household and taking care of the children. Mrs. Cross was the heart of the family, and she believed in being strict and tidy, though she was not much of a housekeeper herself. She had daughters to do the cleaning. She expected them to do their share around the house and more. When her girls loitered and came home late from school, there was a paddling waiting for them at the back porch.

"She was a lady who apparently came up the hard way, was a hard worker, and thought her children should be the same way," said Noreen Harvey, Charlotte's mother and a neighbor of the Cross family when they lived on Oak Lane. "She did say to me one time, 'Both of the girls have got to learn to work!' "

Heike McGinnis remembers Mrs. Cross behind the wheel of a car more readily than she remembers her laboring over a hot stove. Mrs. Cross was the one who carted the girls around before Rosemary got her driver's license, and Heike remembers that a trip with Swannie Gay was a wild ride at the very least.

"She was a crazy driver," she said. "She'd speed up and then hit the brakes, speed and hit the brakes."

When Charlotte wanted to play, she had to go to the Cross home because Mrs. Cross never allowed Theresa and Rosemary to leave their own yard. Charlotte would go to the fence that separated her own parents' property from the Cross's and screech a high-pitched secret signal that she and Theresa used to call each other. Then the girls would rendezvous by the swing set, between the house and the barn.

"I can remember being in their house on a Sunday and listening to the radio, back when there was still radio programs on," said Charlotte. "I heard an episode of *Nick Carter* and it was about somebody being murdered with a poison dart when they were on the telephone. For a long time after that, I remember not wanting to pick up the phone."

When their infrequent visitors dropped by, Mrs. Cross was the hostess while Mr. Cross remained somewhere in the back of the house. To the neighborhood children, Mr. Cross seemed like a more sinister version of the mute *American Gothic* farmer of Grant Wood's famous Depression-era portrait of Midwestern America. James Cross was a hardworking man who drove a milk truck to the dairy where he labored each day and never did say much to the neighbors. Even on weekends, when he wasn't at work, he wasn't especially talkative.

"It seems to me like they had a cow that Mr. Cross used to lead around so he could feel like he was doing something when he watched his wife working outside," said Esther Davis.

Like Esther, Larry Hafner remembers the Crosses as a quiet, easygoing family who kept up their modest two-bedroom home and did a little small-time farming on their own half acre to make ends meet. Mrs. Cross was honest, ebullient, and generous. When she canned or baked, she shared with the neighbors.

"I remember one time Mrs. Cross brought an apple pie over to the house and it was terrible—just terrible," said Larry. "But my mother would never say anything bad about it. Mrs. Cross came over the next day and asked, 'How was that pie?' And my mother told her it was wonderful. 'You're a liar,' she said. That set my mother back on her heels because she thought Mrs. Cross was being serious. Then she laughed out loud and told my mother she forgot to put sugar in the recipe."

Actually, Mrs. Cross avoided putting sugar into anything. Her doctor warned her years earlier that her weight had been affecting her heart and she had taken to sweetening everything with saccharine, except when she forgot.

"I was only eight or nine at the time, but I can remember Theresa's mother using saccharine in the Kool-Aid because she had heart trouble and how awful the Kool-Aid was because the saccharine left a very bitter taste," said Charlotte Harvey.

Rosemary and Theresa were the only other girls on the block and quickly became Charlotte's best friends. Though she was three months older than Rosemary, and nearly three years older than Theresa, it was the younger of the Cross girls that Harvey became closest to.

"She was a sweet little girl," said Harvey.

She frowned, reflecting on what Theresa's life would become years later.

"I can't imagine what went wrong."

James Cross had been a confirmed bachelor until he met Swannie Gay in the early 1940s, but it was Mrs. Cross's second marriage. The Tennessee-born housewife had given birth to two other children during her previous marriage, to a Kentucky railroad engineer named Harry Tapp. When he lost his eyesight in a boiler explosion on the railroad in the mid-1930s, Tapp and his family became tenant farmers. He refused to accept charity, and they scratched out a living until his death in 1939.

His widow was not too proud to take welfare, however. With what little she got from the state, Swannie moved from the farm closer to the city. She and her son, William Hart Tapp, and daughter, Clara, moved into a converted chicken coop in Broderick, northwest of Sacramento. Then she began looking for a new husband.

Swannie Gay Tapp was getting a little old to start another family, but when she met a confirmed bachelor who wanted to have a son to carry on his family name, she agreed. By the time she and Jim Cross drove to Reno to get married on July 11, 1942, Swannie was thirty-four. He was thirty-seven.

Jim Cross was a good catch. He was too old to be drafted during World War II, but he had studied at the California Agricultural College at Davis and had a steady job. He was an assistant cheesemaker at Sacramento's Golden State Dairy, which billed itself as the home of "dependable dairy products."

For the first few years of their marriage the Crosses and Swannie's two children bounced around from one rented home to another. By 1944, the Crosses had moved to a two-bedroom house on Sacramento's rural southeast side and Swannie gave birth to Jim's first child: Rosemary Cross. Two years later they bought a small house in the Del Paso Heights neighborhood north of downtown Sacramento. There, Theresa was born in 1946.

Clara Tapp became surrogate mother to her two half sisters, caring for them while Swannie worked. Sometimes she was forced to stay home from school for weeks at a time. Clara also worked as a waitress and a short-order cook, from age fourteen until she graduated from high school. Jim Cross demanded sixty dollars a month from her for room and board, a stiff sum in those days.

"My stepdad was out for every dime he could get. If he knew I got tips, he'd a took those, too. But he didn't know it and I didn't tell him," Clara recalled, adding with undisguised contempt, "He was a lovely person."

Her older brother, Bill, paid no such tribute to stay under the Cross's roof. He had been in trouble constantly from the moment Swannie and Jim were first married, but he was a male. Both Crosses placed a far higher premium on sons than they did on daughters.

Clara tells the story of how she was so unimportant that she didn't even officially have a name until she was an adult. She made the discovery when she had to furnish her employer with a birth certificate. While William Hart Tapp's identity was clearly typed across his birth certificate, Clara found that she had only been identified on hers as "Baby Tapp." Her mother had never bothered to name her legally until an indignant twenty-year-old Clara went to her and demanded that she sign the papers necessary to grant her a full name on her birth certificate.

Jim Cross was so disappointed that he had fathered only girls that he considered adopting Bill as his own. As the only son growing up in the Cross household, Bill Tapp—or Hart, as his mother liked to call him—was constantly forgiven his failings. When he was caught taking things that did not belong to him, which was often, Jim scolded him and Swannie made excuses for him. Even after he became a teenager and graduated to burglarizing neighbors' houses, breaking into cars, or shoplifting from nearby stores, Swannie would passionately defend him to those outside the family while privately upbraiding Hart for breaking the law.

William Hart Tapp was a smooth, handsome young man whose easygoing manner and good looks masked a deeper character flaw. Put simply, he was a con artist, even as a youngster. His mother's excuses were never viewed as second chances. Bill interpreted the lack of consequences for his thievery as a license to remain irresponsible. Jim Cross was a devout Roman Catholic who had made Swannie convert from her Presbyterian faith when they were married. When Bill began getting into trouble, Cross tried to get the boy to make amends at confession and Mass. But Bill always slipped back into the kinds of activities that called for easy money.

He had a similar predilection for easy women. The same year Theresa was born, Bill turned eighteen and came close to being charged with statutory rape after he drove a fifteen-year-old girlfriend to Reno, lied about her age, and married her so that he could get her into bed. The girl's parents had the marriage annulled, but Jim Cross had had enough. He encouraged Bill to join the navy and get away from his hometown, where his name had become synonymous with loose morals and petty crime. Maybe the military would do the boy some good.

By then, the war was over and life was better all the way around. Jim had been promoted to foreman at Golden State, which subsequently changed its name to Foremost Dairy. Jim took to calling himself "cheese-maker" instead of "pasteurizer." It sounded better, though it didn't increase his salary. Swannie had also found a job, with Essex Lumber Company, operating a machine that made pencils.

Bill returned home early from the navy, discharged for stealing, according to Clara. He didn't remain back in Sacramento long, though. Somehow, he managed to talk his way into the army and was gone again, though not for long. Once again, Bill was discharged early. Again, he was bounced for stealing, according to his sister.

Bill lived off and on with the Crosses until he got married, moved away, and fathered three sons. Rosemary and Theresa didn't often see their older brother as they were growing up. In fact, the next time Jim, Swannie, or any of his sisters heard much about him at all, Bill was divorced and in jail—a place where he spent much of the remainder of his life.

But the rest of Swannie Gay's family prospered. The Crosses were finally doing well enough in the early 1950s to sell their first home and buy a bigger house on a half acre in Rio Linda. Clara married and left home in 1950, but she would often return to baby-sit her two younger sisters for her mother.

Even then, while the girls were still small, Clara saw a marked difference between Rosemary and Theresa. Rosemary was big and stocky, like her mother. Like Clara before her, Rosemary was the family workhorse: a "Cinderella" who did all the work and got minimal appreciation. Theresa was puny: a thin wisp of a child, clear through puberty. She was also the favorite daughter, receiving the same kind of indulgences her brother Bill had been so often granted. Swannie doted on her at the same time·that she was haranguing Rosemary.

The Cross family's good life in Rio Linda crumbled by the end of the 1950s. The Crosses hadn't lived at the Oak Lane address for too many years before the first of several disasters struck. First, Jim Cross became disabled: stricken with Parkinson's disease, he could no longer work and, following an unsuccessful brain surgery, had to retire early from the dairy. The crippling nervous disorder that brings on a terrible, uncontrollable, and irreversible trembling to head, hands, and body dealt a devastating blow to the Crosses. The family began to fall on hard times. The more his health deteriorated, the more angry and frustrated James Cross became. The Hafners came to believe years later that he may well have been taking out that anger on his wife and daughters behind closed doors.

"I want to stress this: Mrs. Cross and those two girls were mighty fine people," said neighbor Howard Hafner. "There was no indication of any potential for anything going wrong whatsoever."

Jim Cross was a "no-nonsense person" who did not

like any display of loose morals by either of his daughters. He might slap a child who got out of line, but he never seemed mean-spirited or physically abusive, according to Robert Knorr, who lived in Rio Linda, went to the same schools as Theresa, and was fated to become her second husband.

"He'd been a hardworking man all his life and worshiped the ground his wife—Theresa's mother—walked on. But he didn't have a lot of time for the girls," said Knorr. "It struck me that his whole life had been his job. When he lost that, he lost everything."

While they were still young teens Rosemary and Theresa showed promise of becoming dark-haired beauties. Rosemary was the taller and more buxom of the two, but that was partially because she was older and had a more athletic build. Because she was well developed for her age, she walked with a slight stoop so that she would not appear taller than the boys, according to her friend Heike.

"Rosemary didn't date much at all, and she wasn't boy crazy either," recalled Heike. "Theresa was the one who was boy crazy."

Indeed, one of Theresa's closest friends during her high-school years remembers her preoccupation with males dating as far back as junior high.

"She was always talking about sex," remembered Janet Kelso.[1] "She was obsessed with it, and she seemed to know everything. I was in awe just listening to her."

She seemed to be competing constantly with her sister, too. The natural rivalry that often develops between sisters was especially tense between Rosemary and Theresa.

"Rosemary was more serious," remembered Heike. "She was the assistant director in the drama club, and I

---

[1]Not her real name.

think she planned to go further in her education after high school."

Still, Rosemary attracted her share of boys, especially after she got her own car: a gasping old Studebaker with a radio that barely worked.

"It looked like a torpedo. It was a riot," remembered Heike. "We'd drive over to the Jolly Kone in Rio Linda after school or go down to Mel's Drive-in in Sacramento, and one of us would have to get out of the car, stand on the pavement, and hold a wire to ground the radio to get it to work so that we could get the boys to come over and talk to us."

Skinny little Theresa, with her slight overbite, shock of Shirley Temple hair, and big brown eyes, was never asked along on these boy-hunting missions. She was only two years younger, but that was enough to drive Rosemary nuts.

"Theresa was the pest. The younger sister who wouldn't go away," recalled Heike.

Theresa was also her mother's favorite.

"You couldn't ask for a better person [than Mrs. Cross], but she favored Theresa over Rosemary," said Bea Howard, who knew the older of the two Cross girls from the Rebekah lodge, a local women's auxiliary of the Oddfellows. Mrs. Martha Hafner sponsored her next-door neighbor's older daughter for membership in the Rebekah's youth group—another source of the growing rift between Rosemary and Theresa.

Where Rosemary was social, Theresa tended to be more of a loner, recalled Bea Howard. Like several other women in town, she now believes that the sisters turned out the way they did in part because of Swannie Gay's bias toward Theresa.

"She was always saying, 'Oh, my beautiful Theresa!'" recalled Mrs. Howard. "But I'll tell you this: Theresa was a very selfish person. Rosemary wasn't."

Theresa basked in her mother's praise. In fact, she

used to boast to school friends that Rosemary was jealous of her because Mrs. Cross openly admitted that she liked Theresa best.

"Gay walked on water, to hear Theresa tell it. Her mother was a living angel," said Bob Knorr.

It was for that reason that the blow that befell Theresa outside the Hiland Market in nearby North Highlands on March 2, 1961, was as haunting as it was devastating. Gay Cross had a history of heart trouble. She was diabetic and dangerously overweight. But even so, her death was unexpected. It was only afterward that the coroner confirmed that she also suffered from arteriosclerosis—hardening of the arteries.

"She loved her mom to death, and when her mom died, I think that had a lot to do with her mental state," said Knorr. "Her mom picked her up from school one day, they went shopping, and as her mom was walking out of the grocery store, she just collapsed."

Theresa was standing at her mother's side at 3:45 P.M. on a Thursday afternoon in March when her mother's heart gave out. Bob Knorr said that she fell so hard against the doorjamb at the store entrance that she broke the frame. In later years Theresa would often repeat the awful story of how she caught her mother in her arms and helplessly watched as she went glassy-eyed and gasped before she died, waiting for the ambulance.

"All I remember is just crying," said Charlotte Harvey. "I just remember going into their front room and seeing several people gathered there and really not knowing what I was doing. And we just hugged and cried."

Swannie Gay Cross was fifty-three years old when she died. She was buried at Sunset Lawn Cemetery three miles south of Rio Linda on March 6, 1961, one week and one day before Theresa's fifteenth birthday.

"It seemed like Rosemary became the mother after her mother died," remembered Heike. "During that time Theresa wasn't much help. She was at a difficult age, a junior-high age. Rosemary was the strong one and had to take over. She held down a part-time job and went to high school. Basically, she had to grow up overnight."

Mrs. Cross's death hastened the dissolution of the Cross family. At seventeen, while still a junior in high school, Rosemary took her mother's place as nominal homemaker and quasi-mother to her little sister. She took a job as bookkeeper at the Thrift Way Market in order to help make ends meet. The carefree days of driving her old Studebaker down to K Street in Sacramento to flirt with the boys were now history. So was any hope of her going on to college.

Theresa was not sympathetic, and the teenage rivalry between them escalated. Her grief metamorphosed into depression and desperation while Rosemary was trying to keep the family together and carry on.

It was near Easter, just weeks after Mrs. Cross's death, that Theresa convinced Janet Kelso to run away with her

"She had a way with guys and she found this one who wanted her to run away to Arkansas with him and she wanted me to come, too," remembered Janet. "We had thirty dollars and he had a car. She talked me into it."

They didn't get far. On the road east, somewhere near Sparks, Nevada, Theresa's boyfriend fell asleep at the wheel, left the road, and rolled the car three times before it came to a stop. He had to have thirty stitches, but both girls emerged unscathed.

"Before the police came, she told me, 'Whatever you do, don't say we're runaways or they'll put us in juvenile hall,' " said Janet. "All she could talk about was, 'They're going to find out I had sex. They're going to find out I had sex.' I said, 'How? How are they going to find out?' They could just tell, she said.

"Well, the first thing I said when the police came was, 'We ran away!' and sure enough, they put us in juvenile hall. But it wasn't bad. We played bingo and watched TV. I kind of liked it. But, boy, was I in big trouble when I got home."

Theresa wasn't, though. Her father was a shaking shadow of his former self, now deeply grieved by the death of his beloved Swannie. The only one left to scold her was her big sister, and Theresa simply refused to listen to her. With rare moments of truce, the split between them began to expand into a lifelong gulf.

"The whole time Theresa and I were married, I saw Rosemary twice," said Bob Knorr. "It seemed like there was this big rivalry—a hatred between them when they'd see each other. They were very standoffish, very short with each other. One would say, 'How ya doin'?' The other would say, 'Fine.' And that was it."

Rosemary became secretly engaged to Floyd "Joe" Norris the following autumn. She had to, according to her half sister Clara. Though she would miscarry, Rosemary had become pregnant by Norris, a tall twenty-two-year-old apprentice carpenter from Rio Linda who was already losing his hair. He was unemployed at the time and lived at home like she did, with little prospect of a career. But Rosemary seemed happy enough when she was with him.

"He was nice and gentle with her, and we were all so happy that Rosemary found somebody like that," said Heike.

Rosemary took the necessary classes to graduate mid-year, ahead of her classmates, so that she could move out and marry Floyd Norris. She asked Heike to stand up for her at the wedding as her maid of honor.

A Roman Catholic priest married Floyd and Rosemary on January 6, 1962. It was a typical overcast Sacramento Valley day, but the most unusual thing Heike remembered about the ceremony wasn't the weather. When she looked around at the handful of guests, Heike realized she was the only representative from the bride's side. Neither Theresa nor James Cross, nor any other member of Rosemary's family or friends showed up.

The reason was simple, according to Clara. Rosemary hadn't told anyone from her family that she was getting married. In fact, she continued to keep it secret for several weeks afterward because she knew that Jim would not approve, even though it was a Catholic ceremony. In the photos from Rosemary's wedding day, Heike stands out as the only one dressed in bright colors. Everyone from the groom to the priest to Floyd's deaf older brother, William, who served as best man, seems to be wearing somber, dark clothing. In the photos, even Rosemary's dress looks gray.

After Jim Cross discovered Rosemary's deception and Floyd had to find them a place to live, the newlyweds moved into a trailer behind Ken Green's home on Tenth Street in Rio Linda. They remained there for at least the next half-dozen years—through a series of Floyd's lackluster jobs, through Rosemary's budding career as a bookkeeper for the state of California, and through the birth of their two sons, Joseph and Daniel.

"They were not the type of people who went and pushed themselves off on people," said Green. "They didn't have friends over too often. No real visitors."

The mysterious absence of Rosemary's father and sister from her wedding and her life didn't last long. Although their visits were infrequent, Green remembers Theresa Cross and her father stopping in to see the Norris family.

By that time James Cross had become totally unemployable. He had been able to collect disability and some welfare for his two daughters, but when Rosemary married and left home, the state cut his income. He had to put the family home up for sale shortly after Swannie's death and sold it for a lower price than it was worth, according to Larry Hafner—probably because Cross was desperate for the money. He spent the rest of his life relying on his daughters to look after him.

In the months following her mother's death, Theresa watched helplessly as her whole world quickly collapsed—first, with Rosemary's departure, and next, the forced sale of the only home she had ever really known. It didn't take long for her to follow Rosemary's lead and begin looking around for a man who would be willing and able to take care of her and her disabled father.

After her ill-fated attempt to run away, Theresa met an Alabama farmhand who had followed his older brothers and sister to California in 1959 to cash in on the post–World War II construction boom.

Clifford Clyde Sanders was five years older than Theresa and easy prey for the blossoming young dark-haired beauty. When he met her during one of his cruises past North Highlands High School near his brother Tom's house, where he was living at the time, Sanders was instantly smitten. Theresa quickly wrapped him around her little finger and taught him the meaning of the term "heavy petting." He wanted her. She made him beg.

"She always had a big ego and bragged about herself," said Janet Kelso. "She liked to have this power over other people, especially men. So she made him get down on his knees and ask her dad to give his consent."

James Cross reluctantly agreed and accompanied his willful daughter and her anxious fiancé on a weekend trip to Reno, Nevada. Theresa married Sanders on September 29, 1962, with James Cross's shaky "X" marking the marriage license at the spot where parental consent is required. Mrs. Theresa Sanders did not return to North Highlands High for the fall semester of her junior year.

"I stayed friends with her and used to go over to their apartment to visit," remembered Janet. "Once, they asked me to spend the night. Now, I was only sixteen myself and still pretty naive about things, and they had only one bed. They told me to get in with them and I did. Along about the middle of the night, Cliff's hand crept over and got me. Well, I flew out of bed so fast.

But I didn't give it too much thought because I thought he was asleep and just thought I was Theresa."

But Clifford was twenty-one and not so naive.

"He was a player," said Bob Knorr, who never met Clifford Sanders himself, but heard the stories about him years later through their mutual circle of drinking buddies. "He liked the ladies. Theresa made him out to be the toughest guy in the world, but my friends who knew him back then—they said he wasn't. He did keep her in line, though."

The tall, gawky Alabama farm boy was easygoing enough when he was sober. But Clifford fit the classic mold of a Southern good ol' boy when he'd had a few. His taste for liquor and barroom brawls did not mix well with Theresa's fear of losing her meal ticket to booze or another woman. Their marriage became a formula for disaster almost from the beginning.

Even if he did want to chase after other women, Cliff Sanders was neither rich nor handsome. His buckteeth, hunched shoulders, and sheep eyes gave him a hayseed appearance reminiscent of TV's Gomer Pyle. The chances of Theresa losing her grip on him to another woman were exceedingly slim.

"She was jealous of him, but I don't know why," recalled Clifford's older brother.

Tom Sanders, who took his younger brother under his wing when he came out to California from Alabama, maintains that Clifford was no more wild than any other young man his age. He liked fishing, beer, and a little mix-it-up now and then at the local cocktail lounge. Tom took a dislike to Theresa instantly.

"I told him not to marry her, but when [young men] got their mind set on what they're going to do, they do it. They don't listen to nobody," he said.

Like his brother-in-law Floyd, Cliff Sanders had drifted from job to job since coming to California. But once he was married, he tried harder to find a vocation. Tom got him a job helping to put up a water tower near

Sacramento State University. Clifford might have been an unskilled day laborer, but he saw to it that the rent was paid and food was on the table.

Shortly after they were married, Cliff and his new bride moved into a rear one-bedroom unit in a duplex on Q Street in North Highlands, a few miles from the trailer on Tenth Street where her sister and brother-in-law lived.

The rivalry between the two sisters persisted after they were both married—even into the maternity ward. On July 16, 1963, almost ten months after their wedding, Theresa gave birth to Howard Sanders, her first son. The very next day in the same hospital, Rosemary bore Floyd Norris his first son, Joseph.

Cliff and Theresa had been married over a year before he was eligible to join the Carpenters Local 586 and gain some of the medical, pension, and insurance benefits that go along with union membership. He hired on steady as an apprentice carpenter at the American Safeway Scaffolding Company on West Capitol Avenue in Sacramento. Though he had no education and only his hands to make a living, the rawboned and rowdy Cliff Sanders worked hard to support his young wife and infant son. He named the boy Howard after his own father and gave him his own middle name, Clyde.

"Clifford thought the world of that boy, and he was just starting to do well with his job and all," recalled Tom Sanders.

Though they hired baby-sitters and still went out together on occasion, the happy young couple clashed in private. As well as he appeared to be doing on the outside, Clifford was having a tough time adjusting to domestic life with Theresa.

She was convinced that he was philandering and constantly confronted him with her suspicions. She told friends and family that her big ol' six-foot, 150-pound husband often bragged about the women he'd bedded, before and after their marriage. The jealousy, touched

off by one too many beers, often led to hand-to-hand
domestic combat in which pint-sized Theresa was inevitably the loser.

"When Theresa married that first guy, Sanders, she
started doing strange things," said Esther Davis. "At my
mom's house one night Theresa came over and asked to
hide because she was scared to death of him. He threatened her."

There were truces for a time, but a split between
twenty-two-year-old Clifford and his fiery young wife
seemed inevitable.

In the spring of 1964, while Howard was still nursing, Theresa became pregnant for a second time. Now it
was Clifford's turn to scream infidelity. He questioned
whether the child she was carrying was his

She had had enough.

It was June of that year when eighteen-year-old
Theresa and young Howard Clyde Sanders moved out
of the house on Q Street and into a tiny white house in
the Swiss dairy town of Galt, some twenty miles south
of Sacramento.

Galt was as flat, rural, and dirt-poor as Rio Linda.
One of its chief sources of municipal revenue was traffic tickets, issued with regularity to motorists on nearby
State Highway 99 after they failed to see the reduced-
speed-limit signs as they zipped past the town. Outside
of its reputation as a notorious speed trap, Galt was best
known as a dairy settlement at the north end of the San
Joaquin Valley wine country that produced milk, not
wine.

"Galt was fairly quiet in 1964," said Ysabel May,
widow of the longtime Sacramento County sheriff's
constable stationed in Galt. "In fact, Galt was fairly
quiet all through the sixties."

The whole southern half of Sacramento County was
so placid back then that her husband, Resident Sheriff's
Constable Fred "Buster" May, would take the drunk-

and-disorderly calls at his home as well as at his one-man office—sometimes, in the middle of the night. He'd roll out of bed and go to a bar where a donnybrook had turned serious or to the home where spouses were pounding each other with tire irons and rolling pins. The threat of violence to a law enforcement officer was not as commonplace as it is today, Ysabel May said. Buster would simply "storm in like a bull in a china shop and haul them in," she recalled.

"The backseat of the squad car got splashed with blood once in a while when people got drunk and knifed each other," she continued, remembering the worst of the violent crime committed in and around Galt. Anything more serious, like murder, simply didn't happen. Few people had guns, explained Ysabel. Drunks and madmen with knives could be dangerous, but rarely lethal.

"There were a lot of knifings in those days, but not too many shootings," she said.

After a cooling-off period, Clifford had finally followed Theresa to Galt and reconciled—to be with the son he adored, if for no other reason, according to his brother, Tom. But the war between him and Theresa quickly erupted anew.

James Cross had moved in with his daughter and grandson when they relocated to Galt. Now totally disabled by Parkinson's disease, he remained powerless to referee the battles that exploded between Theresa and his son-in-law with increasing frequency. While Clifford was mild-mannered and sober most of the time, Theresa remained willful and stubborn whether she had been drinking or not. After a few drinks Clifford could be taunted into an eruption. When things got too bad, Clifford would bat his wife down and simply walk out. At the beginning of the marriage he'd leave for only a few hours, but by the time they had moved to Galt, he would sometimes leave for days.

On June 22, 1964, Clifford came home to the little

house at the end of Elm Avenue, just a dozen yards from the railroad tracks. He drank, argued with his wife, and threw her purse against the living-room window, breaking the glass. Then he hit her, she later told police. But this time she took action. On the advice of Constable May, who lived across the street, she went to the Galt police. She showed them the bruises around her wrists and neck, told them she wanted to make a citizen's arrest, and filed assault-and-battery charges against her husband. But when it came time to book her husband, she refused to press charges. Clifford was released before the first paperwork was ever completed.

Two weeks passed.

"On July 4, I went fishing up at Lake Barryessa and Clifford was supposed to go with me," recalled Tom Sanders. "I wish he had."

Clifford stayed home that holiday weekend. On Sunday, July 5, he celebrated his twenty-third birthday, but it was far from a happy one. Things had continued to deteriorate between him and Theresa. Theresa accused him of whoring around. Clifford ratcheted up the tension between them another notch when he questioned again whether the baby she was carrying was even his. He silently made the fateful decision to move out of the house at 586 Elm Avenue once and for all.

The next morning, Monday, July 6, he packed his bags. But he never got past the front door.

Clifford had beaten Theresa before, and he told her he was going to beat her again. Then he was going to take what money they had and leave her. He had already packed a brown suitcase and a cardboard box when she went to the bedroom, got the Winchester lever-action deer rifle, and returned to the living room. Just as Clifford was about to leave she aimed the gun and held her finger against the trigger.

"I grabbed the gun to make him keep from hitting me

and it went off," she later told authorities. That was all she said she could remember.

A single .30-.30 cartridge penetrated his heart. The coroner said that Clifford apparently held up his left hand to fend off the bullet because it shattered his wrist before striking him in the chest. He took several staggering steps toward the back door before he tripped and fell, landing flat on his back, staring straight up at the ceiling.

Shocked at what she had done, Theresa set the rifle up against the door frame next to the mop, gathered up her purse and baby Howard, and raced outside to the car. She drove no more than a hundred feet down Elm Avenue before stopping in front of Fred and Ysabel May's house, at 603 Elm.

It was 9:20 A.M. when the Mays' eleven-year-old son answered the door and confronted a hysterical Mrs. Sanders, holding her baby in her arms. She sobbed over and over that she had shot Clifford in the arm and needed help. The boy roused Ysabel and Fred out of bed, and Ysabel called for an ambulance while Fred sat the girl and her baby down in a rocker in the front room.

While Fred May was across the street investigating, Ysabel tried to comfort Theresa.

Where was her father? she asked.

His '54 Chevy was still in the driveway, but he had gone to the post office and hadn't seen any of what had happened, Theresa replied.

" 'I did not think it would do that much damage,' " Ysabel remembered Theresa babbling. " 'I didn't think it would hurt him that bad. I didn't think that old gun would hurt him that bad.'

"She kept saying she hadn't meant to shoot him. She said it over and over. She was such a pretty little thing," Ysabel remembered.

But Ysabel also remembered Theresa coming to the house two weeks earlier, to complain to her husband, the town's deputy sheriff, about Clifford's abuse. She remembered Theresa telling Fred that Clifford slapped her around and then left her to take care of the baby and her invalid father all by herself. It was Fred May who first saw the bruises inflicted by Clifford's heavy hands, and it was Fred who recommended that Theresa go to the Galt police to file the assault charges that she never followed through on.

Theresa dropped the charges because she thought he'd learned his lesson. But Clifford had not stopped abusing her. He was trying to hurt her again when she went to get the rifle, she said, rocking hypnotically back and forth with baby Howard in her lap.

When a grim-faced Fred May returned from the Sanderses' home, he went in the other room to call the police. Then he asked Ysabel to come back to the house with him.

"I went and saw the body," Ysabel recalls. "It almost sounds like a TV movie now: blood splattered all over the wall and little bits of skin. I probably would've just noticed the blood, but my husband, he points out the little pieces of skin stuck to the wall and ceiling."

A trail of Type-A blood ran through the tiny house, from the front porch to the back, where Clifford's dead foot propped open the screen door. Inside, the house was sparsely furnished, but clean and orderly in the front room, except for a shattered plaster-of-paris horse atop the TV set that had apparently been hit by the same bullet that killed Clifford.

The bedroom and the kitchen were a mess. The Sanderses' double bed was unmade with unironed laundry at its foot, income tax forms and other documents piled on one end of the mattress, and toys and a blue diaper bag strewn across Howard's crib. In the kitchen, dirty dishes, empty soft-drink bottles, and watermelon rinds littered the dining table. A clock radio played low.

Clifford was dressed in khaki trousers, black shoes, and a white T-shirt. A tattoo on his upper right arm identified him: CLIFF. He had $1.70 in one pocket and two money orders in his wallet, totaling $62.14.

Theresa still didn't know the awful truth when an ambulance pulled up outside her house across the street. She kept rocking in the Mays' front room, asking if Clifford was going to be all right and whether she had just grazed his hand. The Mays kept her questions at bay until a squad car showed up in front of their house for Theresa.

After Galt Police Chief Walter Froelich helped her into the backseat and started off toward the police station, he finally broke the news to Theresa. Ysabel still remembers her scream.

"It was bloodcurdling," she said. "I'll never forget it. Chilling. A chilling scream."

Ysabel May heard the screams all the way down Oak Street, until the squad car turned the corner and headed in the direction of the county jail.

II

Chief Froelich could not calm his suspect or her child and detoured to a local doctor before booking her. Once she had been given a sedative, the next order of business was what to do with baby Howard. Theresa gave him an address in Rio Linda and instructions to take the baby there.

Then she went to jail in Sacramento, not Galt.

The snobs from Sacramento liked to compare Galt to Mayberry R.F.D., saying Chief Froelich was a regular Sheriff Andy Taylor and his right-hand man, Captain Clyde Lee, had to be another Deputy Barney Fife. Chief Froelich worked the day shift and Lee worked nights in their two-man police department. They had volunteers who worked as police reservists, but Froelich and Lee were the only ones on the city payroll. While the two lawmen handled everything from barking dogs to corralling the town drunks in Galt, neither the captain nor the chief could remember the last time a woman had shot her husband to death.

They were quite proud of the fact that they ran a decent town, and they resented imported violence, even the domestic variety. It was some small relief to Captain Lee in particular that Cliff Sanders was an out-of-towner who had only recently settled down in Galt with his wife and child. In later years he would be quick to point out that these were *not* Galt folk shooting each other.

Theresa's attorney asked permission for her to attend her late husband's funeral three days after her arrest. Judge Raymond Coughlin ordered the sheriff's department to escort her to and from the three P.M. burial at East Lawn Sierra Hills Cemetery. According to Clifford's brother, Tom Sanders, Theresa paid for the funeral out of the life insurance money she collected from the Carpenters' Union policy that Clifford had taken out on himself just a few weeks earlier.

The obituary in the classifieds of both the *Union* and the *Bee* told of the death: *In Galt, July 6, 1964, Clifford Clyde Sanders, beloved husband of Theresa Sanders, loving father of Howard Clyde Sanders....*

The case attracted the press immediately. Petite, pretty, pregnant, and penitent, Theresa was as sympathetic a defendant as ever stepped into a Sacramento courtroom. She also attracted first-rate legal talent as her lawyer.

"They used to describe Bob Zarick as Sacramento's answer to Jake Erlich," said Donald Dorfman, the deputy district attorney assigned to prosecute the Sanders case.

Robert A. Zarick was a Yugoslavian with a cynical sense of humor about everything legal.

"He was charming, almost courtly, with a very well-deserved reputation as a sharp lawyer," said Dorfman. "He used to give a grin and a wink while he was filing his probate cases and say in his booming voice, 'The wills you do as a young lawyer come back to support you in your old age as probate.' "

Zarick's biggest problem was with the bottle.

"When I met him, he was at the tail end of his career as an active trial lawyer," Dorfman continued. "He was an alcoholic. I used to pick him up at his house and take him to court in the mornings, and when I showed up, he'd be down in the basement drinking right out of a bottle. Heavy liquor. He'd offer it to me, and when I'd say no, he'd say, 'What'sa matter? Can't you handle it?'

"I had trials with him where he was actually drunk in the court, and he'd nod off and wake up and do something brilliant in between, in his moments of lucidity. That's the way he was. Heavy drinker. But he didn't kill anybody, and he lived to be eighty years old."

Drunk or sober, Zarick had his hands full with Theresa Sanders. Even if she had been the most sympathetic client in the world, the fact remained that she had shot her husband to death in an era when terms like "diminished capacity," "temporary insanity," and "battered-wife syndrome" were unknown or would have been utterly meaningless in a court of law. Any hope he or Theresa had that she might be set free on a simple claim of self-defense vanished two weeks after her arrest, on the evening of July 21.

Beginning at 7:30 P.M., the Sacramento County Grand Jury heard testimony in the matter of Theresa Jimmie Francine Sanders. The first witness called was Dr. Arthur Wallace, who had performed the autopsy on Clifford Sanders.

There were no powder burns on the body, Wallace testified. Whoever shot Clifford Sanders did it from several feet away. What is more, he had died sober. Blood alcohol tests turned up negative.

In fact, Clifford Sanders was the very picture of health. The only thing physically wrong with the dead white male lying on Dr. Wallace's examining table was a bullet lodged in his heart and a shattered wrist that appeared to have been raised to fend off the bullet.

"Both bones were shattered and the wrist was almost amputated," Wallace told the grand jurors. "It was hanging by a few shreds of muscle."

And there was a chest wound, one inch left of the sternum at the level of the eighth rib.

"It was my assumption, and I believe this is very correct, that the deceased apparently had his hand in some position in front of his chest," said Wallace.

"Maybe like this, or like this," he continued, demonstrating for the jury how Sanders might have held up his hand to protect himself from the bullet. Regardless of how he held his hand, it slowed the bullet down, but not enough to save his life. Normally, a .30-.30 slug would have gone right through Sanders and lodged in the wall behind him, said Wallace.

"The fact that it lodged within the soft tissues of the heart shows that its momentum was considerably slowed when it struck the chest."

Wallace finished his description of Clifford Sanders's death in less than ten minutes. He was followed by the deputy coroner who hauled Clifford to the morgue, and by a state-certified criminalist who tested the rifle. Both men spent even less time on the stand, corroborating Wallace's testimony.

Then Buster May was sworn in.

"Directing your attention to the sixth of July of this year, sometime around nine A.M., where were you at that time?" asked Deputy District Attorney Dorfman.

"I was sleeping," said May.

"Did something unusual occur at that time?"

"Yes. My little boy, eleven-year-old, he came in the bedroom and shook me and he says, 'Daddy, get up! There is a woman out here crying. Says she shot her husband.' "

"What did you do then?"

"I jumped out of bed, put on my uniform that was right side of my bed, went out, and the woman was in the living room. She had a little baby. She says, 'Hurry, hurry.' She says, 'Stop the bleeding. His arm is bleeding.' And I asked her where he was at. She says, 'He is lying by the back door, inside the back door.' So I asked her, 'Where is the rifle?' She told me she had shot him with a rifle. I says, 'Where is the gun?' She says, 'I threw it.' She says, 'Maybe it is in the car.'

Well, I went over to their house and I seen the rifle, sitting right side of the door on the right side."

Ysabel May followed her husband to the stand and backed up everything he said. Yes, the young woman came to the house, baby in her arms, hysterical that she might have hurt her husband's hand. Yes, she had been to the house two weeks earlier, complaining that her husband had beaten her. Yes, she had left the rifle with which she shot him propped up against the wall, next to the back door at 586 Elm. Ysabel could have gone on, but Dorfman thanked her and told her that what she had told the grand jury was plenty.

By 8:10 P.M., the grand jury had heard enough. After Mrs. May, testimony in the Mrs. Theresa Jimmie Sanders matter came to an end. Deliberation began.

Less than two and one half hours later the fifteen mostly white, professional, well-educated, and upper-middle-class jurors voted an indictment of first-degree murder against the eighteen-year-old widow, mother, and high-school dropout from dirt-poor Rio Linda, for willfully and maliciously shooting her husband to death.

At 10:40 P.M., the grand jury adjourned.

When the district attorney's office proposed moving the trial of Mrs. Theresa Sanders to downtown Sacramento, the Galt police did not object. Chief Froelich felt a certain sympathy for the thin little wisp of a girl and her baby boy. On the other hand, Galt didn't need all the attendant bad publicity a murder trial would bring.

"I think [Deputy District Attorney Donald] Dorfman thought he had a clear-cut case against her," the chief said years later, underscoring his own belief as to why the DA moved the case out of Froelich's jurisdiction.

Dorfman had other reasons. Clear-cut or not, neither he nor his boss, Chief Deputy DA Ed Garcia, wanted the case muffed by a small-town police operation notorious for losing evidence, alienating witnesses, and overstepping the lines of its authority.

"We used our own investigators from the DA's office and the coroner, and moved the case up to Sacramento because, frankly, we didn't want them screwing it up down in Galt," said Dorfman.

For the young woman standing trial, however, it might have been better if she had been tried in Galt. A move from sympathetic peers in the rural outback to the relatively urbane metropolis of downtown Sacramento did not appear to bode all that well.

It was a different, and far more conservative time in California. A thirteen-year-old was suspended from school in Escondido for six days for having a Beatle haircut the same week Theresa was arrested, and fathers were forbidden by law from being in the delivery room when their wives gave birth.

In addition to the socioeconomic differences between country dwellers and city folk in the state's capital, there was the troublesome fact that women—whether they were accused of a crime or simply seeking a job—were a rarity in the downtown Sacramento court system of the sixties. Women were to be ogled, but not heard.

The same week Theresa's trial was to begin, for example, the Sacramento Christian Women's Club held a luncheon featuring two speakers: San Francisco lawyer George Hardisty and local fashion maven Mrs. Nancy Green. Hardisty's topic was "An Attorney Views Tragedy and Success." Mrs. Green spoke on "How to Be Lovely This Fall."

Generally the only women employed by the courts at the time were secretaries or court reporters. Spittoons and cigar smoke in the clerks' offices and courthouse corridors have long since been replaced by floral arrangements and "no smoking" signs. But in 1964, the Sacramento Superior Courthouse, built at the turn of the century at Sixth and I Streets like a medieval fortress, was still very much a haven for the county's "old boys' network." Women—especially women criminal defendants—were not particularly welcome.

Mrs. Theresa Sanders, the plucky little housewife who blew away her abusive oaf of a husband, had already become a cause célèbre before she ever set foot in a courtroom. The photo on the front page of the *Sacramento Bee* depicted a frail, haunted young woman, barely beyond puberty and clad in prison clothing as she was transferred from Galt to the Sacramento County Jail prior to her first court appearance. When a sad but unbowed Theresa was finally arraigned four weeks later, all the local media were there.

At nine A.M. on August 4, 1964, a county jail matron escorted Mrs. Sanders down a dimly lit corridor on the ground floor of the county courthouse and into Judge Albert Mundt's courtroom. The atmosphere was perfunctory, even if the interior design was not. The railings that separated the bench from the jury box and the counsel tables from the court watchers were made of carved and polished hardwood. The squeaky seats in the gallery, behind the bar, were as hard as Puritan church pews. The clerk's voice echoed off the shiny marble floors and walls as he read the charge: murder in the first degree.

Theresa's rosebud mouth turned down in a resolute frown. She was neither repentant nor remorseless. With Robert Zarick at her side, she offered a plea of not guilty. It was self-defense, after all.

Judge Mundt accepted the plea without comment. He assigned her a trial date of September 10 and a freshman judge who had been on the bench for less than a year: Charles W. Johnson, up in Department 11, on the third floor of the courthouse.

The matron escorted Theresa past reporters and out of the courtroom, back to her cell in the county jail.

* * *

Though new to the bench, Superior Court Judge Charles Johnson had a long career on the periphery of the courts. A 1936 graduate of Stanford Law School, Johnson was a native Californian with a long legal career, steeped in politics. Nearly thirty years before Governor Pat Brown appointed him to the Sacramento County Superior Court in September 1963, Johnson had begun his career as a legal secretary. Later, in the 1940s, then–Attorney General Earl Warren hired him as an assistant attorney general. He had been a professor at McGeorge College of Law, a deputy to the California legislative counsel, a cabinet secretary under Governor Brown, and, most recently, a municipal court judge in northern Sacramento.

Johnson was also a staunch Democrat and a loyal ally of the governor. Some attorneys said that was the chief reason he was rewarded with the judgeship in the first place—that he had made a gift of a color TV set to the governor and good fortune followed. For all of his education and experience, Johnson was not much of a legal scholar. In fact, he had been an administrator and executive throughout his career, but had never actually practiced much in a court of law.

"He did not know the law," said Dorfman. "But in his effort to appear brilliant, in his effort to pull it off and look professional for the jury, he invariably picked on somebody to make himself look good. He was a bigwig in the Democratic party and so was Zarick. Zarick was an older, respected attorney, and I was just a young-kid DA. The Theresa Sanders trial was an opportunity for Johnson to pick on the weak one and ally himself with the strong one. Guess who he picked on?"

In preparing Theresa's defense, Robert Zarick worked with his nephew Marko Zarick, an aspiring trial lawyer who had just passed the bar when his uncle invited him to assist on the Sanders case. Like his uncle, Marko drank heavily and, when he did, had an eye for anything in a skirt.

"Both of them liked to drink," said Dorfman. "Marko ended up stealing from clients, got disbarred, became a cook in a Basque restaurant up in Auburn, and died a few years ago. During the Sanders trial, the joke around the DA's office was, 'If she's really pregnant, Marko did it.' "

Marko and his uncle zeroed in on Theresa's pregnancy immediately as a surefire way to elicit sympathy from a jury. If they dressed her right and had her play up the maternal angle on the stand, they figured they had a shot at a reduced sentence at the least and maybe even an acquittal.

Marko himself was no fashion plate. He was as disheveled in the courtroom as he was in the barroom. But his uncle Robert Zarick was a dandy. He wore his hair thick and slicked straight back, not a strand out of place. According to Dorfman, the courtly old defense lawyer looked the way Moe Howard of Three Stooges fame might have looked had he worn a double-breasted gabardine suit and combed his hair back instead of letting it lie atop his head like a black mop. In the courtroom, Robert Zarick looked and acted like a force to be reckoned with.

Dorfman, who was a couple of decades younger than Zarick, knew he faced stiff competition. Still, he saw the Theresa Sanders assignment as a golden opportunity. He was convinced she had pulled the trigger on purpose and all the evidence seemed to be in his corner. If the nine-man, three-woman jury just kept its eyes open and Judge Johnson was even moderately fair in his rulings, Dorfman had a winner.

The trial began on a sticky Thursday morning when the temperature was already in the eighties before noon. In his opening statement, Dorfman told the jurors he would show that Theresa Sanders did willfully, knowingly, and with malice aforethought go to the bedroom

of the Sanderses' tiny home out near the Galt City Yard
and fetch a deer rifle on the morning of July 6—a rifle
that she cocked, aimed, and cold-bloodedly fired directly into Clifford Sanders's heart.

His first witness, Buster May, recounted the tale of
Mrs. Sanders, still clad in her nightgown, coming to his
front door that morning, clutching her baby in her arms.
He described how he found Clifford, lying on his back
in a pool of blood at the back door of the little house on
Elm Avenue.

After Buster stepped down, Chief Deputy Coroner
Ray Thielen took the stand and picked up the tale: how
Clifford's body was taken to the morgue for autopsy;
how the crime scene was sealed off and photographed;
how Thielen found the murder weapon leaning against
the doorjamb, along with the expended cartridge shell;
and how Chief Deputy District Attorney Ed Garcia visited the crime scene and made the decision to put his
agency's own investigators on the case rather than leave
it to the Galt Police Department.

Things seemed to be moving along smoothly. Dorfman got his first wake-up call the first time that he and
Zarick met with Judge Johnson in chambers.

Zarick wanted to tell the jury that Clifford Sanders
had once been arrested for car theft. He held up a complaint from the state of Alabama and asked to enter it
into evidence as a defense exhibit. Dorfman objected
long and loud. When Clifford Sanders hot-wired a car
for a joyride back on the farm, he wasn't even eighteen.
Besides, a teenager's car theft was about as far from a
violent crime as jaywalking or shoplifting, said Dorfman. What was the point? What did stealing a car six or
seven years ago have to do with his wife shooting him
to death with a deer rifle?

Zarick shrugged. It illustrated Sanders's bad character
and showed why she had reason to be afraid of him, he
explained.

And Johnson agreed.

When Dorfman exploded, waving his hands and saying that there was no legal precedent for allowing such irrelevant nonviolent criminal history into a murder trial, Johnson said he didn't care.

"I'm looking forward to the possibility of appeal and I know the People won't appeal and I don't want to be overturned on appeal, so I'm going to rule in favor of the defense," Johnson told the young deputy DA.

Dorfman recalled his reaction: he was speechless.

"What was the relevance?" Dorfman asked. "One: It happened before they were married. Two: What's it got to do with the fact that she killed him?

"And his comment was: 'I want the jury to know what kind of a guy he was. And I can't make an error on the side of the defense.' And he allowed that in. There's no *way* that should have been admissible. All it did was introduce a factor into the case that had no relevance in an effort to do something that I could have *never* done as a lawyer: to try to show that somebody's *like* a criminal because he was a criminal in the past!"

Dorfman bit his tongue, accepted the ruling, and carried on with his case. He still felt he had the upper hand.

On Friday, September 11, the second day of trial, Thielen finished testifying and was followed to the stand by Dr. Arthur Wallace, who described the autopsy results. Firearms expert David Burd was next, detailing his test of the deer rifle, which proved that it had, indeed, been the murder weapon.

Despite Judge Johnson's peculiar ruling in chambers and an increasing tendency to overrule Dorfman and sustain Zarick in open court, Dorfman went into the weekend believing he had laid a solid foundation for a finding of guilty on the first-degree-murder charge. He returned to court on Monday, September 14 at ten A.M., recalling Ray Thielen to the stand.

Thielen, a former Army Counterintelligence Corps

officer who had enrolled in law school at nights while
he worked in the coroner's office days, was as incredu-
lous about Judge Johnson's rulings as Dorfman. More
than once, Johnson announced to witnesses, lawyers,
spectators, and jury alike that he was purposely ruling
more favorably for the defense than the prosecution because he did not want the California Court of Appeals
overturning any conviction that came out of his courtroom.

"Charlie Johnson was a lousy judge," said Thielen.
"He'd never practiced law, and he looked up to Zarick
as having knowledge of trial law. Bob Zarick was trying
to show this was self-defense, and even as a first-year
law student, I could see Johnson was going along with
it."

Thielen was followed to the stand by one of Clifford's sisters, who attested to her brother's good character. Aside from the youthful car theft back in Alabama,
he had had no run-ins with the law and worked hard to
support his wife and child, she said.

Ysabel May was next, with a revelation that Dorfman
believed would swing the jury to the prosecution. Before taking the stand, she had told him about a puzzling
statement Theresa had made to her while the two of
them waited in Ysabel's front room for Buster to return
from the death scene that morning. Theresa told her that
Clifford was preparing to walk out the door, never to return, when she shot him. She said she didn't think the
gun would do that much damage.

But before Ysabel could tell the jury what she had
heard, her testimony was ruled inadmissible by Judge
Johnson. His reason: a recent California Supreme Court
decision that required that police read a suspect his or
her rights, like the more famous Miranda decision that
the U.S. Supreme Court would hand down two years
later. When Dorfman pointed out that Ysabel was not a
police officer, Johnson waved him off. It didn't matter,
he said. She was married to a deputy.

"The judge ruled that Ysabel was actually an agent for law enforcement when Theresa came over and confessed to her because she was the deputy sheriff's wife and [Theresa's confession] had been made in his house!" said Thielen.

Thus, the jury heard Ysabel tell of the brutality Theresa said she suffered at the hands of her husband and how she cradled her baby in her arms while she waited for Buster's return, but they never heard Mrs. May's report about Theresa's angry remark that Clifford would not get away with abandoning her.

Ysabel stepped down and a frustrated Dorfman called James Cross to the stand.

He was not there to talk about his daughter, or her relationship with Clifford. Dorfman called Theresa's father to the stand to talk about the deer rifle.

In his quavering voice, Theresa's increasingly frail father testified that the rifle was kept loaded in the bedroom, but that the safety was always on. Cross would not lie under oath. In order to fire the rifle, he said, his daughter would have had to click off the safety, deliberately cock the hammer, and pull the trigger—a three-step procedure that Dorfman said precluded any notion of an accidental discharge of the weapon.

After Cross left the stand, Dorfman called Thielen's partner, Bruce Hrabak, to testify as to how he loaded Sanders's body into the coroner's station wagon once the autopsy was finished, and hauled it to a mortuary. Then he rested his case.

Dorfman entered ten photos of the crime scene and autopsy into evidence, along with a diagram of the house at 586 Elm Avenue drawn by Galt city surveyor Clifford Gatzert, the deer rifle, the two live and one expended cartridges, and the slug that Dr. Wallace had removed from Sanders's heart.

Zarick began Theresa's defense in a barely suppressed rage. He told the jury his client had been a victim of Sanders's vicious attacks for months. Theresa wasn't just slapped occasionally, the way some wives were, he explained. She was punched in the face. She was burned with cigarettes. Pushed to the floor and kicked like a dog. This was not a case of murder, he said. This was a case of self-preservation. This was a case of simple survival, not just for Theresa, but for her little boy, Howard, and for the unborn child she carried inside of her.

Clifford Sanders was a brute, pure and simple, Zarick thundered. He was a bully who beat his wife the way a cruel hunter might beat his hound. When his client plucked up the loaded deer rifle and aimed it at her husband that July morning, it was not out of anger or a desire for revenge or any of a host of other emotions. It was out of cold fear that he would beat her yet again. She didn't aim to kill. The weapon went off in her untrained hands. Why else would she run to the nearest neighbor with the story that she had shot her husband in the hand? Why else would she blurt her fears that he might be hurt? Wouldn't someone who aimed to kill simply run from the scene of the murder without worrying whether or not the victim had proper medical attention?

No, Mrs. Theresa Sanders was no murderess. Theresa Jimmie Sanders was a victim. If the jury didn't believe it from Zarick, perhaps they would believe it from the victim herself. He called as his first witness Theresa Jimmie Sanders.

Zarick made much of the fact that Howard Sanders was barely a year old and that Theresa was three months pregnant when she was put on trial for murder. Though her pregnancy barely showed, Zarick made a point of having Theresa wear maternity clothing each day.

"He had her in a pregnancy smock from the word go, and he created a battered wife defense when none existed, Zarick did," said Dorfman. "That this poor girl, instead of killing the man because he was leaving her, she killed him in self-defense. And none of that existed in the facts! It was just a completely fraudulent thing!"

With a cracking voice, Theresa promised to tell the truth and then tearfully entreated the jury to believe her when she told them that she had only feared for her safety and that of her babies. She had never meant to kill Clifford, she said. In fact, she had never even threatened to kill her husband before the day of the murder.

For two hours she reeled off details of the beatings she endured at the hands of Clifford Sanders.

By Tuesday, September 15, the tide seemed to be turning in Theresa's favor.

Martha Hafner told the jury about the thin, spindly limbed little girl who used to play out back of her place on Oak Lane in Rio Linda. Mrs. Hafner spoke of the tragic dissolution of the Cross family with two sick and prematurely aging parents, one of whom literally died in her daughter's arms. The Theresa that she had watched walking to the bus stop each morning in order to get to school on time was not a cold-blooded murderer.

After Theresa dropped out of school to marry Cliff Sanders, Mrs. Hafner rarely saw her, but she did recall for the jury one night when Theresa came to her house to hide from her husband. He beat her, she told Mrs. Hafner. He hurt her and she feared for herself and her baby.

The psychologist who carried the title "mental health counselor" for the county jail and sheriff's department was next up. Dr. Leroy Wolter had interviewed Theresa in jail a few days after the murder and testified on the stand that, in his opinion, she was not a danger to herself or to anyone else. Again, the jury heard Theresa described as anxious, remorseful, and frightened, but not a vengeful and calculating killer. After the soft-spoken psychologist left the stand, Zarick entered Wolter's report into evidence.

DA investigator Ellsworth Frank testified on Theresa's behalf, too, stating for the record that his investigation had turned up no damning evidence of a woman bent on criminal intent to kill. Even the police officers who arrested her testified for the defense.

Chief Froelich took the stand and told the jury about a frightened, hysterical young woman he'd taken into custody following the shooting, how he had to get her to a doctor just to calm her down, and how concerned she seemed to be that her son be placed in good hands until her ordeal was over.

Froelich's assistant, Captain Clyde Lee, followed the chief to the stand and told the jury about the night of June 22, when he responded to a domestic violence call at 586 Elm.

"I had had a call on her prior to this shooting because her husband had came there and abused her and took her money and threw her purse through the window and one thing and another," Lee recalled telling the jury.

"Her and her father and the baby was there at the Elm Avenue address, and I went there and talked to them. I asked her if she wanted to sign a complaint and she said yes. But her husband, Clifford, he had left. So she signed a complaint and I went and got the warrant and then I picked the man up, out in front of the A&W Root Beer stand. I was going to take him to jail, but he wanted to talk to his wife first.

"And I said, 'Well, now, I'll have to see if she wants to talk to you. I don't believe she does.' Anyway, I contacted her, and she says, 'Well, yes, I'll come down and talk to him.'

"So I let them talk there while I had him in the squad car and finally she says, 'Well, I'll drop the charges on him. But I never want him around me again.' And I said, 'Well, I have the warrant. I can't ignore this warrant. I'll have to get the judge to withdraw it.' So I saw our local judge and he said if she wanted it that way, then let it go. So I did.

"But she flat out told him, 'If you ever bother me again, I'll kill you.' Apparently she meant it."

Zarick recalled James Cross and Ysabel May to the stand, this time to testify on behalf of the defense. In his halting voice, Cross backed up his daughter's claims of abuse. Clifford did, indeed, smack her around. Ysabel, too, testified to the truth of Theresa's plea for protection from Clifford two weeks before the shooting. It was Ysabel who advised her to see Captain Lee and swear out a warrant for her husband's arrest.

Ysabel stepped down and Zarick rested his case.

Now Dorfman faced a dilemma. He could see sympathy swaying the nine men and three women in the jury box, but he was certain they weren't getting the full picture. Despite the fact that Clifford was in the process of leaving the house and despite the testimony from Theresa's own father that she had to deliberately cock the rifle and aim it before it would fire, Dorfman feared the jury was buying her battered wife defense. Dorfman smelled another motive. He believed Mrs. Sanders shot her husband out of jealousy, because he consorted with other women.

He called Dr. Wallace to the stand again as his first rebuttal witness, to reestablish for the jury how Clifford Sanders was trying to leave the house that morning and the defensive way in which he held up his hand to protect himself from the bullet.

Then he asked that Mrs. Lydia Hansen, Clifford's older sister, take the witness stand. Zarick objected.

Mrs. Hansen was a new witness, not a rebuttal witness, he argued. If she took the stand, she could only address the points that Dorfman had made earlier, before he rested his case. The judge ordered Zarick and Dorfman into his chambers while he pondered this point of law.

"Lydia Hansen would have testified to the threats,

showing a predisposition to do harm," Dorfman said. "If Theresa expressed animosity against the guy in the past, it would certainly raise questions about this being a killing in retaliation for a beating."

But this logic didn't wash with Judge Johnson. Dorfman had presented a case for second-degree murder at best, he said, and he would not allow Mrs. Hansen to testify as a rebuttal witness. The threats she planned to tell the jury about were threats that Theresa had made one to three months before the shooting. They were threats that were too old to be admissible in testimony, he ruled. "Such icing on a cake" might cause a perfectly sound conviction to be reversed on appeal, he told a dumbfounded Dorfman.

"Here I had evidence the wife made an earlier threat against the deceased and the judge refused to allow me to bring it in!" Dorfman recalled.

Judge Johnson told the young prosecutor that the only way he could put Mrs. Hansen on the stand was to convince the court that he should be allowed to reopen his whole case. To do that, Johnson wanted Dorfman to show him legal precedents that would justify Mrs. Hansen's testimony.

"I've got proof that in the past she made a threat!" said Dorfman. "It's pretty damn obvious that if I got a prior inconsistent statement where Theresa denies under oath she ever made a threat, I should be able to call in my witness to impeach that. In fact, the law is now in California that it not only becomes evidence of the impeachment, it becomes the evidence itself! But Johnson, he forced me to write briefs!"

Dorfman kept a secretary on overtime and worked all night. He met Judge Johnson's challenge with a four-page brief citing five cases, plus two sections of the state penal code and the code of civil procedure, as reason enough to let him reopen his case.

Johnson remained unsatisfied. He let Zarick put Dorfman, Dorfman's court reporter, and his chief investigator on the witness stand and grill them as to the pertinence of Mrs. Hansen's testimony before he would rule on Dorfman's request.

Finally, Johnson grudgingly reopened the prosecution's case, but not without forcing a stipulation that the jury disregard all but the most specific of Mrs. Hansen's testimony. Before Clifford Sanders's sister ever took the witness stand, Judge Johnson had made sure that the jury understood that she might very well be committing perjury.

After the jury returned to the courtroom, Johnson had the clerk read the following instruction to them:

"You are about to hear evidence of statements by the deceased Clifford Clyde Sanders that the defendant threatened his life. This evidence is being received for the sole purpose of showing the state of mind of the deceased, and it must not be considered by you for any other purpose. Evidence that the deceased made these statements is material to the issue of self-defense, to show who was the aggressor, that has been raised in this case, but it does not in any way tend to prove that the defendant made those threats."

When Lydia finally got to testify, she described her brother as a hard worker who never drank, gave his wife all of his money, never threatened her, and never hit her. While Dorfman questioned her she nervously tapped her feet. Theresa, facing her from the defense table, did the same.

"I believe with all my heart that Theresa Sanders planned to kill my brother," she testified.

She said Theresa always drove Clifford to work because she wanted no other women looking at him. She kept him in threadbare work clothes for the same reason and allowed him only fifty cents for lunch money so that he wouldn't go to a restaurant where other women might size him up.

Two months before Clifford died, Theresa had told

her sister-in-law that she would shoot Clifford before she would let another woman have him.

"She said that she had a gun loaded and he'd better walk a chalk line or she'd kill him," she testified.

Furthermore, Mrs. Hansen said that this was not the first time that Theresa had shot at her brother. Before he died, he had shown his sister a bullet hole in the floor of the home where the couple had lived in Sacramento. Theresa had shot and missed, said Mrs. Hansen.

"She said she'd thought of using ant poison but that an autopsy would show it and that she wasn't 'stupid' and she'd get a gun and shoot him and make it look like an accident," Mrs. Hansen said, adding this direct quote from her sister-in-law:

" 'He's a man, ain't he? Why not kill him?' "

Throughout her testimony, Zarick objected, calling Mrs. Hansen "a prejudiced witness trying to discredit my client on trial for first-degree murder," but Judge Johnson overruled him and let her speak. When he got his chance to cross-examine her, however, Zarick pulled out all the stops.

"You loved your brother, didn't you?" he asked.

"Yes," replied Mrs. Hansen.

He accused her on the stand of threatening defense witnesses, being removed from the courtroom for causing a scene, and using obscenities to describe Theresa's own two hours on the witness stand.

He also asked her if she knew whether her brother had beaten or mistreated his wife. All Mrs. Hansen could remember was Clifford slapping her once.

"You have no interest in convicting Theresa Sanders, do you?" he asked.

Oh yes, she testified, she did not want Theresa to get off scot-free. But despite her unwavering belief in Theresa's guilt, Mrs. Hansen added one more paradox to a trial that—from the jury's point of view—seemed to be loaded with contradictions.

Mrs. Hansen asked the jury to acquit her sister-in-law

of the murder of her brother so that she would "be allowed to raise my brother's children."

"I was miserable," Dorfman recalled. "I wanted to get rid of Johnson if I could. Still, I was told that just wasn't done. Today there are fifty to sixty DAs and fifty to sixty judges and they're constantly challenging each other. The prosecutors have as much flexibility as the defense does. But one did not challenge judges in those days. It just was not done by most lawyers, and the DAs *never* did it."

On September 17, Zarick pressed his newfound momentum and, in the absence of the jury, asked Judge Johnson to set bail for Theresa.

She had a little boy who missed her, he said, and, besides, the county jail was no place for a pregnant woman. To underscore his point, he told Johnson that Beatrice Howard, a Rio Linda woman who had been taking care of Theresa's baby, would give Theresa a place to stay while her trial wound down. Mrs. Howard was a capable woman, but little Howard Sanders needed his mother, said Zarick.

Dorfman railed against the unprecedented and questionable request for bail for a murder defendant, especially in the middle of trial, but again, Judge Johnson ruled against him. He granted Theresa's freedom in exchange for $4,000 bail.

Mrs. Hansen was followed by Tom Sanders, who ranted from the stand that his little brother had, in fact, been murdered "by that bitch." It didn't matter that he was admonished for his language. Tom was angry and didn't care who knew it. In his heart, he knew that Clifford had been gunned down.

"I'm gonna get a gun! I'm gonna get a gun!" he shouted, storming from the courtroom. His sister ran after him, shouting "No, no, no!"

Dorfman called for a recess and caught up with both

of them on the street, where he calmed Sanders and warned him how his behavior might influence the trial. At the same time, Judge Johnson openly proclaimed before the jury and everyone else in his courtroom that Clifford Sanders's relatives, particularly his brother, Tom, were an unruly bunch. He stated that they might be as dangerous as Sanders himself had been. He assigned two extra bailiffs to the trial after Tom's outburst and ruled that Zarick would be allowed to carry a loaded gun into the courtroom each day for protection.

"Each day he would take the loaded gun out of his briefcase and cock it and turn back to the deceased's family, in the presence of the jury," said Dorfman. "As if he were saying, 'You people are as dangerous as he was, but you're not gonna get me like he tried to get little Theresa here.' "

Dorfman found three coworkers who were willing to take the witness stand and testify about Clifford's fears of what his volatile young wife might do to him. He also put Lydia Hansen's husband, Edward, before the jury, to give his version of his dead brother-in-law's escalating warfare with Theresa. Like his wife, Hansen maintained that Clifford had reported more than once that Theresa was a jealous, violent woman, capable of plotting and carrying out her husband's demise.

But Zarick countered by putting Theresa back on the stand in the afternoon, along with Martha Hafner. Mrs. Hafner recalled the night Theresa and baby Howard came to her home in abject fear of what Clifford might do to them. At the end of the day Theresa was released on bail.

The trial continued. By Friday, September 18, Tom Sanders had calmed down, but the two extra bailiffs remained in the courtroom anyway, just in case. Zarick put Martha Hafner back on the stand, followed by her brother-in-law Floyd Norris, and a surprise witness for the defense: Dr. Stanley Weitemier, a physician who testified that he had treated Theresa for facial injuries in 1963—injuries she claimed she received when Clifford hit her.

And there was more.

"I remember the torture that the husband had put her through," recalled juror William Hanson. "He'd taken cigarettes and burned her behind her knee. She had several scars there, and that was one of the things that I remember.

"She [Theresa] was dressed pretty well. I remember she got her excuse to go into the judge's chamber and take off her stockings to show him the burn."

Then the defense rested and Judge Johnson recessed for the weekend.

On Monday, September 21, Dorfman went first with closing arguments. Theresa deliberately killed her husband, he said. There was passion. There was the heat of the moment. But she went to the bedroom, cocked the gun, and shot her husband. It was clearly premeditated first-degree murder by a jealous wife, he told the jury.

There was Ysabel May's testimony about Theresa claiming that she didn't think shooting the gun would "do that much damage." Did that sound like the statement of a woman whose gun went off accidentally?

And what of Lydia Hansen's testimony that she had heard Theresa say she had a gun loaded at home and would shoot Clifford before she'd let another woman have him?

"Not every murderer can look like the witch in 'Snow White,' " said Dorfman, pointing at Mrs. Sanders. "It would be easier if they did. She is eighteen and pregnant, but that doesn't overcome the fact she maliciously shot and killed her husband without provocation."

Zarick's closing argument could be summed up in his "Defendant's Proposed Instruction No. 3," which he wanted read to the jury before they retired.

"A homicide is justified and not punishable when committed by a person in the lawful defense of herself," he wrote. Reasonable grounds included imminent "danger of death or great bodily injury," Zarick argued. "To justify taking the life of another in self-defense, the surrounding circumstances must make the danger of great bodily harm apparent, present, and imminent, or must appear, at the time of the homicide," he concluded.

It was an instruction that, ultimately, Judge Johnson did not formally deliver to the jury, but the jury, nonetheless, got that message.

"I remember the case all right," said Jennie Cullers, one of the jurors who, thirty years after the trial, could recall little else about it except her gut feeling at the time. "I remember the girl who was acquitted of shooting her husband. She was abused and pregnant. That's about the extent of my memory."

On Tuesday, September 22, Judge Johnson instructed the jury on what it could and could not consider in deliberating behind closed doors. Among other things, they were to disregard much of Lydia Hansen's testimony.

The jury retired at 11:03 A.M. and returned at 2:45 P.M. "There wasn't too much dissension as I remember," said juror William Hanson. "She really blew him all over the room. She struck me as a young woman who had gotten into a marriage she couldn't handle. Abuse in those days was a big word. Now everybody's abused."

Wearing a baby-blue maternity smock, Theresa waited calmly for the jury to shuffle into the jury box. She put her hand to her lips, fingers quivering as the foreman stood.

Dorfman knew the verdict in his gut before foreman Gary Harrison even handed it to the court clerk.

"Not guilty," read the clerk.

When Johnson asked him if he wanted to poll the

jury, Dorfman waved his hand and spoke no for the record.

Johnson clapped his gavel and ordered Theresa Sanders discharged and her bail lifted. After a twelve-day trial, it had taken the jury just one hour and forty-five minutes, with an hour off for lunch, to set Theresa free. She approached the jury box to thank the jury, but could not stop crying. One female juror put her arm around the young mother, but neither of them spoke.

James Cross led his daughter out into the hall, rushing past the waiting reporters. Zarick later told one newspaper that his client had only one thing to say after she had left the courtroom: " 'All I want to do is go home and take care of my baby.' "

But she did not go home immediately.

"The next day, after the acquittal, she comes to my office and retrieves the gun she shot her husband with," Dorfman said. "No emotion. Just, 'This is mine.' She was petite and pretty, but she's got a very cold heart to her."

Dorfman blamed the judge for a miscarriage of justice, but kept the silence that the DA's office demanded of its junior members. Within a year or two, however, he wearied of the iron grip that all judges—both good and bad—had on the district attorney. He quit, went into private practice, and followed the example that Zarick and other trial lawyers had set for him. Early in his career he became so well-known for defending Sacramento's prostitutes and pimps that he was nicknamed "the King of Tarts." In later years Dorfman gained a reputation as one of Sacramento's better-known criminal defense lawyers.

He never did question the jury members in the Sanders case as to how they reached their decision.

"She was just a simple gal, was married and abused, and not too smart," said juror Hanson. But shooting her husband, and then being acquitted of murder, may well have been a turning point in Theresa's life, Hanson conceded thirty years later.

Hanson has no regrets about the verdict, regardless of what happened later. "I never kept in touch with any of the other jurors," he said. "At the time it just seemed like the right verdict. I just felt sorry for the poor little bunny."

III

"I guess I was a sophomore in college when she was arrested for murdering her first husband," said Charlotte Harvey. "I remember I sent a note to the jail. A good-luck note or something, asking if I could see her.

"But she didn't want to see me, not then and not after. I felt we'd just gone off on different paths. I was just too much of a reminder of something she couldn't do. I just knew that was why she didn't want to see me."

Rosemary and Theresa were not yet twenty-one and their lives were already twisted and stunted in ways that would keep many of their dreams out of reach forever. While Charlotte, their childhood friend, was off at college, Rosemary was living in a trailer in Rio Linda with an out-of-work husband who listed his occupation as "encyclopedia salesman." And Theresa? Theresa was now a pregnant mother, fighting a murder charge.

When the younger of the Cross sisters had first been arrested in July, Chief Froelich followed her instructions and drove her baby some fifty miles north, to a trailer at the rear of an address on Tenth Street in Rio Linda. There, he handed Howard over to Floyd and Rosemary Norris.

Theresa's sister reluctantly took the child, even though the young couple had problems enough of their own. Rosemary had her differences with her younger sister, but Theresa was family after all. Nevertheless, Rosemary really didn't have time for a second child. For one thing, she had to work. From the start of her marriage, Rosemary's meager bookkeeper's salary had been their only steady income. Floyd could not seem to find and hold a job, but neither was he enamored of the idea of becoming a full-time baby-sitter for his sister-in-law's child.

Now, besides their own son, the Norrises had another mouth to feed. Theresa's prospects of getting out of jail anytime soon did not look promising. And even if she did go free, she was due to have another baby in a few months. Rosemary and Floyd were simply not prepared, financially or emotionally, to add two more babies and a sister-in-law to their tiny household.

Rosemary immediately began looking around for a more permanent home for Theresa's baby. She found it with Bea Howard.

Mrs. Howard ran a beauty parlor out of her home at 6608 Cherry Lane, just a few blocks south of the Norrises. She had grown children of her own by her first husband, but she had remarried at forty-one. Now, six years later, it was clear that she and her new husband, Craig, would have no children of their own.

"Since Craig and I were married, he often said he'd like to adopt a little boy," Bea recalled.

Mrs. Howard casually mentioned to a neighbor once that she and her husband had thought about taking the leap and word got around. Within a day or two of Chief Froelich's visit, Rosemary was on the phone asking her if she would consider keeping little Howard Sanders for a weekend. Bea panicked.

"I was going to a twenty-fifth wedding anniversary celebration on that Sunday and I didn't even have a playpen," Bea remembered. "I told her I was busy and that I didn't have any of those things you need for children. I really didn't want to get mixed up in it."

Rosemary was insistent, so Bea relented. She knew the story of the Cross family well enough: their father's illness, their mother's heart attack, and the hard luck the two girls had struggled to overcome following her death. Bea had been Swannie Gay's casual friend and remembered her as a fine woman who had died too young. Mrs. Howard took pity on Rosemary as well as her sister.

"I thought maybe I better keep him," she said.

Just five days after Theresa's arrest for murder, Rosemary handed the towheaded toddler to Mr. and Mrs. Howard. According to Bea, Theresa's first child looked like a Holocaust survivor.

"He was hollow-eyed, slightly potbellied," she said. "I think Theresa loved him, but you could see how thin he was. Every time we'd pass a hamburger joint, he'd say, 'Coke!' I suppose that's all he ever knew, was hamburger joints."

As much as they wanted the child, the Howards were ill-prepared. They were middle-aged, past child-rearing, and had long ago given away any baby clothes Bea had left over from her own children.

"When Rosemary dropped him off, he had only three diapers and nothing more," Bea remembered. "She said, 'I'll leave you the playpen for him to sleep in,' but she didn't even bring that down. We went out and spent about a hundred dollars for clothes 'cause he didn't have any. He didn't even have shoes. I think he had a couple bottles and that was it."

The boy fit right into the Howard household, though, and shed surprisingly few tears when his aunt drove away. Like a scared koala bear, he clung for dear life when Craig carried him around the yard on his shoulders, but he got used to it and giggled the next time his new dad gave him a ride. When the weekend was over, Rosemary did not return to pick Howard up as promised. Instead, her brother-in-law, Bill Norris, phoned the

Howards with a plea that they keep the baby just a little while longer.

"He said if I needed anything for the little boy to just call," Bea recalled. "I said, 'I don't intend to keep track of what I spend and surely the little boy has a check coming. If I'm gonna keep him, the check's mine. Come and get him if you want him!' "

Nobody came and no check arrived. Eventually, Social Security would kick in with a monthly allotment—the legacy of his dead father. But Theresa would be getting those checks by then and using them as much for her own wants and needs as for Howard's.

For the moment Howard's mother was still in the county jail and the youngster was strictly on his own, depending solely on the kindness of strangers. For the next three months Howard Sanders literally became Craig and Bea Howard's son.

"We got so involved. He was such a lovebug," said Bea. "I got him on the eleventh of July, and on the sixteenth he was a year old. We had a playpen, and he was everybody's love child. He was just adorable. Just a lovebug."

A photo album from that time shows the boy's transformation from a thin, ragged wisp with spaghetti limbs and protruding ribs to a robust youngster, mugging with an ear-to-ear grin for the camera.

"We had a granddaughter the same age as Howie and they played together," Bea recalled. "We always called him Howie. Little Howie followed me everywhere. When I went outside, he went outside. We would've loved to have adopted him. Oh, he was a sweetheart!"

But by autumn, Bea Sanders's hopes of becoming a mother again ended with Theresa's acquittal. She was coming home to Rio Linda and her baby. She was also coming home to problems. She might be a free woman, but Theresa was four months pregnant, homeless, jobless, and broke. Furthermore, her son had already started to forget her, according to Mrs. Howard.

"When she came home, I said, 'God, I don't know what to do, Theresa. I hate to turn the little boy over to a total stranger, and you are a stranger to him,' " Bea remembered.

The Howards remember Howard clinging to them and shying away from his mother. Bea offered to let Theresa stay with them until she got reacquainted with her son and back on her feet again. But she put strict conditions on the stay: no dating, help around the house, take care of her baby, and re-enroll in school.

Theresa agreed, but began breaking the rules that same week.

"She didn't make her bed unless I stripped it. Then she'd make it, just to get back in it," said Bea. "She didn't cook a thing. She didn't do a thing."

"She was the laziest human being you ever saw," agreed Bea's husband, Craig. "She'd sit in a rocking chair and rock and rock and rock. I just couldn't hardly stand her. But she was a good-lookin' gal."

And she was not going to let those looks go to waste. It was during this period that Janet Kelso remembers her talking about having an affair with an art instructor at a local college who paid her five dollars an hour to pose in the nude for him.

Theresa wanted her social life back more than she wanted a high-school diploma or motherhood. She began hanging out at the American Legion hall and having her old friends over to the Howards' to visit. One of them was Janet, who brought along a young army veteran confined to a wheelchair.

"I'd been home about a year and a half when I met Theresa," said Estell Lee Thornsberry, an ex-soldier who had been stationed in Germany before falling victim to a paralyzing accident. While on leave at a beach in Holland one holiday weekend in 1962, he ran into the surf and dove into unfamiliar waters headfirst.

"He dove right into the sand. It just squished the fourth and fifth vertebrae and he almost drowned," said his sister, Virginia Herron. "I remember the trauma that we all went through when he came home. It was almost like having a death in the family."

The accident made Thornsberry a quadriplegic, unable to control any of the muscles in his body below his shoulders and confined to a wheelchair for life. He returned to Rio Linda with full disability.

Lee, as he preferred to be called, tried to pick up where he left off, but found his life changed forever when he went to the dances at the American Legion hall or tried to tag along with friends who were out barhopping. Although the government provided a generous monthly living allotment, he couldn't spend his money on sports or fishing trips or cocktail lounges the way his able-bodied contemporaries did. So he bought himself a car. It was a dark blue 1965 Pontiac Bonneville two-door hardtop, especially outfitted so that he could drive it with his limited upper body movement. Theresa fell in love instantly with the Pontiac.

"She and I started talking, one thing led to another, I took her to a burger stand, and it seemed to go from there," said Thornsberry. "I let her drive the car around town and gave her money and things."

If she was brazenly taking advantage of a handicapped man, Lee didn't seem to notice or care.

"She was caring. She was not an abusive woman," he said. "She didn't yell, and we got along. She wasn't a bad-looking woman either."

To make sure her good looks were at their very best, Theresa spent lots of time in a beauty parlor . . . but not Bea's. She slipped away from the Howards' house as often as she could manage and had her face, nails, and hair done. She bleached her shoulder-length brown hair blond and took pains with her makeup, spending what seemed to Bea like hours preening in front of the mirror.

Bea Howard knew Theresa was breaking her "no dating" rule. Even though the young widow had just shot and buried her first husband, been tried for his murder, and was four months pregnant with his child, she spent no time grieving. Both of the Howards felt powerless to enforce their dating ban, though, because they knew that if they did so, Theresa would take little Howard and leave.

Bea kept after her, however. Theresa ignored her, knowing the kind of spell her son had cast over the Howards. Finally, after it was clear that Theresa had no intention of going back to school and her relationship with Lee Thornsberry and his Pontiac had become a minor scandal in Rio Linda, Bea Howard issued her ultimatum.

"I heard the baby fussing one night and went in there," said Bea. "She was shoveling food down his mouth as fast as she could. I said, 'What are you trying to do? You're choking the little guy!'

"She said, 'I'm in a hurry. My ride is waiting.' I said, 'If you're in that big a hurry, leave him here!' When I went to take the spoon from her, I saw a big diamond on her finger. I said, 'Where in heaven's name did you get that?' She didn't answer me.

"So the next morning I got up and I told her: 'You get an apartment. You have not done anything I asked you to do! You're on your own!'"

Theresa moved into a one-bedroom apartment on Rio Linda Boulevard. She no longer made any pretense about her relationship with the paralyzed veteran or the money and gifts he showered on her. She bought a whole new wardrobe and spent as much time as she could out on the town in Rio Linda, trying to recapture some of the adolescence she sacrificed when she married Clifford Sanders. She reclaimed some of the missed dances, partied in the bars and lounges that catered to servicemen and veterans. But she was never able to recapture her laughter.

"I don't know that she did laugh much. In fact, I

don't remember her ever laughing or joking all that much at all," said Lee.

His younger sister, who occasionally watched Howard when Theresa and Lee went out at night, put Theresa's lack of joy in blunter terms.

"She had no sense of humor," said Virginia. "I don't ever remember her being in good humor. After she shot Cliff, I think she may have felt real guilty for it, even though she knew she could get away with it. That might account for part of it."

Nevertheless, in Theresa Sanders, Lee Thornsberry had found a rare soul mate: a pretty young woman whose life had been as crippled emotionally as his own had been crippled physically. They both had their youth cut short and they both tried anything—drink, TV, party crowds—to escape the pain. In Lee's mind, they were made for each other.

"She didn't seem to me like she was any more daffy than any of the women I knew at the time, [but] she was different," Lee remembers. "She seemed to me like she had been through more than most people ever should have to. It seemed like she was going through some tough times."

Lee moved in with Theresa and helped her through her last few months of pregnancy. When her water broke, Lee and his mother drove her to a hospital in nearby Roseville to deliver her second child. On March 13, 1965, Sheila Sanders was born. Theresa gave her the middle name of Gay, after her mother.

But instead of going home with Lee following Sheila's birth, Theresa returned to Bea and Craig Howard's place to recuperate.

"I let her stay a week or ten days because, otherwise, they wouldn't release her from the hospital," said Bea.

Mrs. Howard's husband was happy to be able to toss little Howard up on his shoulders again, but a week of Theresa was about all he could stand. Theresa took full advantage of her new motherhood and demanded that

Craig and Bea wait on her as well as feed, bathe, clothe, and entertain little Howard and the new baby. When Lee called to let Theresa know that he had rented them a house on Madison Street in the northeast Sacramento neighborhood of Citrus Heights, the Howards braced themselves for another round of separation anxiety.

"Howie was only a year and half old, but, boy, he wouldn't let go of me," said Craig Howard. "He said, 'I stay with you! I stay with you!' It took two people to pry him off me. He wouldn't let go. That's how bad he didn't want to go with his mother."

Theresa and the children moved in with Lee, and this time the future for this odd couple looked a little brighter. They started buying furniture and appliances and setting up permanent housekeeping. They were going to get married, they told friends. And, for the first time since her murder trial, Theresa began to open up to her fiancé about what had happened between her and Clifford.

"She talked about how Clifford had abused her and beat her," said Thornsberry. "She got into detail about it, and I figured if that's what he was doing to her, he pretty much had it coming to him."

Janet Kelso remembered a different edge to Theresa's recounting of her tragedy. "She wasn't sad," she said. "It was as if she was gloating when she'd threaten a guy and say she'd shot one man and she wasn't afraid to do it again. It seemed to empower her. You could feel it when she talked about it."

She never broke down in tears during her tirades against her dead husband. Her voice broke with defiant anger more often than it did with distress.

"She said that he had shoved her head through the wall," said Lee. "She found the dentist that had wired her jaw together again after he had broke it one time, and she brought him into court. He testified, and she said that's how she got off."

Lee believed her, but then he believed everything she told him. He wanted to believe her.

"She lied pretty good, too," he recalled with a bitter chuckle. "She was going out with other guys and saying that she wasn't, even after I found out that she had."

The way he discovered Theresa's infidelity was especially hurtful. Like the wheelchair-bound singer of the Kenny Rogers hit song "Ruby, Don't Take Your Love to Town," Lee would watch Theresa doll up in a low-cut dress, smear lipstick across her permanent pout, and walk between him and the television set, letting the screen door slam behind her. Then she trolled the bars in Thornsberry's big, beautiful Bonneville.

" 'Course, I was half in the jug most of the time back then, too," said Thornsberry. "I just wish I could remember clearer, but those days went by in one big blur."

But he knew in his heart where she had gone at night, regardless of her stories about going out with girlfriends. His worst imaginings were confirmed one morning when Theresa was inside, sleeping off a hangover, and Thornsberry wheeled himself onto the front porch and down to the Pontiac to drive to a store. In the front seat he found used condoms and underwear.

"I found odds and ends in the car that just kind of jump up at you and call you a stupid sucker," said Thornsberry. "I never caught my best friend doing it with her, but he was doing it. I know it."

Theresa's attitude toward her children had been changing, too. In one way, she was becoming a better mother. In another way, she was becoming much worse.

"Physically, she took good care of the kids," said Thornsberry's sister, Virginia Herron. "They always had clean clothes. They were always clean, diapers always changed. She took care of them that way, and they were always well fed. It was just the emotional side where she didn't take care of them the way you would expect."

Virginia started to come around more and more to help her brother as well as to baby-sit the children while Theresa was on her jaunts. She remembered an odd difference between Theresa's treatment of Howard and Sheila.

"Sheila and Howard were real cute kids," she said. "Everybody loved them and had a good time with them. But it was obvious that Theresa favored Howard and neglected Sheila, even when she was tiny.

"One day Sheila had gotten in trouble for something, and Theresa scolded her. Sheila was crawling around crying, looking for somebody to pick her up. I wanted to get her, but none of us were allowed to pick her up. Theresa just wouldn't allow it.

"After this whole thing was over, I felt really bad 'cause Theresa had treated Sheila so bad, and she was such a cute little girl. So I asked her why? And Theresa told me that she intended to raise these two kids exactly the way that her mother had raised her. Her mother had favored one sibling over the other. She told me she was going to favor Howard and neglect Sheila just the same way her mother had done.

"I thought it was strange, and I never forgot it. I just remember the day she told me that, and I always worried about Sheila after that."

Bob Knorr, who had become one of Theresa's mystery suitors by this time, got another explanation from Theresa as to why she cuddled Howard and spurned Sheila. "Theresa hated her from day one because she was pregnant with Sheila when she killed Clifford," he said.

According to Knorr, Theresa somehow managed to blame the fetus in her womb for starting the chain of events that led to the shot that ended Clifford's life and changed Theresa's forever. "She blamed a lot of that on Sheila," he said. "Clifford accused her of sleeping around and said that Sheila wasn't his. He told her when Sheila was born, he was gonna have blood tests done. He had threatened to take Howard and leave."

Now it looked as though history was on the way to repeating itself. The arguments between Lee and Theresa began increasing in volume and frequency as they had done between Clifford and Theresa. But Thornsberry didn't pay them much mind. After the shouting match, he'd simply buy a bottle and drink away his despair while Theresa took off with his money for a night on the town.

"Theresa was living with my brother, and meanwhile she was carrying on with Bob," said Thornsberry's sister, Virginia. "I remember thinking how horrible that was. She'd get dressed to kill, put the kids in the car, travel around to bars, and sometimes leave the kids locked up in the backseat, out in the car for hours at a time."

Lee withstood the humiliation of being a cuckold for the better part of a year, but he finally broke up with Theresa when her neglect, profligacy, and extravagance pushed him over the edge.

"I think he moved back home because he wasn't getting the proper care," said Virginia. "He was a quadriplegic, so he really needed somebody around all the time."

Lee moved out of the house on Madison Avenue near the end of 1965, but Theresa stayed on through the first of the year, until she had to move. When Lee returned to retrieve his few remaining things, both they and Theresa were gone.

"I remember the washer and dryer had miraculously disappeared out of the house," he said. "Everything else, too. It was after we'd split up. I'd went back to get my stuff and everything was gone except for junk."

It seemed that Theresa had found a new place to live. She'd found a new father figure, too: a six-foot, blond, and blue-eyed marine, two years younger than herself, who followed her around like a puppy and cut a strapping figure in his dress uniform.

Bob Knorr had joined the marine corps a year before he and Theresa met. He was hopelessly naive about women, but was nonetheless a restless, cocky tenth-grade dropout from North Highlands High, just like Theresa. And, also like Theresa, he wanted something—anything—other than the future that his own parents had opted for.

"You gotta realize I was growing up on a pear ranch in Placerville, with my mom and dad, working farm-work. I joined the marine corps to get away from home," Knorr recalled.

The youngest of three sons who lived at the edge of poverty much of their lives, Knorr had neither the discipline nor the aptitude for school. He preferred driving a tractor on Gus Winkleman's ranch, where his father worked as a mechanic and general handyman. Despite his disdain for school, he had no desire to step into his father's shoes and become part of a world where men settled for any kind of job—fruit picker, fry cook, tractor driver, gas-station attendant—just to make the rent payment. He was young, but not so young that he couldn't foresee a time when the end of the week might roll around and all he'd have left from his paycheck would be enough for a few beers at the corner bar.

From the day he enlisted in December of 1964, shortly after his seventeenth birthday, Knorr began building his self-confidence. Following boot camp, he flew off to the naval air station at Kealakekua Bay in Hawaii for nine months of jungle warfare training with the 1st Marine Brigade.

"He was kind of a dreamer," recalled Duke McIntyre, one of Knorr's closest friends during his time in the marines. "No offense to Bob, but in a way, he didn't have his act together."

Knorr was still a minor and very much a youngster to the other enlistees, who, like Duke McIntyre, were all at

least two or three years older. Nevertheless, he was a
marine, determined to keep up with the others. Despite
the difference in their ages, he and McIntyre hit it off
right away. They both loved fast cars and Southern
Comfort. Just like his peers, Bob carried out orders,
bitched about discipline, and drank and partied when
his platoon hit town on liberty. What doubts he had
about himself as just another Sacramento high-school
dropout began slowly slipping away.

But even after a year in the corps he was easy prey
for a willing woman when he flew home for Christmas
leave in 1965. Drinking and smoking and partying
aside, one aspect of Bob Knorr's youth was still very
much intact. When he got home to Sacramento and his
oldest brother offered to set him up on a date with
Theresa Sanders, Bob Knorr was still a virgin.

Bob's brother was friends with Larry Hafner, who'd
grown up next door to Theresa in Rio Linda. Hafner's wife, Carol, knew Theresa was taking care of
Thornsberry at the time, but she thought the relationship
was strictly business. Theresa took care of Lee and got
paid for it. There were rumors that this was not the
case, but Carol Hafner refused to see it that way. Pair-
ing up with a handicapped man was no life for a lovely
young woman who had had some tough breaks of her
own, reasoned Carol. She took it upon herself to play
Dolly Levi.

"She needed someone to take care of *her*," said
Carol. "She'd had a very hard life, I know that."

Carol's own brother had dated Theresa several times,
but he wasn't "in her league," Carol said. Robert Knorr,
on the other hand, fit Carol's matchmaking criteria to a
tee: a tall, handsome young marine with a crooked grin
and piercing pale blue eyes.

To say that Bob Knorr and Theresa Sanders kissed on
the first date is an understatement, according to Knorr.
"She kissed me on the first date. Boy did she ever!" he

recalled. "And she kept on kissing me, everywhere she *wanted* to kiss me!"

For the remaining two weeks of his Christmas leave, Knorr was in heaven. What is more, he was no longer a virgin. "She was my first," he said. "I was a big young dumb farm boy, she threw the shit on me, and I liked it. What can I say? I'm not gonna tell you no stories. That's exactly the way it was."

Together, they hit the bars in the Sacramento suburb of Citrus Heights almost every night. And, again, almost every night Knorr got lucky.

Knorr knew nothing about Theresa beyond what she wanted him to know. Bob never heard that she had two children, that she'd been acquitted of murdering her husband, that she was living with and engaged to a quadriplegic, but even if he had, it probably would have made little difference.

"My mother could see right through her," Knorr said. "My parents told me, even before I went to Vietnam: she's no good for you.

"I'd say, 'Oh, I wanna marry her!' And my dad would say, 'You wait, son. Wait till you get back.' I was ready to disown my folks 'cause I was underage and couldn't marry her without their approval."

Following Christmas leave, Knorr returned to Kealakekua Bay to finish up his guerrilla training before being shipped off to Vietnam. But he hadn't been back in Hawaii three weeks before he heard from Theresa.

"She calls me and tells me she's coming over," said Knorr. "She borrowed some money from friends and told me she was flying over."

Sure enough, Theresa was on the next plane to Hawaii. For the next three weeks she moved in with friends of Knorr's marine pals who lived in an apartment just off the base. By now, Knorr knew Theresa had two children and that they were staying with friends while she came to see him.

But Knorr didn't care. His hormones were howling

and any discretion he might have possessed was dulled by alcohol or orgasm. Every chance he got, Bob made a beeline to the apartment where Theresa was staying. By the time his unit left for Vietnam in February of 1966, Theresa let him know that she was carrying his child.

After Knorr shipped out, Theresa stayed on in Hawaii awhile longer. She was in no hurry to get home where all she had waiting for her were two babies, no job, and no car. Besides moving out of the Madison Avenue house they once shared, Thornsberry had taken back his Pontiac.

Returning to Thornsberry was out of the question, even though she probably could have patched things up. Despite all the humiliation, he would have taken her back. But Theresa was finished with him. If he didn't believe it when she flew off to Hawaii to be with Knorr, Lee Thornsberry believed it when he got his final phone bill from the house on Madison Avenue. There were several hours' worth of person-to-person charges between Citrus Heights and Hawaii. The bill was for more than five hundred dollars.

IV

Bob Knorr was in love.

His future with the woman of his lustiest, loftiest dreams was secure. He had everything to live for. For that reason alone, he radiated self-confidence when he s'hipped out for Vietnam in the winter of 1966. No chance *he* was coming back a corpse.

He had second thoughts almost from the moment he arrived.

"I got there in February and got shot in March," he remembered. "The first time I was machine-gunned. I was hit from quite a ways away and it felt like bee stings in my shoulder. It hurt, it burned, it stung. The thing is, you don't really hear the ones that hit you."

The bullets just broke the skin. The flesh wounds were enough for several days at a field hospital, but not worth a trip to a bigger military hospital on the coast. Within a few days Knorr was back on patrol.

Less than a month later he was hit again.

"The second time I was sniper shot in the fatty part of my side," said Knorr.

Again, the bullet barely penetrated the skin, but this time he spent a while longer recuperating. He was young and able-bodied, though, and after a week or two he was again sent back with his unit.

Despite his months of training in tropical Hawaii,

Knorr found adjustment to Vietnam trying. On its surface, the country was primeval green and disarmingly peaceful. But those marines who let the picturesque rice paddies lull them into nonchalance did so at great, and often fatal, peril. The Mekong delta mesmerized, but death was ever-present in the form of snipers, booby traps, and bloody ambushes. Throw in the incessant paranoia of never knowing who was an innocent civilian and who was a Viet Cong awaiting just the right moment to kill, and the daily routine became unbearable psychological torture.

Far from fearing the prospect of more bullets, however, Bob talked himself into believing he possessed a kind of invulnerability. He'd cheated death twice and had only scratches and Purple Hearts to show for it. Besides, he had a drop-dead blonde waiting for him back home who pined for him as much as he did for her. Theresa wrote regularly, repeating that Knorr *had* to come back to see his first child born.

Bob believed Theresa's letters. It was his destiny to return home safe and soon. He had a loving woman carrying his unborn son or daughter, and he was fated to get back to marry her, to give their child a name. Following his second discharge from the hospital, Bob's self-confidence soared once again.

He didn't twist his newfound faith into bravado. Bob settled into a more cautious daily routine and tried to stay alert during patrol. But with Theresa constantly on his mind, he sometimes forgot his vow of vigilance in the rice paddies and lapsed into automatic pilot, ignoring the worst of Vietnam while daydreaming about his girl, the end of his tour of duty . . . and his return to the States.

Each night he marked off the calendar, counting the days until he could get back. Over the next two months his platoon roamed a section just south of the demilitarized zone in the Mekong delta, some forty miles outside of Saigon, keeping the peace and trying to flush out an elusive enemy nobody seemed to be able to recognize.

The monsoon season began around May. The heat was overpowering and everything smelled of swamp water. What was more, the villagers that Knorr and his fellow marines met during their patrols seemed sullen and steered clear of the Americans. They weren't especially hostile, but they never seemed very friendly either.

As a low-level grunt, Knorr had no way of knowing what U.S. policymakers had in store for the men on the frontlines, but since his Christmas leave it had become more and more apparent that troop strength in South Vietnam had nearly doubled. New marines and army infantrymen poured in every day.

Back home, Washington painted the military buildup as a humanitarian effort welcomed by the grateful South Vietnamese. It was 1966 and the organized campus protests against the war had only begun to blossom in most parts of the United States. Where Bob and Theresa came from, near Sacramento, demonstrations were still muted. Besides, the buildup had created thousands of defense jobs at the military bases that surrounded Sacramento. If anything, most of the folks back home saw the war as a boost to the local economy.

But to the Vietnamese along the DMZ, it was a foreign invasion. Knorr discovered the depth of their resentment one day late in June, when the monsoon season was at its height and the hot wet winds from the Indian Ocean made patrolling the delta especially miserable, particularly for a marine decked out in full fighting gear.

"We were passing over a bridge and the only thing to hold on to was a steel rail, so we were holding on like we were walking on a tightrope," Bob recalled.

His platoon was halfway across when the bridge exploded. Instantly, Bob Knorr no longer thought himself invincible.

"One minute I'm walking. Next minute I'm dangling off those rails, almost ready to go down into the river," he recalled. "There was five of us hit with that one mine. The guy behind me got both his legs and half his butt blown off. Another got his privates blown off. Another guy got his ear completely blown off, just like they'd took a knife and severed it.

"And I got shrapnel in my arms and legs and back. Just blew me completely out of my combat boots. The soles were gone and my feet were just dangling through the tops."

This time Knorr wasn't patched up at a field hospital and sent back on patrol. Instead, he and the other casualties were flown to Okinawa for emergency surgery and skin grafts, then were shipped back to the Oakland, California, Naval Hospital via Clark Air Force Base in the Philippines. Their war experiences were over.

"Off and on I was in the hospital almost nine months," said Knorr.

"I'd be released, then something else would go wrong with a wound and I'd have to go back. I've got thirty-seven holes in my body from shrapnel and bullets. And it hurt like hell—nothing like you see on TV, that's for damn sure. I still got metal in me and permanent nerve damage in both my hands and arms."

The first call he made when he arrived in Oakland was to his brother, who came to the hospital and took him home to visit his mother and father. In his euphoria at being back, he completely forgot about calling Theresa. But he already knew her well enough to know there would be hell to pay for that mistake. Even before they got married, he appreciated the wisdom of lying to his fiancée.

"She was the type of woman who didn't get pissed. She got enraged," Bob said. "I went back to the hospital a few days later, and *then* I called her. And I told her I'd just gotten in."

Theresa was at his bedside in a flash, fussing over

him, kissing him, possessing him. By now, her pregnancy was showing and she wanted to get married right away. So did Bob, only now there was nothing to stop him. He didn't need his parents' approval. He was over eighteen, head over heels in love, and as deaf and blind as passion can make a man.

"My folks told me, 'You're making the worst mistake of your life. Don't marry this one.' But I bitched and bitched," he remembered.

Bob's father was especially wary. He warned his son that Theresa acted like a woman with something to hide, but Bob was adamant. Even though he didn't need their permission, he still wanted his parents' approval. So, on the second weekend of July, he convinced his mother and father to drive him and Theresa to Nevada and act as witnesses at their wedding at the courthouse in Carson City. Reluctantly, the Knorrs agreed.

On Saturday, July 9, 1966, Mrs. Clifford Sanders became Mrs. Robert Knorr.

"She was six or seven months pregnant when we stood up in front of the judge," said Bob. "He even made the comment, 'Not a minute too soon, huh, kids?' "

There was no honeymoon. By Sunday, Bob was back at Oakland Naval Hospital, having the dressings changed on his wounds, and Theresa was out driving their '61 Pontiac around north Sacramento, looking for a place to set up temporary housekeeping.

"From the time we got married, it was pure hell," said Knorr. "Before that it wasn't bad. But from that point on, it was like, once I said 'I do,' she said 'You will.' "

Theresa found a place built over a garage in a low-income housing project at the edge of north Sacramento. One of her first orders of business was moving James Cross out of a convalescent home where she had put him while she tracked down a new husband. From the day Bob and Theresa were married, James Cross lived with them. Theresa added his monthly retirement check to those she was already collecting from the Social Security Administration on behalf of Howard and Sheila. Under federal law, both children were to receive monthly allotments until their eighteenth birthdays. Bob remembers her collecting over four hundred dollars a month in allotments for Howard and Sheila during the late 1960s. With cost-of-living increases, that amount climbed over the years.

In addition to this income, Theresa took charge of Bob's paychecks.

"She had all our money," said Bob. "She had control. But I'd been that way all my life. I just didn't want to be bothered with paychecks and stuff. I'd just say, 'Here's the money. You take care of it.' "

While she awaited her third and Bob's first child, Theresa looked around for a new baby-sitter for her other two children. At first, she left them with Bob's mother. But Mrs. Knorr had fallen ill with the cancer that would eventually kill her, and Theresa had to turn to Knorr's other relatives for assistance.

Bob's aunt and uncle, Evie and Pat Works, told the young couple that they would be happy to help them get on their feet. Evie even offered to do for Theresa what Bea and Craig Howard had done: act as surrogate parents for her toddlers until she and Bob got settled.

Evie Works, who had sons and daughters of her own, had firm rules for raising children. From the very first, she sensed something very wrong in the way Theresa behaved toward her own children. To begin with, Bob's young wife clearly played favorites. She might yell at Howard, but it was Sheila who really caught hell. Every time Sheila moved or made a sound, Theresa fixed her with an icy glance. The little girl didn't dare cry.

"We had seen her sit Sheila down in front of a blank TV as punishment," said Evie. "All the little girl would have to do was try and eat her breakfast, and if she'd pick up a glass of milk and spill it, Theresa would jerk her up by one arm, take her from the kitchen, spank her, and sit her in front of a blank TV. She'd order her to just sit there and watch it. Now, mind you, Sheila couldn't have been more than eighteen months old!"

Actually, the petite, dark-haired child seemed far younger when Evie first got her. It was as if both her growth and behavior had been stunted. While Sheila was slow and fearful, Howard was bright and unafraid. He was Theresa's "pet," according to Mrs. Works. Theresa made it plain to both Evie and Pat that she cared a great deal about her son. Even though she could be just as quick to lash out at Howard as she did at Sheila, there was a real difference in the degree of severity with which she punished her daughter.

"Howard could get away with almost anything, but Theresa was downright cruel to Sheila," said Evie.

She was careful about letting strangers get a glimpse of that cruelty, too. The children might get the tar whipped out of them behind closed doors, but out in public she insisted on maintaining the illusion of a perfect family.

Appearances were extremely important to Theresa. Evie recalls her spending as much as thirty-five dollars a week at the beauty shop just to maintain her nails, complexion, and champagne-blond coiffure—all at a time when Bob barely earned that much in salary. Theresa was equally exacting about the appearance of her house. It had to be immaculate and everything had to be in its place. Her obsessive attention to perfection extended to her children.

"Anything cute the kids did, she could not see as cute," said Evie. "My sister had given Sheila a bowl of peaches once and Bob's shoes was right there, and I guess she spilled the whole bowl of peaches in his shoes. Everybody else in that place laughed, but it was *not* funny to Theresa. It was embarrassing to her. And probably Sheila got her butt beat again."

Mrs. Works remembered one disturbing incident before she and her husband had taken Sheila full-time. She drove over to pick the child up at Theresa's apartment and found her head completely shaved.

"The minute I walked in the room, the little girl ran over to me, and there were little cuts all over the top of her head," she recalled. "And I asked, 'Theresa, what's the matter with her head? Is she digging at it?' And she said, 'No, I sat her on the chair and shaved her head. And every time I pulled that razor, I wanted to go down into her brain with it, but I just didn't have the guts to.' "

Instead of criticizing Theresa, the Workses learned to hold their tongues. They quickly came to understand that if either of them spoke up, their chances of getting to keep Sheila with them would disappear and the little girl would wind up being punished. When Theresa went into one of her rages, the Workses felt powerless.

"She'd yell, 'She is my child, and she is going to mind!' " Mrs. Works recalled. "I'd try to explain that you can make a child mind, but not under those circumstances. And she said, 'That's the way *I* make her mind!' "

As her pregnancy reached its final stages Theresa reluctantly relinquished Sheila's full-time care to the Workses. They took the girl to a doctor when they first got her because they found abrasions on her ankles and the backs of her feet. The doctor told them that Sheila suffered from bedsores. He explained that her feet and ankles were rubbed raw from being forced to stay in bed, beneath the sheets all the time, not unlike an immobilized hospital patient.

During those first few weeks with the Workses, Sheila sat and stared most of the time. The only time she showed much initiative was at mealtime.

"As a little baby, Sheila had better table manners than any five-year-old child I had ever seen," recalled Evie. "She would not pick up food with her hands. She had to have a fork. Sheila could not get dirty. She could not embarrass her mother in no way whatsoever.

"Theresa demanded all of this of this little baby. And if she was embarrassed, Sheila was reprimanded for it. She would really go after her. Spank her. Slap her across the face. There was no part of her little body that Theresa would not go up against. She'd go after her like you would a ten-year-old kid."

For the first six months with the Workses, Sheila remained mute. Then, one warm spring evening Pat Works drove her along with one of his own daughters, Candy, to a nearby convenience store for a soda. Sheila evidently had something else in mind.

"The first words that little girl ever said were 'Daddy Pat, buy me an icee,' " recalled Evie. "My husband was so shocked. He turned around and looked at Candy and said, 'Did *you* say that?' And Candy said, 'No, Dad. Sheila said it! Get her an icee.' " You can bet she *definitely* got her wish.

"Evidently she knew how to talk, but she just wouldn't say nothing. After that, she'd call me Mama Ev and she talked up a storm. That is, she'd talk until Theresa walked in. Then you wouldn't hear a word out of her. She'd just clam up."

On September 27, 1966, while Sheila and Howard remained with the Workses, Theresa traveled to the military hospital at Mather Air Force Base just north of Sacramento and delivered her third child, a girl. She named her Suesan Marline Knorr.

Bob got a release to visit his wife and daughter, but had to return within a few days to the Oakland Naval Hospital, where he was treated as an outpatient and assigned temporary duty status. His military doctors had determined that his wounds had partially disabled him, but not enough to warrant a medical discharge. He could continue serving as a marine. He was awarded the Bronze Star and put back to work.

Meanwhile Theresa changed their residence. By the

time she was ready to bring the baby home, she had arranged to move her father and herself out of the low-income apartment in Sacramento and into a house on Tioga Street in San Francisco so that she could be closer to Bob. It was a move prompted as much by jealousy as by love.

Though they'd only been married a few months, Bob already felt a subtle shift in her attitude. Knorr the Boyfriend was a very different proposition from Knorr the Husband. He was now a possession. Despite his combat wounds, he still cut a dashing figure in his dress blues and Theresa wanted him nearby so that she could keep an eye on him. If a nurse was too attentive or Theresa caught her husband making flirtatious eye contact with a female patient, he got a taste of her fury.

"She'd say, 'If I ever catch you fooling around on me or if you try to leave me, I wouldn't hesitate to shoot you,' " he remembered.

By this time Knorr and his entire family were fully apprised of the way Theresa's first marriage had ended. Bob's father tried not to rub it in, but he did point out to his son that he had tried to warn him more than once that he was absolutely certain that Theresa was hiding something from them. Bob defended his wife, though. When she first told him, he believed Theresa's tearful version of the events—how she was regularly pounded into submission by the brute and how it led to her picking up the deer rifle to defend herself. It wasn't until later on, when she threatened in the heat of their arguments to do to him what she had done to Clifford, that Knorr began to have second thoughts about his wife's account.

In the autumn of 1966, though, they were still riding on the euphoria of being newlyweds. They went bar-hopping together when they could, even though Bob was still only nineteen and Theresa was just over California's legal drinking age of twenty-one. Once again, he played champion to her damsel in distress. Bob was a reluctant warrior until he had a few beers in him, but Theresa usually arranged a pitched battle for him.

"She just loved to see me fighting over her all the time," he said. "When we went out, she was always trying to get me to fight someone about her. Being young and stupid, half the time I'd do it."

While Theresa settled in at the Tioga Street apartment, Bob's superiors assigned him to the marine barracks at Treasure Island, where he stood guard at the main gate when he was not flying off on his new limited-duty assignment. For the remainder of his time in the military, he was told, Bob Knorr was to be a burial escort.

"You'd take the bodies out to the plane and make sure they got loaded properly, fly to the proper destination, make sure the funeral home picked up the coffin, and stay with the remains until after the funeral," he said.

It was a grim but interesting job that took Knorr all over the United States. For the next two years he accompanied the increasing number of marines who came home in coffins to virtually every state in the country: New York, Oklahoma, Texas, Illinois. . . .

While he enjoyed his new job, Theresa hated it.

"When the military tells you you've got a job to do, you better do it," he said. "During those periods I'd be gone, she'd go nuts. She'd accuse me of going out on her while I was away. She'd have to know the motel I was staying in, the funeral home I was going to be working at, and she'd call every hour while I was gone."

Their frequent quarrels over Bob's absences did not, however, put a damper on their sex life. Less than three months after Suesan was born, Theresa was pregnant yet again. She didn't let pregnancy slow down her social life, though. Leaving her invalid father in charge, she'd get in the car and be gone for hours—sometimes all night long. Pregnancy had never kept her from having a good time and it wasn't going to do so now.

"When I'd come home, she'd go out sometimes and wouldn't come back until five in the morning," said Bob. "She'd come home stinking [drunk]. When I'd ask where she'd been, she'd say she 'went for a drive.' "

When Bob wasn't home and Theresa was gone, care of their new infant daughter fell increasingly to James Cross and his three-year-old grandson, Howard. The Parkinson's disease had completely handicapped the old man by now, but he still retained his full mental faculties. He used Howard as "his arms and legs," according to Bob, sending the boy on errands or instructing him when and how to feed or care for his little sister.

"Howard was an exceptionally quick-learning kid," said Bob.

While Howard was growing up in San Francisco as a silent witness to his mother's unpredictable brutality and quixotic worldview, his cousin Joseph was growing up in rural poverty but with some stability, living with his family in a rented trailer in Rio Linda. Joseph Norris, who had been born just one day after Howard Sanders, now had a younger brother. Daniel Lee Norris had been born on November 7, 1965, eight months after his cousin Sheila Sanders. Though the Knorrs and Norrises never lived far from each other, they rarely visited. The Norris boys grew up vaguely knowing that they had cousins, but almost never saw them. By the time she married Bob Knorr, Theresa was completely alienated from Rosemary.

"Theresa and Rosemary never got along very well," said Bob. "Rosemary was a big woman and a no-nonsense person. By the time I met her, she was also becoming a very successful state worker and that used to irritate Theresa a lot."

Despite being saddled with two sons and an "encyclopedia salesman" for a husband, Rosemary had firmly taken control of her life. She knew Floyd wouldn't.

While he floundered from job to job she was making painstaking progress in a government bookkeeping job, climbing the career ladder despite her limited high-school education.

"Floyd was a deduction for Rosemary. Kind of flaky," said Bob. "But Rosemary was successful and Theresa always wanted to be. And she hated that."

The Cross sisters had witnessed poverty firsthand, and earlier than most of their peers. Harsh reality as well as sex, bars, and booze—the cheap escapes from that reality—had always been all around them. While they were growing up, Rio Linda had more than its share of residents who lived at or below the poverty line.

Thanks to the untimely death of their mother and their father's disabling disease, Theresa and Rosemary were plunged into the panic and desperation that comes with having no income, no resources, no home. The Cross sisters saw—or should have seen—what too many children, too many cartons of Kools, too many six-packs of Bud, and too many late-night escapes into too many places with names like the Easy Inn or the Thunderbird Lounge, can do to dreams.

But only one of the sisters did see the correlation. While Rosemary pursued her bookkeeping career after giving birth to Daniel Lee, Theresa continued having children, earning no income, and visiting bars. She depended on her husband to pay the bills.

Less than a year after the birth of her third child, Theresa delivered her fourth. William Robert Knorr was born on September 15, 1967, also at Mather Air Force Base. According to Bob, Theresa named the boy for her older half brother, William Hart Tapp.

By this time Bob was a lance corporal in the marine corps and the family had moved to the San Francisco suburb of Daly City. A month after William's birth Bob's mother died.

"At the end my mom accepted our marriage and seemed to get along with Theresa," said Bob.

But at the funeral, Theresa refused to go near her mother-in-law's body. She wore a deep frown throughout the service and remained outside the viewing room when the rest of the family shuffled by to pay their last respects. Knorr attributed her behavior to the trauma of her own mother's sudden death. Still, he found it hard to forgive her.

Whether it was the fear of losing her own family, prompted by Mrs. Knorr's death, or the fear that she might lose the allotment money to Evie and Pat Works, Theresa suddenly decided after nearly a year of leaving her first daughter with the Workses that she wanted Sheila back. Her reason: They were a bad influence.

"She just blew up one time and we got in a big argument over my aunt and uncle because my uncle came up to visit and had Sheila with him and Sheila had a little fingernail polish on," said Bob. "And Theresa said, 'That's it. I'm taking her back right now.' "

Theresa was certain that Evie and Pat Works were planning to adopt Sheila so that they could collect her Social Security payments, according to Bob.

"But my aunt and uncle had never even *thought* of asking for it," he said. "They were taking care of Sheila just to help. Sheila was slow to potty-train, to talk, and my aunt and uncle had helped a lot."

Evie and Pat cared for Sheila, but they had their own reasons for not fighting to keep her. By now, the entire family knew about Theresa's violent and often irrational temper.

"Before she died, Bob's mother told me, 'If Theresa ever wants her back, give her back, because, if not, Bob will be killed,' " said Evie Works. "My sister died in October of '67, and only a month afterward, Theresa told me she wanted Sheila back. So we packed her clothes, took her up to my brother-in-law's place in Placerville, and we let Theresa have her back."

Bob's trips as a marine burial escort increased over the following year, and he made no secret of the fact that he enjoyed traveling. He got to eat out at restaurants, stay in hotels, and steer clear of his wife's wrath for days at a time. But all his travel only increased Theresa's jealousy—both of the trips and what she believed to be Bob's adulterous liaisons, all over the United States.

"The Christmas of 1967 she made me open every present I bought her so she could see them before Christmas," said Bob. "She thought I was fooling around, cheating on her, and I was buying all these gifts for somebody else, even though they were under *our* tree."

Holidays were a toss-up. Some were good, some bad. But Theresa didn't need a Christmas or Easter for her suspicious behavior to show itself. Whenever Bob had to report back to Treasure Island for duty, she encouraged him to go AWOL and remain at home.

"She almost screwed my service record up for me," said Knorr. "She had me staying home with her and not reporting back to duty. See, she couldn't control me when I was out on base."

Bob blamed Theresa for his failure to climb any higher in the marines than lance corporal. "She just sat around trying to think of ways to harass me," he said. "When I look back on it now, it really wasn't a very good time in my life."

Even the passion that brought them together had cooled. According to Knorr, "She used sex as a tool. If she wanted something and she couldn't get it no other way, she'd get it that way. Or if she thought there was something in it for her, she'd use sex to get it."

She could be remarkably cruel, calling the ugly scars left by Bob's war wounds disgusting disfigurements that made him less of a man than the one she had first slept with.

She rarely smiled and never laughed. The good times they'd had together before they were married simply evaporated. Even when they went out, Bob and Theresa were no longer really a "couple." Wherever they went, they took the kids. There was little opportunity for them to spend time alone. By the summer of 1968 they had four children between them and a fifth on the way.

Theresa liked the idea of motherhood, according to Bob, but she hated what it did to her looks. After four pregnancies, she still hated the bloating, the sleepless nights, the aches and pains that appeared in lines across her face. And she felt that Bob didn't show the proper attention to her while she was pregnant either.

Bob maintains that he stayed true to Theresa throughout their marriage, despite the boredom that set in near the end. When he was on duty in the marine corps, there was simply no time to fool around, even if he had wanted to. But Theresa didn't believe him. The longer they were married, the more volatile she became about her husband's alleged adultery, until Bob came home from the base one night and found her, the children, the furniture . . . gone.

"Theresa was supposed to pick me up from the base when I got off duty, and I called the house and I told her, 'I'm pretty tired. I'm gonna take an hour's nap. Why don't you pick me up then?' And she said, 'No problem.'

"I never did see her. When I got to the house, she'd had everything loaded and moved out. That's the way she did things."

Theresa simply packed up all four children, James Cross, and the furniture and moved to a house in Rio Linda. Bob tracked her down by going to Rosemary's— the second and last time he ever saw his sister-in-law.

"I just wanted to find out what I did to make her move," he said. "She said she wasn't gonna put up with my cheating anymore."

When he finally convinced her to give it one more try, they moved back in together just as Bob's enlistment in the marines was winding down and he was about to become a father for the third time. Just before midnight on New Year's Eve of 1968, Theresa gave birth to the third of Robert Knorr's children, and his namesake: Robert Wallace Knorr Jr.

"He was the last baby born at Mather [Air Force Base Hospital] in 1968," recalled Bob.

A new baby may have brought Bob and Theresa back together again, but it didn't make things any easier. With five children to feed, the Knorrs' only steady income was James Cross's retirement checks and the two monthly Social Security allotments for Howard and Sheila. Bob went job hunting, but until he could get a good job and/or qualify for Veterans Administration disability payments, he had to be satisfied pumping gas at a local service station.

Theresa worked as a nurse's aide when she worked, earning about fifty dollars a month after taxes. Their new financial crunch didn't dampen her spending habits, though. She used credit cards to buy everything from appliances to clothing to jewelry.

"She wanted everything to be name-brand labels. Christian Dior and all that," said Bob. "Yet she never really had [name-brand products]. She just made people *think* she did. Shortly after I got out of the service, she ran up the credit cards and buried me so far into debt, I wasn't never going to get out."

Despite their bleak financial picture, the Knorrs bought a brand-new 1969 Plymouth Roadrunner with payments of $116 a month. Theresa got to drive it while Bob drove his old 1959 Chevy pickup truck.

But buying her a new car didn't help. By June of 1969 things had deteriorated between them to the point that Bob moved out of the family home. Theresa filed for divorce on grounds of extreme cruelty.

In her court declaration, she said that she was the fit parent, *and it is in the best interest of the minor children that I have custody, subject to rights of reasonable visitation of the defendant.*

With the help of her lawyer, she went on to describe in detail the pitched battles she and Bob had been having:

> On numerous occasions, the exact dates of which I do not now recall, the defendant has threatened me with great physical violence and, in fact, carried out that threat at least once a day during this period. During the first week of June, 1969, defendant did strike me upon the lower extremities thereby causing injury to the body and shock and injury to the nervous system. [On] June 10, 1969, while I was driving the family automobile, with the defendant in the front seat, he attempted to force the automobile off the roadway and when prevented from doing so, he commenced beating me about the head. Based on the foregoing, I believe that the defendant intends to and will—unless restrained by order of this court from doing so and ordered to vacate the family residence—continue to annoy, molest, and injure me.

According to Bob, the divorce suit was just one more example of Theresa taking extreme action to control him. He had moved out over her objections and vowed not to come back. She didn't get a gun and go after him as she had often threatened, but she did hire a lawyer and asked the court to order Bob to pay $250 a month in alimony and child support.

Bob came back. Despite her dramatic accusations of extreme cruelty in the divorce petition, by the end of the month Theresa dropped her suit. They decided to try a change of locale in one last effort to make their marriage work.

The court clerk had barely stamped DISMISSED on the Knorr divorce before Bob and Theresa packed up their belongings and children and left the state.

V

Duke McIntyre hadn't seen Bob Knorr since he watched him leave Vietnam on a stretcher back in the summer of '66. When "Bubbles" Knorr called him one day nearly three years later, it was "out of the blue," Duke recalled.

"He says, 'Hey, what's the job situation like up there in Spokane?' And I said, 'There's jobs up here.' And he said, 'Well, I'm on my way up!' "

At the end of June, just days after Theresa dropped her suit for divorce, Bob loaded all their worldly goods in a trailer, hitched it to the back of Theresa's brand-new Plymouth Roadrunner, and drove his wife, five children, and father-in-law nearly a thousand miles to Spokane to start a new life.

It was Theresa's idea, he said. If they got out of town and started all over in a new place, maybe their marriage would work out.

But Bob and Theresa weren't simply in the market for new opportunities in Washington State. They were also on the run from bill collectors back in California.

"Our credit rating was shot by the time we left Sacramento," said Bob. "She bought clothes, furniture . . . just anything and everything. Instead of making the payments, I guess she was spending the money, because nothing ever got paid."

But Bob was no wizard when it came to handling money either, according to the man who helped the Knorrs resettle in Spokane.

"He seemed like he always lived above his budget," said Duke McIntyre. "He was kind of a dreamer, always trying to measure up to her expectations."

Bob's dreams always exceeded his ability to achieve them, even during their days in the corps together, according to McIntyre. If reality wasn't quite to his liking, Bob was not above inventing a little fiction. He may not have meant for it to happen, but Knorr tended to shine up the unvarnished truth about his humble roots and how he planned to conduct his life, particularly after a beer or three.

While they were still in training in Hawaii, for instance, McIntyre says Knorr told him that his father owned a food-processing plant in Placerville that manufactured C rations for the military. When Theresa flew over to see him, Bob left Duke with the impression that his wealthy father had paid for the trip.

When Bob "Bubbles" Knorr came rolling into Spokane looking like a latter-day Tom Joad, loaded down with kids, ragged clothes, and boxes of bric-a-brac, McIntyre began questioning everything that Knorr had ever told him. "Bob was a nice enough guy," said McIntyre. "He just really didn't have his cards all together."

Shortly after the Knorrs' arrival, McIntyre threw a welcoming party at his mother's house. Before the young couple arrived, he got an odd phone call from someone wanting to know if Duke knew who Bob Knorr was and where he might be.

"They said, 'He had a car involved in a hit-and-run, and we'd like to talk to him.' So I said, 'Well, he'll be here at my mother's house tonight at ten P.M.' "

Bob did show up at ten, just as he promised, but the mystery caller didn't. Bob and Duke reverted to old times, recalling how they used to hit the bars in Hawaii and the settlements outside of Saigon, drinking sweet Southern Comfort until everything that had gone wrong in their lives seemed right again. All went well until about two A.M., when Bob went outside for a smoke and returned a few moments later, as agitated as a snakebite victim.

"Duke!" he yelled. "Duke, call the cops! My car's gone!"

When he called the Spokane police, McIntyre was told that they already knew about the car. It hadn't been stolen, it had been repossessed. The Knorrs had bought it half a year earlier, he was told, and hadn't made the required $116-a-month payment on the $3,600 purchase price for several months.

Their Plymouth Roadrunner now gone, Bob needed a job more than ever. He found two, both at little more than minimum wage. "I was working two jobs up there: delivering for a furniture store and working in a service station in the evenings," Knorr recalled.

He worked himself to exhaustion, but it didn't help. Even twelve-to-sixteen-hour days, six days a week, could not keep up with Theresa's new spending, let alone the outstanding bills.

"They were living about one step above welfare," said Duke.

In his job hunting, it didn't help that Knorr was a Vietnam veteran. By the summer of '69, the war had come home, even to Spokane, and it was inadvisable to advertise the fact that you had once been a gun-toting GI in Southeast Asia.

"They classified Vietnam as a conflict, not a war," said Bob. "We had no heroes' welcome. And the people more or less treated us like we were in conflict with them. They treated us like we were warmongers."

McIntyre tried to help, but there was only so much he could do. Bob was a great drinking buddy, but he had few marketable skills and only a tenth-grade education.

He did have one helluva wife, though, according to McIntyre.

"She struck me as the type of lady who expected the guy she was with to take care of her," he said. "He'd have to have a good job so she could buy clothes. If she wanted fifty different colors of lipstick, she expected the guy to provide it. It looked to me like a mismatch between her and Bubbles. He was in love with her, head over heels. And she used him for, like, whatever she could get."

McIntyre, who insisted on calling Bob by the nickname he'd given him during their marine days, nicknamed Theresa "Mrs. Bubbles." She didn't grumble about it like her husband.

"She thought that was cuter than shit," McIntyre said.

And though he was recently discharged from the marines and newly married, McIntyre found Mrs. Bubbles pretty cute, too.

"Terry was a beautiful blonde back then. She would always wear sweaters to show off her boobs," he said. "She knew she was looking good and wore tight slacks, too. Kathleen, my ex-wife, was a little jealous of her because Kathleen was short and stocky and kind of all business. She wasn't quite as beautiful and stunning as Terry. She'd say, 'Gee whiz, that sweater's about two sizes too small for her!' "

As a couple, the Knorrs might not have had a lot of things in common, but one mutual interest they developed in Spokane under Duke's tutelage was drag racing.

"I had a '34 Ford coupe painted with purple primer that I used to race," said McIntyre. "It had six carburetors and an Olds engine in the front seat with eight flames shooting out the exhaust. I used to run it at the drag races up at Deer Park and Bob would tow it to the track for me."

Duke remembered Bob's eyes widening and his mouth hanging open as he waited on the sidelines, watching Duke's purple chariot shoot off the line. With exhaust flames scorching the dust of the racetrack, the squarish old chassis of the souped-up coupe appeared jet-propelled. After that first time Bob confessed what McIntyre had already read in his friend's eyes: Bob had to have a dragster of his own.

Bubbles Knorr wasn't the only one turned on by Duke McIntyre's speed machine. Mrs. Bubbles was equally smitten. "Terry saw me as the master of this fire-breathing animal," Duke said with a chuckle.

After they lost the Roadrunner, Bob went shopping for a new car. At a used lot, he found a 1940 Ford that he thought he might be able to bring up to the hot-rod standard set by McIntyre's coupe. Bob paid too much for the old heap and brought it home.

"It looked like shit," said Duke. "It was not exactly what you ought to have as a family vehicle. Three hippies had driven it in from New York, and it looked like they painted it canary yellow with a broom. But the car bug just kind of bites you sometimes I guess."

McIntyre helped Bob work on the engine, and Theresa had become enough of a crash-wagon buff herself that she helped her husband tinker with the jalopy whenever she got a chance. During one of their engine overhauls, Theresa got so involved that she fell and broke her leg, according to McIntyre.

The Knorrs' joint enthusiasm for auto mechanics amounted to little more than a truce, however. The level of warfare between them escalated by the winter of 1969, even though Theresa appeared to outsiders to be utterly devoted to her family.

"The facade Terry put on for me was [that of] the very loving mother," said Duke. "She loved Bob and her kids. I never saw any abuse. I saw them correct the kids—whack 'em on the ass like normal parents. But that was the most I ever saw."

The manner in which she ran her household was a little out of the ordinary, though. Theresa kept her house spotless and would not tolerate insubordination from her children. McIntyre remembers the Knorr family performing chores like a miniature marine platoon. "The sergeant major was the tough guy in the marine corps, the guy who snapped the troops into readiness," he said. "And Terry was like that. Whenever Bob would come home, Terry would say to the kids, 'Get in line now. Your dad's home.' She was like that."

But around McIntyre, she was all softness and giggles. As she had done in San Francisco and Sacramento, Theresa tended to leave her father and Howard in charge of the younger children while she went out visiting. One place she liked to visit was McIntyre's apartment.

"I was very attracted to Terry," Duke admitted. "Back then she was a very attractive lady. She was a good-looking gal. But there was nothing between us. You know, she was my buddy's wife.

"There was a time she came by my apartment and Kathleen, my wife, was gone, and we could've had an affair, but it didn't happen. Not that it couldn't have and not that she didn't want it to. Had I not been just freshly married, I'd've been very attracted to her."

Bob was never so sure that something didn't happen between his wife and his best friend. "I didn't want to argue and fight," he said. "It seemed like that was all we were doing. But yet, when I came home from work one night while we were living in Spokane, Duke was laying in my bed, and she come downstairs in a nightgown."

Bob never accused either of them of the obvious, but he did harbor the belief that it was the first time in their marriage that he had almost caught Theresa red-handed. He puzzled over the hypocrisy of her constant accusations that *he* was having affairs until several years later, when he took a junior-college psychology course and learned about projection. Only then did it seem clear to him that what his wife was doing was accusing *him* of promiscuity when, in fact, *she* was the one sleeping around.

"She was like a reverse-psychology person," said Bob. "When she was out fooling around with somebody, she'd come home and try to accuse me of everything in the book.

"By that time I didn't give a shit anymore. I just wanted to get back to California."

But it wasn't his suspicions about his wife that prompted his sudden homesickness. It was the weather.

"Shit, I grew up in California and I wasn't used to snow," he said. "I was trying to hold a job down and the first snow came and the streets were covered up. That's when I said this place ain't for me. Get me back to California!"

For months Bob had been writing, calling, and visiting the Veterans Administration, trying to qualify for military medical disability. As soon as it came through, he planned to return to Sacramento. "They didn't figure my injuries were bad enough to medically discharge me," he said. "I'm over 75 percent disabled, but to get a retired military ID card all you have to be is 50 percent disabled. Yet they say I don't rate one."

Finally, with the snow still falling outside his window, Bob got confirmation that his disability benefits had come through. And all he could think about was going back home to sunny, dry Sacramento. He went to Duke and offered him his only two assets: the partially restored '40 Ford coupe and a '44 Dodge he'd purchased with the hope of turning it, too, into a dragster. He hated to part with them, he said, but he needed cash to get his family back to California.

"I said, 'All I got is this paycheck here for three hundred dollars," remembers McIntyre. "So he took it. And that's the last I heard of him."

By now, it was 1970: new year, new decade, fresh start. Bob and Theresa reconciled and made one more try at staying together. They moved back to an apartment at 1380 Morse Avenue in Sacramento, and shortly after their return, Theresa announced to Bob that she was pregnant once more.

Bob got a job as a service-station attendant. In addition to his veteran's disability, he earned $650 a month pumping gas, changing oil, and lubing cars at Jerry's Shell. Combined with the Social Security money Theresa got for her father, Howard, and Sheila, they were making a fair living.

But the jealousy persisted. Bob was sure she was sneaking off and having affairs and Theresa was accusing Bob of the same thing.

"She was so jealous of me I couldn't watch TV programs that had women on them," he said. "She'd come in the living room and shut it off."

She insisted on driving Bob to work each day instead of letting him drive.

"We had two cars: a Chrysler station wagon and a '64 Chevy," he said. "But she had to drop me off at work. She had to have control of both cars. If I had a car at work, I was gonna go fool around."

Even without a car, she was sure he had a girl on the side.

"Where she thought I was fooling around during the day, I don't know," said Bob. "Maybe back in the lube room or something."

Returning to Sacramento got him out of the snow, but it didn't save his marriage. The war of words escalated into fists and slaps, and by the spring of 1970, the marriage was over.

"The day we split up for the last time, I went to work that morning," said Bob. "A friend of hers came by and gave me a note from Theresa. It said, *Your car is parked around the corner on the street with your belongings in it. Do not come back to the house.*

"She'd packed up my clothes, put them in the backseat of the Chevy, and left it parked down the street from where I was working. Left it with the key under the mat. That was the final straw."

They separated in May and the divorce became final on July 3, 1970. Theresa waived alimony and the court ordered Bob to pay $150 a month in child support. Theresa got the Chrysler and the kids. Bob got the Chevy and his mechanic's tools. Ironically, the judge who signed the interlocutory decree was none other than Charles W. Johnson, the Sacramento superior-court judge who had presided over Theresa's murder trial just six years earlier.

"People say I was a lot of things when I was younger," said Knorr. "I was an asshole most of the time. But, boy, I don't think I ever deserved her."

Knorr had always found a roost in neighborhood bars, long before he ever left Theresa, but this accelerated after they were formally separated and he no longer had a real home. One bar he frequented was called the Bluebird on Dry Creek Road in Rio Linda. There, he met Georgia Desouza, a petite, effervescent brunette with a malleable personality who seemed to be the polar opposite of his ex-wife. Instead of being bitterly cynical, Georgia seemed naive. She giggled and had a sense of humor. She was the same age as Theresa, but she seemed years younger. She also deferred to Bob in all decisions. She let him be in control instead of trying to direct his every move. And Bob liked that.

But he was not yet rid of Theresa. Despite the divorce, she still regarded him as her property and was not ready to surrender him to another woman— especially a Hispanic woman who had graduated from North Highlands High the same year she herself would have graduated had she remained in school. Theresa's imagined jealousies of Bob's affairs were now glaringly real—once the divorce was over—and she couldn't stand it. She began stalking them.

"At first we thought it was our imagination," said Georgia. "But we'd see her in the rearview mirror, and she'd make the same turns that we made. We'd flip a U-turn, and then she'd make a U-turn. We started taking the back roads, just to try to lose her."

The harassment didn't stop there. If she could, Theresa made a scene whenever she saw them out in public together. And she used the telephone like a weapon against her rival.

"She called my parents' house and Bob's folks and his aunt and uncle," Georgia recalled. "She called me a whore, a slut, a dirty Mexican. She said I paraded around in a negligee and I wasn't fit for her husband. And when she'd get Bob on the phone, it was 'oh honey' this and 'oh honey' that."

The children missed Bob as much as she did, Theresa pleaded. If only he would dump the wetback and return, they could be a family again. Bob resisted. He talked to Georgia about how he wanted to see his children, especially his sons, but he refused to go through with visits for fear of Theresa's harangues.

"When I first met him, Bob seemed like he was in the same state of absolute control that his kids were," remembered Georgia. "She worked on him, and if I hadn't shown up on the scene, I think he would have gone back to her."

Even when the last of his children by Theresa was born, Bob refused to go to the hospital. Being with Georgia had made him stronger, but he remained afraid of falling under Theresa's control once more. Besides, he had convinced himself that the infant had been conceived by someone else during one of Theresa's affairs. She was not his daughter, he said.

Theresa Marie Knorr, the last of Theresa Jimmie Francine Cross Sanders Knorr's six children, was born on August 5, 1970, at 10:25 P.M. at Sutter Memorial Hospital in south Sacramento.

Theresa Marie was not only her mother's namesake. Little Terry looked more like her mother than either of her two sisters. Whereas Suesan was slender and fair like her father, and Sheila had the sharp features and swarthy complexion of Clifford Sanders, Terry seemed both delicate and resilient at the same time. From the beginning, she was just as strong-willed as her mother, too. Her hair was light, and her eyes were a ghostly electric blue—so blue, in fact, that they were a perfect match for Bob Knorr's own blue eyes. For years, Bob continued to question her paternity. But to any objective outsider, there was no question.

The same day Terry was born, Bob asked Georgia to marry him. For the next several months he resolved to try to see his children. He suffered rebuff after rebuff whenever he made an appointment to pick them up. They weren't ready. They were sick. Theresa couldn't let one or two of them go without all of them going. And she wouldn't let them go at all if *that Mexican woman* was with him.

Georgia hardened herself to Theresa's vicious verbal attacks and accompanied Bob. Theresa let them in for brief visits, but only under her strict conditions.

"I wanted to show her that I accepted all six kids and that I wanted to get to know her and the kids better," said Georgia.

What she saw was the same rigidity and spiteful abuse that Bob's aunt and uncle had witnessed years earlier.

"She'd be brushing Susie's hair, and Susie would be on her knees watching TV," said Georgia. "And if she moved, her mother would hit her on the side of the head with the brush. She'd yell, 'I told you not to move!' so that any of the gentleness of brushing her hair was gone."

Suesan learned about sex early. Her mother made certain all of her children knew what the male penis and female vagina were for. Georgia overheard Theresa lecturing Bob once about Suesan's precocious sexuality: how, at the age of four, she provocatively took her clothes off in front of her brothers.

"She's just a little girl," said Bob. "All little kids do things like that."

Theresa disagreed. It didn't seem to matter that Theresa herself taught promiscuity by example. Suesan's behavior was sick, and she told her ex-husband that she intended to teach the child to hate men. Georgia wasn't sure why Theresa hated men so much, but she was certain that her anger against all men—not just Bob—went back a lot further than their marriage. She tried to tell Bob as much when he needed consolation for his failed marriage. Whatever anger Theresa harbored came from someplace deep inside that had little to do with the four years she spent as Bob Knorr's wife.

Despite Theresa's continued harassment, Bob married Georgia four months after Terry's birth. On December 13, 1970, they made the obligatory matrimonial trek to Reno and moved in with Georgia's parents until they could earn enough between them to get a place of their own.

Georgia's first priority was convincing her new husband that not all women were like Theresa. "When we were first married, there was no trust," she said. "If I hugged a friend, he'd get jealous. I said, 'Look, I'm *not* your ex-wife! These are just good friends.'

"I had to exercise a lot of patience to convince him that I was a different person. For a long time after we were first married, he would be home right after work—not out of love so much as out of fear of losing me."

Bob persisted in trying to see his children. One day Theresa called and told him to come pick up his youngest son. "She said she had no control over little Robert," Georgia remembered.

Theresa told them Robert's pediatrician had pronounced him "mentally slow." For that reason, she said, she kept him confined to a playpen. Though he was already over two years old, Robert could neither walk nor talk. He had most of his teeth, but gagged on anything but baby food. "He couldn't eat regular food. He almost choked on it. Even when I strained spaghetti for him, he couldn't eat it," said Georgia.

According to Theresa, Robert wouldn't sleep and couldn't be disciplined.

"We said we would take him for two weeks," said Georgia. "Theresa had brought him over in his playpen, but he hated that playpen. He'd just start rocking in it and bang his head on the floor, lean against the side, beating his head against it. I'd try to put him to bed in the playpen at night and he would wail. I had to rock him to sleep."

After just a few days the incorrigible baby became a model member of the household.

"While Bob and I were at work, my mom would work with little Robert. She would try to walk him around, rub his legs. His muscles weren't used to walking, so we had to rub his legs down. We'd do the same when we got home from work: walk him around the house at night with his shoes on.

"We bought him junior baby food, and my mom would lash him onto a chair with a dish towel and sit him up straight so that he could learn to eat. My mom got him to chew on crackers. He didn't know what suckers or candy were."

At the end of two weeks Bob and Georgia asked Theresa if they could keep Robert.

"Absolutely not. She wanted him home right away," said Georgia.

Bob was proud of the progress his son had made and wanted to show him off to his mother. He'd stopped rocking in his playpen and banging his head. He wasn't talking yet, but had begun to experiment with sounds to show when he wanted something. He was walking and eating solid food.

Georgia sat silently in the front room as Bob tried to demonstrate Robert's progress. He gripped the toddler's hands and stood him up in front of his mother, urging him to take his first steps for her.

"It was the most awful thing," said Georgia. "This two-year-old boy looked straight at his mom, picked up his little feet, and refused to put them down on the floor. He got down on his hands and knees and crawled away."

Throughout this time Theresa didn't let child rearing and pitched battles with her ex-husband and his new wife interfere with her social life. When she wasn't out at the bars, Theresa and her next-door neighbor, Cherise Kelly, often sat up until all hours drinking and schmoozing about their favorite mutual interest: the occult. As often as possible, however, Theresa persuaded Cherise to assist James Cross and Howard in watching the other children while she went out trolling for a new husband.

Once, she told Bob, she had been to a bar where she had been drugged and raped outside in the parking lot by four or five different men. She even accused Bob of hiring the rapists.

"I never did believe she was raped," said Bob. "She'd say things to make herself look big. She had to be the center of everything."

For a short time she got a job tending bar at a topless lounge called Little Joe Ortega's, according to Bob. She moved from there to other bars, pouring drinks or waiting tables. It was during one of these stints at a blue-collar bar on Sacramento's industrial west side that Bob believes Theresa met Ron Pulliam, a twenty-eight-year-old railroad worker. Pulliam had been married before and had been raised near booze because his mother owned a bar, but he still met with Bob's approval the very first time he met him.

"I always thought he was a pretty straightaway guy," said Knorr.

Three months after Bob married Georgia, Theresa married Ron Pulliam.

On March 27, 1971, just two weeks after Theresa's twenty-fifth birthday, they drove to Reno and exchanged vows at the twenty-four-hour-a-day Starlite Wedding Chapel, located directly across the street from the Washoe County Courthouse, where a divorce can be had for as little time and trouble as a wedding license.

VI

From the beginning, Ron Pulliam took an active interest in Theresa's children. The gruff, brooding railway worker she'd met in a bar turned out to be an ideal father figure. He treated the three boys and three girls, ranging in age from six months to eight years, as if they were his own. They went for family rides in the car. He bought them toys and candy and played catch with the boys. The usual problems a stepparent has with his spouse's children appeared to be minimal.

According to Georgia Knorr, Pulliam even built a special outdoor playpen for Robert so that the toddler could get some fresh air and exercise. Pulliam had taken up where Bob and Georgia left off and worked with Robert daily, teaching him to walk and talk. In Ron Pulliam, Theresa had found what she did not have in either of her first two husbands: a mature, steady man with a good job and a solid future. He only earned $718.48 a month, but it was a regular income and he invested almost all of it in his new family. Finally, it seemed, Theresa had found someone who could care for both her and her children.

"One of my first childhood recollections was of Ronald K. Pulliam," recalled Terry Marie Knorr. "I thought of him as my dad. He was the only man I ever called Dad when I was a little kid. In fact, he was the only man I ever remember being there with me at all when I was little, besides my brother Howard."

More than twenty years later Terry Knorr still remembers the tall, muscular railroad man with the mustache and the strong arms and shoulders as the only man in her mother's life whom Terry could ever love or respect. "He used to throw me around," she remembered. "I was his kid, and he treated me like his kid. He'd say, 'How's Daddy's little girl?' and he'd pick me up and throw me up in the air when he'd get home from work. I remember going places with him in his big shiny red convertible."

Terry's older brother Bill remembers Pulliam taking the family on camping trips to the Sierra foothills and to the beach. With Pulliam, it looked like Terry's mother had a real shot at settling down. He recognized right away that his new family needed a permanent home and acceded to Theresa's demands that they go looking for a house to buy soon after they were married.

It was Pulliam, Georgia is convinced, who finally curbed Theresa's desire for vengeance against her ex-husband and pushed her into granting Bob and his new wife more time with the children, including a full-fledged weekend visit. In the spring of 1971, Bob got his first real unsupervised time with his children since the divorce.

"When we first moved out of my folks' house and into our own home, we got to take Howard, Sheila, Susie, and William for a weekend visit," said Georgia. "We were so broke that we had to borrow thirty-two dollars so that we could take them to see *Pinocchio* and drive out to Bob's dad's place in Placerville.

"I got to know Howard and Susie a little, but on the way home the first time I turned around in the car and said hello to all of the kids, William crossed his arms and stuck out his jaw and said, 'My mom says I don't have to talk to you and I don't have to be nice to you.'

"Bob turned around from the wheel and pointed at me and said to William, 'You talk to her or I'll bust your little bottom. And if your mother doesn't like it, I'll bust her bottom, too.' It broke the silence, and we chattered all the rest of the way to our house."

A single weekend wasn't long enough to do any kind of in-depth personality analysis, but Georgia did see marked differences in the four older children. William was stubborn but sensitive, putting on a comical tough-guy facade that melted as the day progressed and he grew tired of poking out his lower lip. Suesan was a typical little girl, full of giggles and curiosity. Once she felt secure, she spouted nonstop questions and requests.

"Howard was Mommy's boy," said Georgia. When the visits were over, Howard was the one who went straight to Theresa with a full report on everything that his brothers and sisters had done while out from under the eagle eye of their mother.

"Sheila seemed smart, but mysteriously silent," said Georgia. "She was a normal enough little girl, but she barely spoke."

Once they got home, things seemed to settle down.

"I pampered the girls, and Bob would make the boys feel comfortable," said Georgia. "I caught the girls once, flouncing a little in front of the mirror with ribbons in their hair and I teased them about it."

When it was time for bed, Bob and Georgia put the children down with blankets and pillows in the front room and told them they were "camping out." Bob collected his good-night kisses from each child and was about to sternly instruct them to do the same for Georgia when she took him aside and whispered that she thought that forcing herself on them so quickly might not be such a good idea. To her surprise, all four of them voluntarily lined up to hug and kiss their new stepmother good night anyway.

"Next morning, Howard told me the breakfast was

good, and in fact, they all acted like it was the kind of breakfast they'd never had before," said Georgia.

After a short trip to Bob's father's home in Placerville, the weekend was over and Bob told the children it was time for them to return home.

"There was a dead silence," said Georgia. "It was like they were scared to go home."

As they pulled up at the Pulliams' place Ron had to come out and coax the kids out of the car. Little Robert was on the front porch, and when he saw Bob get out of the car, he ran from the house wearing his new shoes, shouting "Daddy! Daddy!" according to Georgia. Inside, Terry watched from her playpen as her brothers and sisters shuffled through the front door and sat silently on the couch. As each of them kissed and hugged their stepmother good-bye, Georgia caught a glimpse of Theresa standing in a doorway, her arms crossed and a scowl as deep as Death Valley drawn across her face.

The next day, Theresa called Bob at work. " 'I don't want my kids kissing that bitch,' she told him," Georgia remembered. " 'I don't want you taking them to your scummy father's house either.' "

There were a few more attempts to visit with the children, but they dwindled quickly.

"After that weekend visit, the kids weren't the same," said Georgia. "She tormented us with them. Theresa asked questions when they came back from visits. She wanted to know what we did. I think the kids came home happy, she noticed that, and she was jealous."

From Georgia's point of view, the children were still not getting what they needed, even with Pulliam acting as a father. When Theresa packed for the children's visits, their clothes were "worse than welfare clothes." "I don't know if she was trying to show Bob that he wasn't supporting them enough or what. At the time he was paying her seventy-five dollars a month," she said.

It was only half the support he had been ordered to pay by the court, but it was all that he said he could afford. After leaving Theresa, Bob had qualified for a Cal Vet education loan and enrolled in a yearlong retraining program at the Sacramento Skill Center, where he learned how to rebuild engines and transmissions. In the meantime he and Georgia continued working in order to earn enough to buy a place of their own.

The last straw for Georgia came when Theresa sent bill collectors to Georgia's employer. It seemed that Bob still hadn't paid for his half of Theresa's wedding rings, purchased several years earlier. "She wanted *me* to pay Bob's half of the bill for *her* rings!" said Georgia, who remained aghast at the first Mrs. Knorr's unmitigated gall for years afterward.

In addition, Theresa continued to use the children to torment Bob. She taught them to fear their father, told them that he had developed a drug habit, and that he was prone to violence ... stories that stayed with the children, even after they grew to adults and met with the man they had known only as an ogre who had abandoned them.

"He had a drug problem," said William, recalling his earliest memories of his father. "And when he would get loaded up, he was abusive. . . .

"When I was right around five years old I think was the last time I recall him being anywhere near around. He abused Howard quite a bit. He was real resentful of the fact that my mom had kids that weren't his. He threw me across the bed, into a dresser at one point when I was just a couple years old. Frankly, I don't remember it. Howard told me about it."

Terry Knorr did not remember physical abuse, but she did remember cruel indifference.

"I never had a lot of respect for my father 'cause I watched my father torment my mother for years," she said. "I think he just totally destroyed her when he left her with six kids."

Bob recalls things differently. He admits to having had a drug problem, and he was occasionally stern when his children misbehaved, but he was never abusive. The abuse stories sprang from Theresa's fertile imagination and became a part of the family lore, drilled into her children's memories like a cruel Rosary.

Though she had lost Bob to another woman, Theresa still held the children out as lures to get her ex-husband to do as she wanted: if he didn't pay his child support, pay for her wedding rings, get rid of Georgia, and so on, he wouldn't get to see or even speak with his children. After months of such harassment Bob finally decided to give up.

"He said he had to make a choice so that we wouldn't be hounded. So he didn't bother to call them anymore," said Georgia, fighting back tears. "She had the control. We couldn't afford to go to court and fight. We couldn't afford a lawyer. There was nothing we could do.

"We called Pulliam and told him we weren't going to try to see the kids anymore because it was tearing us apart."

In the meantime Theresa stepped up the pressure on her new husband to buy a house. On August 26, 1971, Ron and Theresa bought a five-room bungalow at 3825 William Way, near Del Paso Country Club in the suburbs east of Sacramento. They paid $18,000 and their monthly mortgage payments were $172. By now, Theresa had her father in a rest home, so it was just she, Pulliam, and the children living together.

All seemed well for a time. Bob and Georgia started their own family with the birth of a daughter, Dodie, in August of 1972. Bob's bitterness about losing his family softened when he was able to start another. He let his child-support payments slide. But Theresa's harassment and hang-up calls faded and any guilty conscience he had about his four children, living under her roof and her control, faded along with them.

Then, one day in the spring of 1973, more than a year and half later, Ron Pulliam came to see Bob and Georgia. He was by himself. He looked haggard, angry, distraught.

"Pulliam pulled up in a car, came to the door, and said he couldn't find Theresa," said Georgia.

The story he told Bob and Georgia didn't surprise Bob all that much. He'd lived through it himself. It seemed that Theresa had a drinking problem and a boyfriend—maybe more than one.

At first, Ron explained, the Pulliams had seemed to be happy enough. They were a family in the traditional sense, with Ron bringing home the bacon and Theresa keeping house, staying with the kids. It was after they bought the place on William Way that things began to get dicey. Theresa would go off to the store or out visiting a friend and be gone for hours. Sometimes she didn't return until long after midnight.

Then it got worse. She would be gone all night long and the kids either became the responsibility of Ron or, while he was at work, Howard. The older children were missing school, and Pulliam himself had to call in sick a lot to work because Theresa wasn't home half the time to watch the little ones. Then, one day, she disappeared altogether.

"He had almost lost his job, trying to find her and staying home taking care of the kids," said Georgia. "He asked Bob if he could borrow some money to help feed the kids."

Pulliam was a tolerant man, but he was not a doormat. He hadn't simply stood by and let Theresa get away with her profligate ways. By the time he showed up at the Knorrs' doorstep with his sorry tale, it had been nearly a year since he had filed for divorce. On March 7, 1972, twenty days short of their first anniversary, the Pulliams had legally separated. A week later, on March 15, Pulliam formally filed for dissolution of the marriage.

Perhaps he believed that the sobering threat of divorce might bring Theresa back into line, in much the same way that Theresa's divorce suit against Bob in 1969, before they traveled to Spokane, temporarily got them back together. Going to court could be a kind of shock treatment that would make her snap out of her impulsive, self-indulgent ways.

But any good that going to court might have done was soon lost. Theresa continued to use the William Way house as little more than a way station between her increasingly frequent absences. The pattern was familiar to Bob: she'd leave, come home with booze on her breath, fight with Pulliam, make up—often in bed—and settle down for a few days before taking off again.

Pulliam was not so fooled that Theresa was able to convince him through pleas or kisses to drop his divorce suit. His suit continued to wind its way through the court system, and on September 27, 1972, the Pulliams were officially no longer husband and wife. Ironically again, it was Judge Charles W. Johnson who presided over the end of Theresa's marriage. Judge Johnson granted the interlocutory decree based on irreconcilable differences and gave Pulliam the house on William Way, plus the furniture. All Theresa got in the divorce was their 1967 Ford Country Sedan—the one she was always using to run off to "visit a friend."

Yet she and the children continued to live with Pulliam. Bob and Georgia speculated that Pulliam permitted this chiefly because he had grown so attached to her children. Terry Knorr has another theory.

"I think Ron really did love my mom, but she didn't love him," she said. "I don't think she's capable of it."

Nevertheless, the divorcees continued to live as man and wife.

Indeed, just before Christmas of 1972, more than three months after the divorce was final, Theresa and Ron went to a Sacramento department store and bought a dishwasher, refrigerator, and stove, signing two separate credit agreements on two separate occasions as Mr. and Mrs. Ron Pulliam, husband and wife. However rocky their marriage had been and however final the divorce decree, Pulliam was still willing to call Theresa his wife and was still keeping house with her at the start of 1973.

But even Pulliam's remarkable patience was pushed over the edge when Theresa flatly admitted one day that she had found a younger man and planned to live with him.

Terry remembers his name as Ron Bullington—a serviceman from New Mexico stationed at nearby Mather Air Force Base in Sacramento. She remembered that her mother had met Bullington the same way she'd met most of the men in her life: in a bar. Unlike Pulliam, Bullington seemed still to wallow in adolescent self-absorption.

When Bob heard about him, he just laughed. "She was going to make him a businessman," he said. "Take him down, get his fingernails manicured, get him well-groomed, haircuts, and dress him right and everything. I said, 'What's the matter? Can't he dress himself?' I guess he was quite a bit younger than her."

All Pulliam wanted now was to be rid of her. Like Bob, he was even willing to sacrifice the bonds he had made with the children in order to shed himself of Theresa's lies and addictions. But Theresa wanted him to pay a higher price than the '67 Ford sedan.

On February 22, 1973, Ron went back to court and signed a stipulation that he would be responsible for $2,350 in community debts that he and Theresa had chalked up during their short marriage. He would pay off Sears, Household Finance, and all the rest of it. Theresa was to be responsible only for two hundred dollars in charges made to Weinstock's, a department store where she bought her clothes. She had recently become an Amway distributor and figured on supplementing her meager income from her children's support checks that way.

But Pulliam was not yet finished paying for his bad

judgment in marrying Theresa. After years of scrimping and saving, her sister, Rosemary, had recently moved her family out of the trailer in Rio Linda and into a brand-new town house in a wooded development in the suburb of Citrus Heights. Theresa wanted her own piece of real estate, too, and threatened to contest the court decision to grant him the house on William Way if he didn't help her get her own place. Her approach was alternately to bat her eyelashes and threaten to return to court.

Pulliam reluctantly agreed to help Theresa buy her own house in the suburb of Orangevale, just a few miles east of Rosemary's new house. On March 5, 1973, Theresa signed a quitclaim deed, granting her share of the William Way property to Pulliam. A month later escrow closed on a four-bedroom, two-bath house at 5539 Bellingham Way, purchased solely in Theresa's name for a price of $21,000.

"That's how she got that house," said Terry. "My mother married for the money."

But it wasn't over yet. Theresa had a new boyfriend and a big new house in a new neighborhood, but she had almost no furniture. On April 20, 1973, while Ron was at work, she had her boyfriend back a truck into Pulliam's driveway and begin removing everything he could load, from appliances like the washer, dryer, and refrigerator down to the ashtrays, flashlights, extension cords, pots, pans, and her toothbrush.

Four days later Ron drove to the house on Bellingham Way and confronted her. From the front door, he saw his TV set and the refrigerator they'd recently bought together. He left in a huff and reported the theft to both the sheriff's office and the Sacramento district attorney. It didn't matter that he had court documents showing that he was awarded the house *and* the furniture in the divorce. It didn't matter that he had helped her buy the new house on Bellingham Way or that he had accepted the burden of almost all of their community debts. Both the sheriff and the DA refused to do anything. It wasn't theft, they said. It was a civil matter.

Ron was furious. He filed a civil contempt charge with the same court that had granted him his divorce seven months earlier. Once again, Judge Charles W. Johnson heard the case.

In her defense, Theresa flatly stated that she and Pulliam had been living together in the same home as husband and wife for over a year since Pulliam first filed for divorce. They had even filed a joint income-tax return for 1972. In fact, Theresa claimed, Pulliam never even *told* her he had filed for divorce until after the interlocutory decree was final.

When they finally did decide to split up once and for all, she said, they had agreed how the furniture and other household items were to be divided. She was to get certain items, including all the furniture that she had taken, and he was to get the rest. It was only after Pulliam discovered that Theresa had a boyfriend that he decided to charge her with contempt, Theresa told the judge.

She had stolen nothing, she said. In fact, some of the items he accused her of stealing from him—an antique telephone, a light fixture, plywood, and a roll of linoleum—*he* had actually stolen from his employer, Western Pacific Railroad, Theresa told the judge.

Other items, such as silverware and mixing bowls, had belonged to her mother. The crystal ashtray that Pulliam had listed in his inventory of stolen goods was actually a gift from Theresa's employer, Amway.

Before the hearing was complete, Theresa brought out the same trump card that had worked for her in the Clifford Sanders murder trial: spousal violence.

Pulliam had listed a missing .22 pistol among the items that Theresa and her boyfriend had loaded into his truck. Theresa's explanation to Judge Johnson was that she felt she had to remove the pistol "to a place of safekeeping."

When husband threatened to kill wife, she took gun to home of a friend, she wrote in her sworn declaration.

Judge Johnson was once more persuaded by the tearful pleadings and the lousy luck of the poor, pretty Rio Linda girl he'd seen acquitted in his courtroom nearly nine years earlier. She did look considerably older, but her life seemed just as out of control as it had been so many years earlier, when she wept on the witness stand about the way Clifford Sanders had threatened to kill her. On May 15, 1973, Judge Johnson found Theresa not guilty of contempt. Furthermore, she got to keep all that she'd taken from Pulliam's house.

Pulliam's disgust with the court system was now as deep as his disgust for the sheriff's department or the district attorney. Even with her track record, a weepy Theresa Cross Sanders Knorr Pulliam stood a better chance of hoodwinking the justice system than a sensible man with a clean record who had treated his wife and stepchildren with kindness and done all the right things. She now had both his car and his furniture, as well as her own house. To make absolutely sure she could not steal anything further from him, Pulliam filed a homestead document with the Sacramento County Recorder's Office on June 13, 1973, officially noting that he was divorced and that the house on William Way belonged solely to him. When he sold the house a year later, he alone got the equity.

Time passed. Ron Bullington was discharged from the service and, like all the other men in her life, eventually left Theresa, apparently returning home to New Mexico. "Bullington was a mama's boy," recalled Robert. "His mom basically ran his life, and when she told him to stop seeing my mother, he did."

Her mother found other boyfriends, but none who ever stayed with her for very long. She took to demanding that they take her to a hotel rather than drive back to her home to spend the night. She did not want her amorous activities to be witnessed by her children, she explained.

Some of Theresa's boyfriends left positive memories with the children. One was a white-haired Lithuanian contractor who installed a shower in one of the bathrooms on Bellingham Way. Another was an Italian named Al who worked in a restaurant and came by the house when Theresa was gone one evening, offering to cook dinner for the kids. The odor of olive oil and artichokes filled the house when Theresa came home, but far from being pleased, she slapped the children around for letting Al in. She never let anyone in her house after her breakups with Pulliam and Bullington. Not neighbors. Not lovers. Not family.

She and Rosemary never visited each other. Though they lived only a few miles apart, Rosemary's two boys rarely saw their cousins. In fact, Theresa and her children saw less and less of any of her old friends from Rio Linda. Her life revolved increasingly around the house on Bellingham Way, which she seldom left except to go to work or visit the bars. Her children had become her chief companions as well as her primary possessions.

In the fall of 1972, as her marriage to Pulliam reached the final stages of disintegration, Theresa had begun paying attention to the newspaper headlines in a way she hadn't since the summer of 1963, when she was awaiting trial for Clifford's murder. This time the murder trial she followed was someone else's: her half brother Bill's.

"My mother always talked about her brother Bill," said Terry. "William Hart Tapp, who is a convict. That generation. They were all a bunch of lunatics running around without shrinks."

On October 8, 1972, a pair of Northern California newlyweds, Jay and Viola Taresh, were found dead on the living-room floor of their farmhouse near the town of Orland, about a hundred miles north of Sacramento.

Their throats had been slashed so savagely that the knife left inch-deep cuts in the wooden floor. In addition, Jay Taresh had been held to the floor while he was shot three times with a .32-caliber gun: once in the chest, once through the top of the head, and once between the eyes. The apparent motive had been robbery: the place looked as though it was being ransacked when the unlucky Tareshes arrived home from visiting friends and happened through their front door at the wrong moment.

Following a weeklong investigation, authorities arrested William and Robert Tidwell, two rowdy brothers in their early twenties with long records of violent behavior and jail time. In fact, both Tidwells had been convicted of murder in 1967, but their convictions were overturned by the California Supreme Court in 1971. They were granted a new trial and acquitted.

A few days after the Tidwells were charged with the Taresh murders, a third suspect was arrested. He was older and had spent much of his adult life in Folsom State Prison, and it was he who police first believed to have been the slasher. A forty-four-year-old Chico auto mechanic who had once worked in a slaughterhouse, the suspect had a twenty-year history of felonies ranging from assault and burglary to armed robbery.

His name was William Hart Tapp.

It wasn't the first time Theresa's brother, Bill, had turned up in the newspapers. Back in the summer of 1967, when Theresa was trying to come up with a name for her first son with Bob Knorr, her notorious half brother popped up in the headlines as a suspect in a bizarre kidnapping/robbery case near Oroville. He may never have known it, but brother Bill became the inspiration for naming her son William Robert Knorr.

According to newspaper accounts from the 1967 case, a thirty-three-year-old waitress at an Oroville tavern told sheriff's deputies that a drunken Tapp had put a knife to her back while she was getting cigarettes for a customer. He ordered her to his car, told her to give him her money, and then made her strip while he held his knife to her throat.

He drove off with her in the car, holding her head down on the seat so that she couldn't see where he was taking her. On the way he tried to get her to take some pills and get as loaded as he was, but she refused. When Tapp arrived at his house in the rural outskirts of Oroville, he forced the naked waitress out of the car and into the living room. When he went to the kitchen for a cigarette, she streaked out the front door.

"I awoke to someone outside screaming, 'He's gonna kill me!' " recalled Leona Kohnke, who lived with her husband next to Tapp's place. "All of a sudden this woman was scratching outside our bedroom window. We went out to the front porch and Tapp was trying to drag her away. And she was stark naked."

Leona and Richard Kohnke had witnessed Tapp's brutality before. They were sure he was a wife beater, a fact confirmed just a few weeks before the kidnapping incident. According to newspaper accounts, Tapp had been charged with breaking his wife's jaw with a sockful of buckshot, but the jury deadlocked ten to two for conviction and he did not go to jail. His wife had finally had enough, however. She took their sons and left.

But Tapp didn't reserve his brutality for humans. For a time after he had gotten out of Folsom Prison and moved in next door to the Kohnkes, he worked for the local humane society. On occasion he'd bring animals home, tie them up, and tease them. Once, the Kohnkes watched in horror as he hamstrung a cat and left it on the front lawn to die.

They were afraid to intervene. Tapp owned a German shepherd that he taught to kill chickens and nip at his neighbors' horses. It was the dog, in fact, that the Kohnkes thought was causing the ruckus on their front porch when they switched on the light that night and saw their drunken neighbor trying to drag off a nude waitress by the hair, as if he were a caveman and she were his naked prey. Richard Kohnke got his rifle and told Tapp to turn her loose.

"He just let go and she ran in our house. She ran all the way through the living room and into the kitchen," recalled Mrs. Kohnke. "She sat down at the kitchen table, shivering. Her feet were all bloody from running over the gravel road to get away from Tapp. He had cut her with the knife, too, it looked like. She was bleeding all over.

"The neighbors all heard the screaming and came over. We called the sheriff. But Tapp got in his car and drove off with his lights out, down the road."

He hid out for three days but, once he sobered up, turned himself in to sheriff's deputies.

Following the kidnapping incident, Tapp went back to jail for a while, but was out on parole in the fall of 1972, when the Tidwells asked him if he'd like to join them in their expedition to the Tareshes' farm. Again, he blamed his behavior on booze and pills. When he was sober, he insisted, he was a different person.

"He was a killer, but he was very personable," said Robert Quall, the prosecutor who put both Tapp and the Tidwell brothers behind bars following a two-month trial in 1973.

Tapp pleaded guilty and turned against the Tidwells on the witness stand, testifying that he held the Tareshes down while the Tidwells slashed and shot them. Tapp remained a charmer, even when it came to making a deal with the prosecution. All he demanded of Quall and the district attorney's office was that his jailers take him out for a steak dinner at the Holiday Inn the night before he was to take the witness stand.

Though he made no deals with the prosecution, Tapp did get one break for confessing. Instead of the death penalty, the judge sentenced him to life imprisonment. In San Quentin, Tapp found religion and became Robert Quall's pen pal. He seemed to regard the man who had put him away for life as·a kind of older brother or, at the very least, a respected friend.

"Tapp wrote me every week," said Quall, who went on to become a municipal-court judge. "He was in the cell next to Charles Manson. He sent me an autographed picture of himself once, along with a poem by Keats that had been signed by Charlie Manson himself. He made purses for my daughters and one for my wife, and he made a mirror for me that said BEHOLD, THE GREATEST JUDGE IN THE WORLD.

"He was really a very charming fellow. He just happened to be a cold-blooded murderer."

VII

A large eucalyptus tree grows on the front lawn of the white stucco house where Theresa and her children lived at the corner of Sutton Place and Bellingham Way. There are dark green shutters and trim all the way around, and a chain-link fence rims the backyard so children can safely play. Schools are all within walking distance, and Pecan Park, with its playground and trees and a creek bubbling through its middle, is a half-dozen blocks away.

Theresa's kids used to catch crawdads down at the creek, just like all the other youngsters in the neighborhood. They loitered after school at an open field across the road from the park, where they discovered wild sauerkraut and fig trees and raspberries. In the mid-1970s, Orangevale was a good place to raise a family.

The neighbors were chiefly hardworking young middle-class families, just like Mrs. Theresa Pulliam's family appeared to be. On Saturday mornings, the sounds of power lawn mowers filled the air. On Saturday evenings, the smell of barbecue wafted over the neighborhood. Sunday mornings, families went to worship, including Theresa and her children, who attended services and Sunday school at the Hazel Avenue Baptist Church.

The rest of the week, children went to school while parents went to work—Theresa among them. For a time she had a line job at a canning plant and, later on, learned to drive a forklift. None of her early jobs could be called a "career." In the days before her children became old enough to escape her control, Theresa was a mother first and a member of the workforce second. If she had been able to keep a man around, she would have been a full-time mother.

"The earliest thought I have of my mother was when she was still pretty," remembered Terry, who was just three years old when the family moved to Bellingham Way.

"She'd put on weight, yeah, but she was still pretty slender, and I remember she used to take me and my brother Robert to Dairy Queen all the time. And she'd buy us lunch. She would make us promise not to tell my older brothers and sisters, because the other kids didn't get to go. They were all in school."

Half a mile to the west of their new neighborhood was a shopping center with a McDonald's restaurant, a Pizza Hut, a pharmacy, a Raley's supermarket, and a half-dozen other stores. To the east, at another nearby intersection, was a Hostess bakery shop where goods past their "sell before" dates went for half price. The neighborhood Capri Market and a martial-arts school where Bill Knorr learned the rudiments of karate, were across the street. Next to Capri was Mr. B's barbershop, where Theresa Pulliam's boys all got their hair cut, and down the block was a place called McHenry's, where her girls shopped for clothes.

But family shopping trips weren't simply happy outings straight out of *Ozzie & Harriet*. They were instructive as well. By watching their mother, Theresa's children learned how they were to behave. "My mom used to write a bad check and cash it at the Capri Market once a month. And she knew it was going to be bad, too," Terry recalled.

She also used a post office box so that bill collectors would have difficulty finding where she lived. Whenever the increasingly reclusive Mrs. Theresa Pulliam needed her PO box checked, or had any other errands that needed running, she would usually send one of her children to do it.

"We were always ducking people serving papers on us from court," recalled Robert. "But I can remember a sheriff's deputy only showing up at the front door once."

In that instance, Theresa had successfully ignored bills from a furniture company for over a year. She bought sofas, chairs, a coffee table, and a pair of china hutches for the living room on credit, and made no payments. When she peeked through the front curtains one day and saw a patrol car pull up front, Theresa dispatched Robert outside to play, with specific instructions as to how he should answer if the deputy approached him and began asking questions.

"The cop asked me my name, and I told him 'Robert Sanders,' " said Robert, even though his last name was Knorr. "So he starts going over his sheet, asking me all of mom's aliases: Did Theresa Pulliam Cross Knorr live there? He had all of her various names except for Sanders.

"Then one of my friends, Gabriel, comes over to see what's going on and the cop points to me and asks Gabriel, 'Is this Robert Sanders?' Gabriel looks at me, I give him a little nod, and he says: 'Yeah. Sure, this is Robert Sanders.' "

With that, the deputy left, whatever papers he had to serve still tucked in his file folder. The furniture company never got its money, and Theresa never returned the furniture.

The walking route to the intersection of Hazel and Madison Avenues where the family did its grocery shopping was a well-worn trail over a sloping, grassy hill. When Terry and her older brothers and sisters were assigned to go to the market, they made sure their mother wasn't watching and then rolled themselves down to the sidewalk that ran along busy Madison Avenue like human logs. They'd wind up dizzy and dirty at the bottom, giggling all the way down.

But much of the time they didn't dare giggle or dawdle or roll down hills. If they came home too dirty, too late, or too giddy, there was often hell to pay. If they tracked mud in the house or smudged up the walls with grubby fingers or tore a hole in a pair of pants or a T-shirt, their mother could go off like a grenade. If they laughed or teased or clowned around, Theresa was likely to explode. If they did not get home on time, they got a hard and heavy dose of Theresa's "Board of Education," a board about an inch thick and four feet long with a grip at one end that she used to discipline the children.

"We couldn't go to the store and [fail to] be within five minutes of her time line [for returning home] without reaping the consequences," recalled Terry's older brother Bill. "I mean, we'd come home ten minutes late, regardless of the circumstances, and we were prepared to take a whipping."

But not always. If Theresa were in one of her self-absorbed moods, she might ignore her children's lack of punctuality altogether. "Zoned out" was how Terry put it. She and her brothers and sisters could come home late, slop around the house like creatures from the Black Lagoon, and Theresa might look straight through them.

Grenade or zombie. It all depended. Theresa was an enigma, even to her own children. Nobody knew exactly what might set her off, or when.

"My mom started out as a normal person when we were real small kids," said Bill. "Then something happened. I don't know. Maybe change-of-life chemical imbalance. She said something about having her pituitary removed when she was like thirteen due to a weight problem she had of some sort. I'm not exactly sure exactly what it was."

Theresa had her scars—both psychic and physical—but she never had her pituitary removed. Like other fantastic tales that would eventually weave themselves into the unbelievable saga of the Knorr family, the pituitary story became part of the rationale for their mother's utterly irrational behavior.

She told her children that she had a twin brother who died at birth because the obstetrician had been drunk, and that was how she wound up with the middle name of "Jimmie"; that she was descended from the biblical tribe of David and her father was the last male in a long line of Crosses that evil spirits were conspiring to wipe off the face of the earth; that her mother predicted terror and tribulation for Theresa and her grandchildren before she died; and that Swannie Gay's insistence that she make a bonfire of her musty old volumes about witchcraft and demonology out in the backyard of their Rio Linda home triggered the gloom and doom that Theresa now had to fight.

Whenever Theresa related one of her stories, it inevitably put her into an emotional tailspin that climaxed in a rage.

Terry, Bill, and their two brothers and two sisters spent much of their grammar-school years trying to second-guess the signs of an impending explosion.

Terry thought she could predict her mother's next tantrum most of the time, but she never became an expert. The cause-and-effect sequence was just too fuzzy. She remembered an unnerving incident at Pershing Elementary that illustrated just how fuzzy.

Mrs. Gallagher, her third-grade teacher, greeted Theresa at a parent-teacher conference with a smile, an arched eyebrow, and a cheery "I've heard a lot about you!" At that same moment Terry walked over to her mother, wrapped her arms around her middle, and said, "I love you, Mom!"

"And she just looked at me," said Terry. "And when I got home from school that day, she locked me in the deep freezer because she thought that I had said bad things about her."

Theresa and Howard sat on top of the appliance to make sure Terry didn't get out.

In a similar jaw-dropping episode, a friend of Terry's who lived a block away had outgrown some clothes. Though secondhand, the clothes were name brand and still nearly brand new, so the girl's mother sent them down to Terry's house to see if she could use them.

"And my mom thought that I was going around telling people that we didn't have enough, that we were so poor that she couldn't afford to buy me things," said Terry.

As punishment, Terry was stripped naked and ordered to stand with her face against a door. Her mother then looped a rope around her neck, tossed the loose end over the top of the door, and had one of her other children hold on to it so that Terry's naked body was stretched upward against the door. Then Theresa got a willow branch from the yard and proceeded to lay into her daughter's flesh.

"She beat me so bad," Terry recalled. "She hit me everywhere she could hit me."

Terry recalls a whipping so prolonged and intense that she very nearly passed out. She was six years old at the time.

"When we were kids, my mom beat the shit out of us a lot," she said. "If we hugged our mom too much, it was like: Who were we trying to convince? That we loved her, or she loved us? On the other hand, if we *didn't* hug and kiss and tell her we loved her, then we didn't love her, and we were evil children. We were demon seeds that had been given to her by Bob Knorr."

Theresa's explosions could be triggered by almost anything. And they grew worse and more frequent with each passing year. Though no one knew what set her off, all her children agreed that alcohol was a major contributing factor. Even while Terry was still an infant, Theresa would leave for hours at a time, often sitting at a neighbor's house drinking until dawn. It fell to Howard to keep order in the house.

"He basically raised me from a baby to a kid to an adolescent," said Terry. "My brother would end up having me sleep on his tummy, 'cause I couldn't go to sleep anywhere else. So he'd have to lay me flat on his stomach before I'd go to sleep."

Money was a constant worry to Theresa and her children. Her job at the canning plant didn't last. She got almost no financial help from her ex-husbands. Pulliam had washed his hands of her altogether, and Bob Knorr stopped paying direct child support, though the Veteran's Administration sent her forty-four dollars a month out of Knorr's disability allotment—eleven dollars for each of his four children.

"Economically, we couldn't keep up with the friends that we did have," said Terry's older brother Robert. "You know, guys would say, 'Hey, you want to go to Wet n' Wild?' Well, we couldn't do that. We didn't have the money for that."

Robert recalled one Christmas when his precocious older sister Suesan got fed up with being poor. "Suesan decided that she didn't get enough Christmas presents and went over to one of the neighbors and said, 'You know, we didn't have enough money for a Christmas tree or any presents.'

"The neighbors got together and called the Salvation Army out there and everyone chipped in," said Robert. "They showed up with a new tree and everything. At that time my mom was working, so we had a tree in the living room and presents, and here they're coming in with a turkey and everything else."

In one of the first dramatic contests of will between Theresa and her middle daughter, Suesan was severely punished for going to the neighbors. It was true that they could hardly afford much of a Christmas, but Theresa's rule about keeping family problems entirely within the family was ironclad.

Theresa hated the financial insecurity. After Bullington left her and she was once again utterly on her own, she sold Watkins Products for a while. She eventually settled into a new career, prompted in part by her visits to the Orangevale rest home where she had put her father. She saw firsthand the inner workings of a nursing home, where helpless seniors like Jim Cross were spoon-fed and diapered. Theresa was an expert at that kind of care. She'd changed children's diapers and spoon-fed them until they were old enough to learn how to feed themselves. Why not get paid for what she had been doing all her life?

In the mid-seventies, Theresa juggled her roles as mother, homeowner, daughter of an invalid father, and ex-wife on the rebound so that she could fit in one more: career woman. Working at various nursing homes and hospitals whenever she needed the money, she slowly moved up from being a convalescent orderly to a nurse's aide. In time, she told her children, she had hopes of going even further.

"She furthered her education by working in convalescent homes," said Terry. "She went from being a candy striper to a certified nurse's assistant."

"She did want to be a registered nurse," recalled Robert. "She took the classes at the convalescent homes, and I helped her study. I remember the little overlays of all the anatomical charts and the paperback pamphlets that they used to give her to read."

But when she wasn't working or studying, which was often, Theresa continued to drink. She relied on the Social Security checks she received for Howard and Sheila and her father, the pittance from the VA, and whatever other money she could beg or borrow from boyfriends in order to make ends meet, and to buy booze.

None of her children characterized her as an alcoholic, because she could go long periods without a drink. But drink she did, and when she had done so, it was not pleasant to watch. After a few drinks, her personality changed completely and her pent-up rage spilled over on anyone who got near her.

Yet, in her own way, Theresa tried to be a good mother to her six youngsters. "She was a good cook!" said Terry, straining to recall something truly maternal about her mother. Even that positive recollection had to be qualified, though. "*When* she cooked, she was a good cook," Terry added.

Much of the time any cooking that was done was done by the children for the children. Same with the laundry, the dishes, and the housekeeping. If the kids found enough change lying around the kitchen sinktop or in the recesses of the living-room couch, they'd walk down the hill to McDonald's for a feast. But usually that was too pricey a proposition for the Knorr and Sanders children.

For family entertainment, Theresa would pack the kids into the car and drive to a nearby cemetery. It stood next to a drive-in movie theater and the screen could easily be seen from the cemetery parking lot. While Terry and her brothers and sisters watched the movie screen without benefit of sound, Theresa sat in the driver's seat and drank.

"When we went to the movies, it was to see things like *The Exorcist* or *Beyond the Door*, or any of the *Omen* movies with Damien," said Robert.

Besides movies, there was the TV in the front room

to keep the family occupied and the children got their weekly dose of *Gomer Pyle, U.S.M.C.*, *LaVerne & Shirley*, and Saturday-morning cartoons. But Theresa's favorites were *Star Trek* and *Kung Fu.*

"She had a thing for David Carradine," said Robert.

Actually, Theresa had a thing for any man whom she thought might save her from her fate. She hit the bars frequently between boyfriends, trolling for new ones all the time. When the children were too small to leave at home alone with the TV set as sole baby-sitter, she took them along with her. She'd park, put Howard in charge, and spend hours at a time in a cocktail lounge, looking for a knight in shining armor—though a lonely soldier or a used-car salesman would do. But men were getting harder and harder to come by. Theresa didn't blame it on her thickening middle, her fading beauty, or her hair-trigger temper. She blamed it on her children.

"Most people would agree that six children was a lot to build into a relationship with a man who just wants to have a good time," said Robert. "Part of that was probably true, because you know how kids are. They're still growing up. There are social fuckups, like spilling the cherry sauce on the guy she brings home for dinner. Kids mess up the house just before a big date. So some of that is valid.

"But we got *all* the blame. It just became a cycle that fed upon itself. Obviously it was our fault that these people were running away, and not her winning personality."

The kids were certain that men figured into the formula that set her off, but they couldn't figure out exactly how. Terry recognized early on that her mother seemed happiest when she had a man in her life—preferably a strong but malleable man who looked good and gave her presents, but didn't protest too much when Theresa ordered him around.

Terry remembered Ron Bullington as such a man. Her mother even took to referring to herself as "Mrs.

Theresa Bullington" for a while, though they were never married. But Bullington hadn't lasted much longer than Pulliam. For a while Theresa dated a man named Ollie. He looked promising, in part because he had a son of his own. The boy was an "obnoxious brat," according to Robert, but his father at least tried to get Theresa's brood to like him and he did seem to have some small understanding of what it meant to be around children.

But for reasons that none of her children ever understood, Theresa decided to end it with Ollie. It came to a vicious climax one night when a shrieking Theresa busted a telephone against his head. He escaped from the front room with his hand covering a gap in his skull, leaving behind a trail of blood that the kids had to clean up the next morning. Their mother offered no explanations as to what provoked her attack.

Still, Ollie came back. Ultimately, Theresa pulled the same trick on him that she later played on tenacious bill collectors who went beyond her post office box and located where she lived: she acted as if no one was at home and refused to answer the door.

"We *never* answered the door," said Terry. "Even if it was somebody you knew, you did not answer the door unless my mom said it was all right. Usually we just sat quiet in the front room, barely breathing until whoever it was got tired of ringing the bell and left."

Despite the cloak of brooding anger that constantly enveloped the house at 5539 Bellingham Way, the 1970s were generally a good time for the three boys and three girls that Theresa Pulliam raised, as a single parent, in the suburbs of Sacramento. It was a good time for Theresa, too. The house might not be the Ritz, and living one step above welfare on minimum wage might not foster a royal lifestyle, but owning her own home and eking out an existence for herself and her children represented at least some version of the American

Dream to a single mother who'd grown up dirt-poor and undereducated in Rio Linda.

Then Theresa met Chet Harris, and everything changed.

VIII

Like George Burns and Ted Kennedy, newspaperman Chet Harris was living, breathing testimony to the fact that abusing one's body did not necessarily guarantee a quick trip to the grave. He was nearly sixty before he became the fourth and final husband of Theresa Jimmie Cross. He seemed to be in wheezing poor health even then, but he went on to live another thirteen years.

Harris was fifty-two when he arrived in Sacramento, having spent most of his early career in the East as a hard-drinking, heavy-smoking cityside reporter for newspapers in Pittsburgh, Long Island, and St. Louis. Pictures taken during his salad days showed the steely eyes and granite profile of a tough young newsman. He wore a snap-brim hat in the Walter Winchell style, delighted in flashing his "press" card when the cops tried barring him from the scene of an accident, and would simply never take "no comment" as any kind of an answer.

But his reporting days had long ended by the time he got to California. He couldn't grab a pad and pencil and run off to press conferences the way he once did. In fact, he couldn't run anywhere. At more than three hundred pounds, he was barely able to scale the three flights of stairs and squeeze into a swivel chair at the copy desk of the *Sacramento Union* each day, where he rewrote other reporters' stories, scribbled captions for photos, and dashed off headlines for the next day's editions.

It had not always been so. Chet Harris had been a real journalist once. He'd written three books and worked on more than a half-dozen newspapers before emigrating to California. He began as a cub on the sports desk of the *McKeesport Daily* in 1936, when he was still in his teens. For the next twenty years Chet Harris was a firebrand with a First Amendment missionary's zeal.

He didn't write stories to please or inform the public. He wrote stories to put miscreants in jail. He was married and had a family, but the newsroom at the *Sun Telegraph* in Pittsburgh, where he spent twenty years, became his real home. The editors, reporters, and photographers who gathered there each morning to put out another edition became more of a family to him than his own wife and children. Harris and his colleagues ended each day with a round of drinks at the bar across the street. Sometimes he didn't get home until way after midnight, stinking of beer. If his wife raised the question of his priorities, family or job, the newspaper invariably won out.

The 1940s and 1950s were Harris's glory days. By the time the rival *Pittsburgh Post Gazette* bought his beloved *Sun Telegraph* from Hearst Newspapers, just so the new owners could close it down forever, Chet Harris's career as a crusading investigative reporter had wound to a close.

In 1960, the *Sun Telegraph* had merged with the *Post Gazette* and Harris found himself out of a job. His wife had divorced him and left the state with their two daughters. And Harris wasn't getting any younger. He had gained a lot of weight, developed a hacking smoker's cough, and increased his alcohol intake to several six-packs a day. But Chet Harris was a stubborn man. It would be years before he came to fully comprehend that drinking could ruin just about everything in a man's life except his dedication to the written word.

He moved on from Pittsburgh to New York and then St. Louis, and to a job as a copy editor at the *Globe-Democrat*, all the while putting away more beer on a daily basis than a hundred Homer Simpsons. In St. Louis, he remarried. He and his new wife, a nurse named Dona Davis Harris, lived modestly but happily for a few years in the suburbs. Inevitably, booze and bad habits bested that marriage, too.

By 1970, the very heavy, very alcoholic, and very grizzled Chester L. Harris left Dona Davis and St. Louis, and set out for yet another new life—this time on the West Coast. Just before Christmas, he showed up as sober as he could manage at the *Sacramento Union*, looking for a job.

"He was one of the last of the itinerent newspaper editors," said Michael Fallon, who worked with Harris at the *Union*. In the 1990s, Harris would never have been able to pull up stakes, get in his car, and drive to another town with any kind of assurance that he would find a job waiting for him there. But in the 1970s, when newspapers were still formidable and flush with advertising money, a skilled copy editor could walk into almost any newspaper office in the land and go to work.

Robert Carney, Harris's old boss at the *Globe-Democrat*, had hired on at the *Union* as news editor a few years before Harris showed up in California. He put Chet to work immediately on the copy desk.

The *Union* was the home of K. W. Lee, a brilliant but incendiary investigative reporter likened by his co-workers to a "crazy Korean kamikaze," who nonetheless wrote the kinds of stories that sent corrupt officials to jail and got wrongly convicted felons released from prison; Wayne Kent, who covered lurid murder trials and delighted in detailing for the young and impressionable women in the office precisely what the killers did to the corpses; Steve Spence, a practical joker and ladies' man who ran the city desk like a check-in counter at a mental-health clinic. In his baggy pants, clownish suspenders, slue-footed shuffle, and potbelly to rival that of Santa Claus, Chet Harris fit right in—drunk or sober.

"Newspaper people are a different breed of people from other grown-ups," explained Patty Williams, a former receptionist for the newspaper. "Chet did not appear to be a drunk, although we all drank a lot at the *Union* in those days. Looking back, I don't know if the pot would know whether the kettle drank or not. We all had our peculiarities."

One of Chet's peculiarities was an unswerving dedication to the men and women of American Legion Post No. 521 of Rio Linda, where Chet's stool at the end of the bar was as sacrosanct as that of the TV character Norm in the sitcom *Cheers.*

"I think of his social life as beginning and ending at the American Legion hall at Rio Linda," said Michael Fallon. "He was really quite a private person as far as the paper was concerned. He was a bit older and kept pretty much to himself. He just sort of did his job and then loped off to Rio Linda each day."

At the American Legion, Harris had his loyal following of conservative fellow–World War II vets who groused about draft dodgers and dopers who'd come back from Vietnam only to become losers, living off the public dole. One of the Vietnam vets who resented the talk about World War II being "the Good War" and the harsh words heaped on those who got strung out on drugs in Vietnam was Bob Knorr. He belonged to the same American Legion post as Harris, had been struggling for years with his own drug problems, and didn't appreciate the rank old copy editor's self-righteous attitude. Of the dozen or so aging, alcoholic vets who gathered at the end of each day at the American Legion bar to complain about the younger generation, Knorr found Chet Harris to be particularly offensive.

Chet Harris no longer wore his Walter Winchell snap-brim hat. He had become grouchy, obese, and smelled of pilsner and body odor. When he rolled in from the *Union* at the end of each day, he expected not one, but two, bottles of Coors to be waiting for him at the end of the bar. He once explained to a fellow customer that he always wanted to be sure he had a cold one waiting for him and the only way to be sure of that was by ordering two at once.

Beer was not his only addiction. He also liked women—or, at least, sex.

"He was married five or six times, which is amazing in itself because I can't imagine five or six women in this world who would want to marry him," recalled Patty Williams. "He was pretty gross."

Gross, perhaps, but a lothario nonetheless.

"He had several wives," said his sister, Mrs. Janet Gentilini. "He went from one wife to another. I don't know whether it was five or six times. His first wife died on their first wedding anniversary. He was married to his second wife—the one who moved to upstate New York—for at least eighteen or twenty years. And he married the next one, Dona Davis, just about a year later. The marriage to Dona might've been another five or six years.

"And then, after that, it just seemed like it was *bing*, *bing*, *bing*! It was one right after the other. I lost track of them after about the first three. In fact, I don't believe I ever met any after the first three."

After Dona, whom he often described as the one true love of his life, Harris married again and again . . . but didn't remain married long.

On January 8, 1973, he married Roxie Chaffin, a petite housewife eleven years younger than he.

"It seems to me that in some people's eyes, she was attractive," said Patty Williams. "They used to fight a lot, though."

"She was a very presentable woman and a very gracious hostess," recalled Robert Carney. "They seemed very much in love when they were first together, but I guess it soured."

And soured quickly. On February 4, Mrs. Roxie Harris filed for divorce and had the papers served at Chet's third-floor office in the *Union* building. She waived alimony and asked only that the name Roxie Chaffin be restored. Because the marriage wasn't even a month old, Roxie didn't get a formal divorce. The court granted her an annulment. None of Chet's close associates ever knew exactly why Roxie left him, but Chet made it clear just how badly he took it.

"Chet really hated that breakup," recalled Carney. "He used to be quite upset because she was living away from him. He wanted to have her back."

In the meantime Harris moved into his dream home. He painted the walls of the interior white and the baseboard and trim red. His collies had the run of the house. When he was married, he had people from the paper out to visit and threw barbecues in the backyard on occasion. But after Roxie left him, he became a hermit, with only his three dogs to keep him company. Alone with his dogs and his beer, he grew larger and lonelier with each passing year.

"After he left St. Louis and he drove out west, I guess he was just a very lonely man," said his sister, Janet. "He'd made such a mess of his life. I guess he figured he'd go out there and start anew. His drinking and carousing got him in trouble, and anyone he happened to meet who maybe had a little sympathy toward his problems, or was easy to talk to, he latched onto. He just liked to have company. He didn't like to be alone."

When he met Theresa Pulliam at the bar of the American Legion hall in the summer of 1976, Chet was twice her age and twice her size. He smoked two packs of filterless Pall Malls each day, and lived on a diet of draft beer, cold cuts, and cholesterol-laden groceries. Theresa had begun to thicken around the middle herself, but she was still a toothpick by her future husband's standards.

"By then, Chet Harris had to weigh maybe 375, 400 pounds," said Bob Knorr. "He was a big man. Over six foot. Had a big nose and lost most of his hair. Really a pretty awful sight to have to look at.

"She met him in the American Legion hall one night. About three days later they decided they're gonna get married. I caught hell from my buddies. 'That's your ex-wife married to Chet Harris?' She was still kind of thin then. Just about that time was when she started putting the weight on."

Theresa and Chet were married August 23, 1976, in Sacramento. He was the fifty-nine-year-old Special Sections editor of the *Union*, earning a salary of $1,600 a month, and she was a thirty-year-old sometimes Watkins Products saleswoman from Orangevale—a mother of six children, ranging in age from seven to thirteen. Her monthly income: $1,000.

"My mother married him for the same reason she ever went out with any guy I ever knew: for the money," said Terry. "She got him, and she got him good."

With her children, Theresa made no pretense about what she was doing and why. "Even before she got married we were all informed that it was a big sacrifice for her because she wanted Suesan to get an education," said Robert. "Since Chester had political connections with the board of education through the *Union*, Suesan would have a better opportunity to get a first-rate education along with all the rest of the kids," Robert recalled his mother saying.

Theresa moved swiftly. Before the ceremony, she put the house on Bellingham Way up for sale and moved herself and all six of her children into Chet's place on Eighth Street in Rio Linda. Once she and her brood were in residence, she declared that the house was too small for eight people and three dogs. She informed her new husband that they needed more room.

"She married Chet Harris, and right away she got him to put a big addition onto his house," said Bob Knorr. "He had to go out and take a second mortgage out on the house to make it big enough to satisfy her."

On September 16, 1976, less than three weeks after exchanging wedding vows, Chet and Theresa obtained a second trust deed loan of $7,000 from Investors Yield of Sacramento. Before he could use a dime of it to build the addition that Theresa demanded, Theresa used five hundred dollars to pay off a three-year-old court judgment against her. She explained to her new husband that she had purchased some appliances on credit back in 1973, after she left Ron Pulliam, and then found that she couldn't pay for them. By paying them off, she and Chet would start out with a clean slate.

The money situation was not going to be a one-way street, however, she assured him. With the equity she had built up in the Bellingham Way house, they would be able to pool their money and turn the Eighth Street house into a veritable Taj Mahal.

But the Taj Mahal was never to be. Within weeks of their wedding Theresa discovered that Chet Harris had a horrid little secret, and Theresa's own double standard in ethical behavior went into overdrive. His hobby was photography, and he had photos on the wall of all of his ex-wives. He had other portraits of them, too, which he did not openly display.

"He had a portrait done of Roxanne that was nude," said Robert. "It was a picture of her with her hands kind of triangled between her legs, outlining her crotch, and the crotch was thrust forward. I remember that vividly because I opened a closet one day and there it was."

Chester wanted Theresa to pose for him, too. According to Terry, he wanted her mother to do it in the nude. Theresa refused.

"He liked pornography," said Terry. "He had naked pictures of Roxie, the woman he was married to before, and when my mother saw them, she went nuts. I mean, *she* did all kinds of shit with men, but when it came to *other* people and *their* sexual kinky stuff, she went off like a firecracker."

Theresa wore muumuus around the house and nothing else. She had to remain naked for Chester, she explained to her daughters. It was all part of her sacrifice for her children.

Most of Theresa's children had no sympathy for Harris. He wasn't abusive and did not appear to get fresh with Theresa's girls at first, but his sheer size and girth combined with years of foul bachelor habits made all the children shudder each time he walked through the front door.

But Theresa was willing to overlook all his faults in furtherance of her grand plan. Besides using him to pay her bills and build a larger, newer house for herself and her children, she saw Chet Harris as a tool to torture and lure Bob Knorr back into her clutches.

"My mom was trying to hook up with my dad again at this time, while she was still married to Chet and he was still married to Georgia," said Terry. "She was making eyeballs at my real dad, Robert Knorr, who lived in Rio Linda then and used to go drink at the American Legion a lot.

"My mom never got over my dad. All our life she had his marine pictures around, and she wouldn't let any of us kids mess with them. She kept them in one box in the cupboard with anything that meant anything to her: dolls, pictures, an old camera, an old Burgermeister beer mug from my grandpa, her geneology book about the Cross family. . . ."

The story Theresa told her children about how she met Chester put the blame squarely on Bob's shoulders. He was the one who introduced them at the American

Legion hall, and he was the one who knew—or should have known—that Chet Harris was evil.

On Halloween, the boys saw—or thought they saw—the real Chester Harris. It was Chester's favorite holiday.

"He called it Hobo Days rather than Halloween," said Robert. "He came out wearing a devil's mask that looked a little too natural on him. And I remember I slid back on all fours about two or three feet and stopped when I realized that the asshole was wearing a mask. My brother William ran out of the house and was in the backyard the second he saw him."

Chester laughed at the two frightened little boys. After that incident he said Bill was the coward and Robert was the one with the balls to stand up to the devil. He would be a killer.

"I remember that to this day," said Robert.

Chester had names for all of Theresa's children. Besides Robert the Killer and William the Coward, he called Terry the Little Stripper and Sheila, who had grown up pretty but slightly retarded, Suesan's Dog.

"It seemed to be a thing that was repeated over and over again," said Robert. Since she was very young, Sheila had always followed Suesan around, patterning her own behavior after her younger, brighter sister. It wasn't just Chester who slapped Sheila with the unflattering name. Everyone, including her own mother, told her she was Suesan's Dog.

Suesan herself, however, was Chester's pet. A precocious ten-year-old with an insatiable appetite for books, she was to be famous and have a harem of men at her beck and call when she grew up, according to Harris. Unlike her brothers and sisters, Suesan was flattered by her hideous stepfather, and found him to be as intellectually intriguing as he was physically repulsive. When Harris was sober, they carried on lively, even stimulating dialogues about everything from mythology to Chet's favorite subject, politics.

"This guy bought my sis a puzzle book for kids four or five years older than she was," said Terry. "My sister was later tested and found to be four years advanced of herself. She was a genius, like my aunt Rosemary."

Suesan's spindly child's body was just beginning to fill out a bit, and she was showing the promise of growing up to be as attractive a teenager as her mother had been. Suesan tested bright enough in school to be placed in accelerated classes, but she remained shy and nearsighted, her natural good looks marred by thick eyeglasses. Chet drew her out of her shell, and for a little while it looked like he would finally become the father he never was to his own two daughters back in Pittsburgh.

But Chet's interest in Suesan was not enough to keep the marriage together. His interest in pornography disgusted Theresa and her interest in other men enraged him. Near the end of their short time together Theresa went through a ritual each night before turning out the lights that absolutely unnerved her new husband.

"When she went to sleep, she put a gun under her pillow," said Terry Smith, Chester's daughter. "It scared the living bejeezus out of Dad because he didn't know if it was because of him or what."

Less than three months after they tied the knot, Chet threw Theresa out of the house and Theresa filed for divorce.

The way Bob Knorr heard it, things finally unraveled when Harris got a call one day from a nervous acquaintance who confessed to Harris that Theresa had gone out drinking with him and wound up giving him oral sex.

Word got around fast in gossip-driven Rio Linda. Surprisingly, sympathies were as much with Theresa as they were with the cuckolded Chester Harris.

"He married Theresa and she wanted to go out two nights out of the week, and he tracked her down and she was going with a new man," said Bea Howard. "So he wanted out of the marriage. I said if he was stupid enough to marry that much of a younger person, that's his hard luck!"

The house on Bellingham Way had been sold, but fortunately it had not yet gone through escrow. Theresa moved back in, derailed the sale, and took the house off the market.

On November 22, 1976, Theresa filed an affidavit with the court in support of her suit for divorce from Chester Harris. In it, she set out her version of the events that led to divorce:

> At the time of my marriage, Respondent promised that we would live together as husband and wife. After the marriage, he instructed me to pose for lewd photographs and pornographic movies. When I refused, he evicted me and my children from the house.
>
> The Respondent has attempted to choke me and I fear possible physical harm. I request that he be restrained from either annoying, molesting, or harassing either me or my children.

Chet had tricked and manipulated her, selling off more than $1,000 of her personal property since she had moved out, she wrote in her affidavit. What was more, she complained, the addition to Harris's Rio Linda home turned out not to have been planned for Theresa and her children at all.

> I learned that he had no intention of living with me as husband and wife and that the addition to the house was not for me but rather to be used by other people for immoral purposes. I request that Respondent be restrained from transferring or otherwise encumbering the title to the real property located at 6936 8th Street, Rio Linda, California, so that the court may decide my separate property interest in it.
>
> On the basis of Respondent's promise that we would live together as husband and wife, I allowed

him to list my Orangevale home with a realtor. Because he evicted me and my children from the Rio Linda home, I, of course, must now live in my Orangevale home. Respondent is still trying to sell my home and I request that he be restrained from selling or ordering the sale of my residence at 5539 Bellingham Way.

The marriage lasted two months and seven days. In addition to her Bellingham Way address, her personal effects, and a lien against Harris's Rio Linda home in the amount of $8,923.86, Theresa also demanded the washer, the dryer, the refrigerator, deep freeze, TV, dishwasher, stereo, furniture, and a statue of the *Venus de Milo*, with pedestal.

There was not much of a fight, though. Chet Harris gave in to almost all of Theresa's demands.

"She got him good. He had to go take a loan out to get his own house back," said Knorr. "He had to pay her off in order for her to sign his deed back over to him."

It wasn't luck or goodwill that won the day for Theresa and her children. She didn't go to court alone. Theresa was no stranger to the justice system and knew the value of a good lawyer. The first thing she did after suing for divorce was to pay a visit to an old adversary.

"A woman named Theresa Harris shows up one day and asks me to represent her in her divorce," said Donald Dorfman, the former deputy district attorney who had prosecuted Theresa Sanders for murder in 1964.

Dorfman, who had left the DA's office to become a defense attorney in part because of his disgust over the outcome of the Sanders murder case, didn't recognize Theresa when she first walked into his office in the fall of 1976. It wasn't until she told him who she was that the usually unflappable lawyer dropped his jaw, made a quick recovery, and asked her why she decided to ask him to represent her.

"I liked the way you came after me at the trial," she said calmly.

Dorfman referred Theresa to another attorney, but she named him in her divorce papers as her attorney anyway, along with Carl Swain, the lawyer who actually did represent her.

As it turned out, Dorfman's wasn't the only name from the past to show up in her divorce suit. In one of his final actions on the bench, Sacramento County Superior Court judge Charles W. Johnson declared the marriage between Chet and Theresa Harris officially ended as of December 17, 1976.

The sixty-four-year-old jurist who had presided over Theresa's murder trial thirteen years earlier had also signed off on her two previous divorces, from Robert Knorr and Ron Pulliam. He never indicated in any of those divorces that he recognized the petite young woman he had once declared innocent of murder.

At the end of 1976, Johnson declared his intention to retire, following a barrage of bad publicity. In the spring, the Sacramento County Bar Association had singled him out in a poll of trial attorneys. Charles Johnson was voted the worst judge in the county.

Johnson refused to acknowledge the humiliation, telling a reporter for Chet Harris's newspaper, the *Union*, that the only reason he had decided to step down from the bench was to "let a younger man devote his greater energy to the task."

He ignored the bar association's accusations that he failed to follow or keep up on changes in the law, showed blatant favoritism toward friends and political cronies, and based his decisions on whim. The vote of no confidence was "merely an expression of pique on the part of a vociferous minority of the attorneys," he said.

Johnson died two years later, exactly fourteen years and two months after setting Mrs. Theresa Sanders free and declaring the murder case of Clifford Clyde Sanders closed.

Whatever else she may have won in her divorce from Chet Harris, Theresa seemed to have lost her last shred of sociability, as well as her taste for men. "She dropped out of sight right after Chet Harris," said Bob Knorr. "That was the last contact I had with her. I never even got to see the kids while she was with Chet Harris. There was always a reason why I couldn't see them. But after that, I didn't see her or the kids at all."

IX

Back at the house on Bellingham Way, Theresa grew more reclusive, more unpredictable, and more violent, but nobody outside of her immediate family knew anything about it. Though she had always been hard on her children, it was her last husband who finally turned her into a monster.

"She really went over the edge with Chet Harris," said Terry. "After Harris, she dated for a little while, but then she got to the point where she wouldn't date or remarry or nothing."

Terry's older brothers William and Robert agreed, recalling that their mother's gradual transformation from angry disciplinarian to raging eccentric took place in the late 1970s.

"Sometime around when I turned ten or eleven or so, she started becoming abusive, real short-tempered," William recalled. "She stopped going out, seeing friends at all, on any level. She got rid of the telephone because she didn't want any people calling. We weren't allowed to have anybody inside the house."

"When I was growing up, I hated *The Brady Bunch* because I knew that nobody lived like that," said Robert. "I knew that because I knew what my family life was like. Nothing could be more different from the truth than that bullshit TV show.

"I grew up in an insane asylum basically, but what's worse is we didn't *know* it was an insane asylum," he continued. "I never really admitted or even knew that I was being abused or that my family was being abused, because I thought it was normal."

And yet as far as the neighbors knew, the Knorr family was no different from any other.

"Not that I want to say that they were private, but they stayed to themselves," said Janet Garrett, who lived next door. "It was difficult to strike up a conversation with the mother. She just didn't want to, it seemed like. You try a few times, and after two or three times you just say, 'Okay.' You just give up."

Theresa's changing behavior even went undetected by the neighborhood kids, who generally had a closer view of their friends' private life than their parents.

"Not having a father figure around—that was the only thing about their family that seemed different," said Janet's son Chris Garrett.

He was the same age as Terry Knorr and went to her house to play from time to time. Once, he went to her birthday party—a party at which he noticed that he was the only non–family member.

"Terry's mom wasn't the silent type," he recalled. "In fact, she was real talkative. Kept to herself, but talkative when you talked to her. Even so, I don't remember her ever saying anything that you could call 'off the wall.' "

But Terry's mom was definitely different from the other moms in the neighborhood. "I will say this about her," Garrett added. "Terry's mom definitely had control of the kids. I didn't see a lot of back talk or argument coming out of any of them. If they were told to be in by a certain time, they were in. If they were told to do something, they did it. They never asked questions. They never made a point to second-guess authority."

Theresa's children may have accepted this dictatorial isolation, but they didn't understand it. They complained about not being able to have friends over, but if they whined too much about it, they were slapped into silence. They did not see the gradual evaporation of their contact with the outside world as the logical result of shutting themselves inside the house. Instead, Theresa's children saw the neighbors' distancing from their mother and themselves as indifference and an unwillingness to get involved.

"Our neighbors backed off," said Terry. "They knew better than to screw with our family. Everybody shuts their eyes, nobody wants to get involved."

The Knorr children's blind obedience to their mother stemmed from a constant state of terror that remained invisible to the Garretts and every one else who lived along Bellingham Way. Even in the early stages, the terror was so bizarre and their mother so skilled at keeping it "in the family," it would have taken more than simple curiosity on the part of the neighbors to uncover what was going on. Had the Garretts or any of the other neighbors known about it, Terry wonders even today if they would have done anything.

"When my mother got drunk, she used to lick the ends of steak knives," Terry recalled. "Serrated-edged knives. And she threw them at us to see if her aim was good."

Knives weren't Theresa's only deadly playthings when she'd had a little too much to drink.

Terry still blanches, remembering the chill in her mother's voice one evening when she went in to say good night. Eyes half-closed, her mother sat in a deep chair in the living room and motioned for Terry to approach. In her drunken stupor, Theresa howled at her shivering but stoic young daughter, boasting of that defining moment nearly fifteen years earlier when she pointed a gun at Clifford Sanders and pulled the trigger.

"She owned two guns, a derringer and a revolver," Terry recalled. "At one point, she took out the bone-

handled old cowboy gun. It looked like a toy, but it was
a real six-shooter. A .22 pistol."

Aiming the pistol at her daughter, Theresa told Terry,
"I shot once and I can do it again."

Terry froze, standing terrified before her.

"And she told me to come to her. And I did," Terry
said with a shudder, remembering. "And she put the
gun to my head, so hard that the next morning I woke
up and I still had a knot from where the barrel had sunk
into my temple."

On the evenings that followed, sobered and sentimen-
tal, Theresa would try to make amends by taking everyone out for a family ride, as if nothing had happened.
She'd load them into the car and drive up Highway 50,
past Placerville, into the High Sierras.

"It was one of those see-how-nice-I-can-be type
things," Bill recalled.

There was no point to it, other than to commune with
nature. They never went to play in the snow or hike in
the forest. It was just a tour through the mountains. Unlike six-lane Interstate 80, which cut through the relatively barren Donner Pass, the Placerville highway had
more vistas, more wildlife, and more trees, which ap-
pealed to Theresa's aesthetic sense. But the family
drives did little to make up for the savagery that went
on back home.

"It was beat us, lock us in our room for days, and
then, she'd be all lovey-dovey," said Terry. "My mom
was so blatantly contradictory. She played the part of a
mother, but she also played the part of a very torturous,
sadistic human being. Oh yeah, she was schizo."

But that information was not for popular consump-
tion. What families did to each other behind closed
doors was private. Underscoring that basic human
"truth" was an incident that happened to Terry shortly
after they returned to Bellingham Way.

While Terry was attending Palisades Elementary, one

of her few remaining friends came to school one day with bruises. She confided to Terry that she, too, had been a victim of abuse: her mother slapped her around. Terry, who had been appointed one of Palisades' "Guardian Eagle" playground monitors, reported the abuse to a counselor. The following day Terry found that she was being stalked.

"The girl's mother followed me home from the bus stop, came in my backyard, shaking me, banging my head against the wall," said Terry. "And my mother was standing in the kitchen window watching. She did nothing. Finally, she calls my brother, whose naked asleep in bed, and tells him, 'Howard, come get this woman out of the backyard!' And all this time this woman is beating me up."

Howard threw something on and did manage to eject the angry woman from the yard, but Terry got no sympathy from her brother or her mother. Instead, Theresa shrieked at her daughter for making waves at school and bringing the crazy woman to their home. As usual, Terry was punished. Then, a few days later, her mother was making amends again.

"I remember, right after the lady beat me up, my mom pawning her ring," said Terry.

It was a platinum cocktail ring that Theresa had custom-crafted from diamonds she'd taken from the wedding sets Clifford Sanders and Bob Knorr had given to her. She used to say that the single-carat diamond at the ring's center was the sun, trailed by smaller diamond stars that encircled a moon.

"To her, that ring had a lot of meaning, and she went and pawned it so I could have some new clothes," said Terry. "I always had to wear hand-me-downs until my mom hocked her ring and bought me brand-new Smurfette clothes. That was a big thing for me. And it was right after that woman came in our yard and beat me up."

Money remained a problem. Theresa continued to work odd hours at convalescent homes, where she claimed to have become something of an expert in moving the addled and the infirm from place to place. She bragged of being able to "curl" two-hundred-pound men, getting them from wheelchair to bed all by herself. But she didn't complain about the nursing homes as much as she had her other jobs. She liked taking care of people—particularly those who were under her absolute control. She took her job so seriously that she enrolled in and completed the necessary classes to earn a certified nursing assistant certificate from the California Nurse Licensing Board.

But one night, her budding nursing career was cut short by a flying fist. A strong but senile patient lashed out at her as she tried moving him onto his bed. He knocked her flat to the floor, wrenching her back and hurting her hip. She never walked the same after that, though her children believed that her growing weight problem was as much to blame for her pained, rolling gait as the back injury.

After that, she began staying home more than she went to work. When she wasn't working or drinking, or alternately terrorizing and being tender with her children, Theresa read aloud to them, as often from *The Stand* as from the Bible.

"My mother's favorite author was Stephen King. I mean she read every freakin' book Stephen King ever wrote, even the ones under his ghost name of Richard Bachman," said Terry. "And get this: *I* like Stephen King today because my mom used to read his books to us when we were little."

When Theresa's readings were from the Bible, the children fell into a fearful silence.

"My mom ... started reading the Bible when she started becoming abusive, and the more she read the Bible the more she twisted ... what the Bible was saying," said Bill. "And she would use that in her beliefs as far as why she was beating us for doing certain things."

Theresa rounded out her library with other horror writers, including Peter Strauss and V. C. Andrews. She also liked true-crime books like *Helter Skelter.*

"One of her favorites was about a prostitute who used to kill her johns with a razor blade," said Terry. "She had a different blade for every day of the week. My mom was the Lorena Bobbitt of fiction. While other parents were reading their kids Mother Goose, my mom was reading to us from *Salem's Lot.*"

But the older her children got, the more difficult they were to control. They wanted to visit friends, not stay at home for readings from *It* or Ecclesiastes. William was among the first to begin plotting his escape.

"When we got to a certain age, we were no longer permitted to go outside," Bill recalled. "We were always grounded. Friends that came over were told by my mom that we were grounded, or asleep, or not there. We had everything taken away from us."

Theresa timed her children's visits to school, to the grocery store, to church—and administered the third degree if they were a few minutes late getting home.

"She would never just go off and beat all the kids just to beat all the kids," Bill explained. "It was, if you did something wrong, or that she saw wrong, like coming back late from the store, that was a beating right there. If I came home late from school, she knew I was out talking to somebody, so I was getting a beating."

But while William dreamed of his eventual getaway, his older sisters were made to understand that they were different. They were girls. For girls, there was no escape.

When the family was out together, Theresa went so far as to make all of her daughters go to the bathroom with her so that she could keep an eye on them. When she warned them not to talk to strangers, there was a cold-steel edge to her voice that made each of the girls understand that she meant "don't talk to *anyone.*"

She was still bigger than most of her children, but wielding the Board of Education was no longer as effective as it had been when they were small. Howard became her new tool of discipline. During her fits of terror, Theresa solicited help from her oldest son.

"Howard was the first one that was made to help hold us down," said William.

The sweet young towhead whom Bea Howard wanted to adopt as her own had grown into a huge, confused, and bitter teenager. He towered over his mother, his constant dour expression matching hers. Even though she had put on dozens of pounds since leaving Chester Harris, her oldest son still outweighed her. He never crossed her, though.

"At the age of six, I was sodomized by my brother Howard," said Terry. "He molested me, but he was expressing his sexuality, so I didn't blame him."

Terry's mother was not so forgiving. When her young daughter and youngest son, Robert, teamed up and timidly approached their mother to tell her what had happened, she was incensed to discover that Howard had been sexually exploiting everyone in the household when Theresa was off at work.

"At that time I didn't even have breasts, but they were, you know, my nipples were sore and they were red and I went to my mom and I told her, 'Well, Howard pinched them, you know,' " said Terry.

Robert described how his older brother traded sexual favors with him for trinkets, making his humiliating submission to Howard a kind of incestuous prostitution. Once, he said, Howard ordered his scrawny kid brother to mount his older sister, Suesan. When Robert refused, Howard raped Suesan and made Robert watch.

Theresa was furious.

"She literally broke a chair over my brother's back over that," said Terry. "She beat him so bad over that, and he never did it again."

But Theresa wasn't through. She sat the rest of the family down and offered up an explanation for their oldest brother's brutal sexual behavior. He had been molested as a small child, she explained. The molester, she said, was none other than their father, Bob Knorr.

And there was more. Bob Knorr's family had been involved for years in witchcraft, said Theresa. The Knorrs practiced sorcery beneath the pear trees of the ranch in Placerville where Bob grew up. His father and mother were actually a warlock and a witch and Bob had been raised in a coven, practicing black magic. An essential part of all that voodoo was sexual exploitation of the helpless, particularly small children and women. It was no wonder, she said, that Bob molested Howard. It was no wonder that Bob had introduced her to that demon incarnate, Chester Harris.

While the younger children listened to Theresa's supernatural rantings in rapt awe, Howard ignored her. In fact, Howard ignored most of Theresa's ravings and demands. He began to refuse to stay at home all the time and hold his brothers and sisters while Theresa thrashed them. He had become as coldly cynical as a KGB hit man before his fourteenth birthday and had no intention of being anybody's stooge. Unlike his brothers and sisters, Howard defied her edict not to have friends and not to leave the house. Howard wanted more. He found it in drugs.

"That's where I first did lines, was with Howard. He gave me my first taste," said Terry. "Howard was doing speed and pot and mushrooms and dropping acid like it was going out of style!"

Howard initiated all of his siblings into the use of controlled substances. For them, it offered a kind of escape from semipermanent house arrest. And, in his own way, it was Howard expressing gruff affection for his brothers and sisters.

"I was doing bong loads of marijuana at the age of seven or eight," said Robert. "He said if I was going to do dope, I had to do it like a man. I couldn't smoke any prissy-assed joints. I had to do a bong load. So I learned how to do copious amounts of marijuana. I'm amazed I have any brain cells left. Howard did that quite a bit. I think that was his method of male bonding."

Through junior high and high school, Howard Sanders developed a reputation as a user and seller of all sorts of pharmaceuticals, from exotic street cocktails to vials of prescription medicines that Theresa often lifted from the convalescent homes where she worked.

"I became his doorman," said Robert. "Howard had a lot of people running in and out of the house buying dope. I answered the door, saw who it was, and told my brother who it was. If he wanted to deal with him, he'd deal with him. If he didn't, I'd tell whoever was at the front door that Howard wasn't there."

Theresa knew he was dealing drugs out of her house, but she could no longer control her eldest son with brute force. Besides, he was paying rent by the time he entered high school and Theresa needed the money. While Howard managed to regularly turn all of his brothers and sisters on to one drug or another, Theresa herself refused to participate.

"My mother distanced herself from it," said Robert. "While he was in his room, dealing, she would be in her room reading her Bible or in the kitchen making dinner."

Yet no matter how often she read the Scriptures, Theresa was never able to find the calming passages that could help her lie down in the green pastures of a soul at peace with itself. She had been permanently infected by the witchcraft bug during her short time with Chester Harris, and remained obsessed with ideas and

beliefs that smacked more of mayhem and Stephen
King than King James and Catholicism.

"My mom thought Suesan was a witch," said Terry.
"She was sure of it because she thought Suesan was trying to pass [into the devil's dimension] when she was
with Chester Harris."

At first, Suesan and her mother seemed to have developed a new and loving bond after Chester Harris.
Suesan even took to doing the readings from the Bible
and Stephen King. At one point, it got to be a shared
activity, with Suesan and her mother sitting together in
the front room, the kitchen, or back in the girls' bedroom, taking turns reading to each other.

But the mother-daughter love fest was short lived.

Whether it was true or just a taunt to make her
mother crazier than she already was, Suesan began confessing to Theresa how Chester Harris planned to initiate her into his witches' coven. Though he had never
had sex with her, she said, Harris showed her how to
use her thumb and forefingers to enlarge her vagina for
the time that he would deflower her in the name of Satan.

She told her mother and her sisters that Harris used to
wear a black robe lined with red satin that he kept hidden in a footlocker beneath his bed, along with a scep-
ter, a signet ring, and a stack of books on witchcraft.
And all of this hocus pocus was not just confined to her
and Chester Harris. Once Suesan was a full-fledged
necromancer, she was supposed to initiate her sisters
into the black arts as well.

Only many years later did Robert, Terry, and the rest
of the children seriously question whether Suesan's
Chet Harris stories really happened or if their older sister was merely spinning fanciful Stephen King–
influenced tales to top the tales their mother told them.

Whether the stories were true or not, even uttering
Chet's name was a remarkably effective way of driving
Theresa nuts, and Suesan used it to full effect. Besides,

Suesan had her own fascination with good and evil, dating back to Sunday school at the Hazel Avenue Baptist Church. A married couple who had a fire-and-brimstone approach to lay preaching for elementary-school children impressed Suesan, but not in the way that they planned.

"Satan was described as this real powerful evil guy," said Robert. "They did discourses on Satan all the time. But rather than deter her, it fascinated Suesan. It impressed upon her more the power of Satan than it did God at that point."

By the time she met Chet Harris, Suesan had a sympathetic picture of Lucifer that more closely approximated Mick Jagger's than, say, Jimmy Swaggert's. "My sister was intellectually superior and curious and she wanted to know did magic work?" said Robert. "There's a lot of instances in history and even in the Bible, you know, where they describe witches and the power of Satan."

Suesan's strong will, quick wit, probing intellect, and growing good looks did nothing to lessen her mother's conviction that she had made some sort of unholy pact during her short time as Chester Harris's stepdaughter. In elementary school, the other kids nicknamed her "Fish" because of her thick glasses, but by the time Suesan was in junior high, even the glasses could not disguise the youthful grace of her growing bosom, hips, and dark blond hair.

"Suesan was a late bloomer," said Terry. "She was beautiful. She looked a little like me, or rather, I look a little like she did. And we both looked like our father."

Suesan was bright enough to be sent to the only school in the district for accelerated students. Not only was she a voracious reader, she was equally good with numbers and served as a kind of math tutor for the rest of her brothers and sisters.

By contrast, Sheila seemed slower and more intimidated. Compared with blond and buxom Suesan, the dark-haired Sheila was petite and dispirited. Theresa had turned her into little more than a scullery maid years earlier, forcing her to clean up after the rest of the family—a Cinderella without hope of a fairy godmother.

Robert described his older half sister as "borderline mentally retarded with severe manic depression." "I remember her saying that her whole philosophy from the time she got into kindergarten was: 'Why should I try? It's only going to get harder,' " said Robert.

She was equally lackadaisical about her chores around the house. Doing the dishes was a daily exercise in futility, she used to complain. " 'Why should I do them? They'll only get dirty again,' " Robert recalled her saying, like clockwork, every night after she and her sisters cleared the table.

Robert maintains that the only time he ever saw Sheila move quickly was when someone offered her sweets or she was doing something that she was not supposed to do and had gotten caught. The rest of the time it took her three times as long as any of her brothers and sisters to accomplish a task.

As an experiment, Robert recalled, Theresa once asked Howard to give his sister a dose of methamphetamine to see if it would hasten her through her housework. "Howard gave her some speed and Sheila went to sleep," said Robert. "She laid there, hyped out, sleeping through her trip. Maybe she did it just to defy Mom, but as far as I know, she really went to sleep. It made Mom mad no end."

Though she was three years older than Suesan, Sheila had the fire beaten out of her from the time she was a toddler, and she rarely spoke unless spoken to. The fact that she and Howard had a different father than the rest of Theresa's kids made her place in the family hierarchy even more tenuous. Coming from Arkansas, Clifford

Sanders apparently had Cherokee blood coursing through his veins, according to Theresa. The result was that Howard and Sheila both had sharper features and darker skin and hair than Bob Knorr's children. At school, while Suesan was suffering the nickname Fish, Sheila was regularly tagged as a "dirty Indian."

And nobody stepped to her defense. Everything conspired to turn Sheila's natural shyness into a sullen powerlessness. She protested by becoming even slower than she seemed to be by nature. She did not have Suesan's fire. In an eerie affirmation of Chet Harris's pronouncements about Theresa's children, Sheila really did seem to tag after her younger sister, almost like a dog. She rarely challenged her mother the way Suesan did.

So when the children became teenagers, the first and most frequent victim of Theresa's beatings while Howard pinned her arms behind her and kept her feet from kicking was Suesan. If she broke free or fought back, Theresa enlisted the help of her other sons to hold her down while Theresa slammed her with fists, feet, and her Board of Education. William and Robert had plenty of incentive for helping Howard wrestle Suesan to the ground.

"If the other ones held that one sufficiently, then that was the only person that got beat at that time," Bill explained.

The boys had far less to fear than Theresa's daughters, though. William and Robert had to break one of Theresa's many rules in order to deserve a slap. The girls, on the other hand, could wind up on the floor screaming for mercy, never knowing what they had done to deserve their punishment in the first place. Theresa saved most of her wrath for her girls, especially Suesan.

"She loved her boys and hated her daughters," said Terry.

If any of the children were given preferential treatment, it was William, or "Billy Bob," as their mother used to call him. The reason, according to Terry, was that Bill most closely resembled his father in appearance. He became almost a surrogate for his father.

"Bill slept with her every night until he was almost twelve years old," said Terry. "Howard didn't. Robert never did. When Bill quit sleeping with her, I started sleeping with her for a little while, until she started knocking me out of bed and I ended up sleeping on the floor."

Bill recalled that Theresa did seem to go lighter on him than anyone else. He still got enough kicks and slaps to want to steer clear of his mother as frequently as possible, but he had a facility for getting along with her that none of his siblings ever seemed to be able to master. Bill learned to mask his true feelings at a very tender age.

Bill also learned early how to get out of the house. At the age of ten, he started working. It wasn't for extra spending money because the family had no extra money. (At the end of the month, William had to turn his earnings over to his mother, who kept track of his income to make sure that he wasn't holding out on her.) It was one of the few opportunities that William had to get out of the house without his mother keeping tabs on exactly how long he was gone. In fact, if he was gone longer than planned, that could be good, because he might be working overtime and bring home extra money.

His jobs began with yard work around the neighborhood and a paper route that Terry remembers at least as well as Bill does.

"My brother William had this *Sacramento Bee* route, and the girls—myself and my two sisters—ended up getting stuck helping him out, if not doing it for him, because he wouldn't get out of bed. He was Mommy's little baby," Terry said sarcastically, years after she had delivered her last paper for her brother.

Once, when Terry refused to get out of bed and Suesan and Sheila wound up delivering the papers, the two older girls found a treasure trove waiting for them on the streets of Orangevale.

"Once a year everybody throws all their trash out, like spring-cleaning day," said Terry. "They throw out all their appliances and everything. One person's junk could be somebody else's fortune or treasure. And this particular morning when they were throwing my brother's paper route, my sisters went searching through all this garbage, and they brought home stuff."

Theresa was delighted. There were clothes that could be washed and worn, appliances that might be rewired and refurbished. She found a hand mixer that looked like it had been used to blend cockroaches, but Theresa patiently took it apart, cleaned it, and put it back together, as good as new. It looked as though her daughters had actually done something that had pleased her for a change.

"But my mom was going through all this shit and found a *Book of Mormon*," said Terry. "To my mom, this was evil. She believed my sister Suesan found it because she was a witch and the devil was giving my mom a sign, because she had brought her this book."

Theresa's delight instantly turned to rage. She howled at Suesan, accusing her of selling her soul to Chester Harris and carting blasphemy into the house under the pretense of digging through the neighbors' trash.

"My mom burned that book because she said it was like a demon book," said Terry. "It was about a bunch of witches and shit. My mom was a trippy woman."

Her sister was not a trippy woman.

By the late 1970s, Rosemary Norris was living proof that hard work, perseverance, goodwill, and a strong heart can overcome even the worst childhood conditions. Even a mediocre marriage to a man who could not hold a job didn't defeat Rosemary's brand of determination.

In May of 1977, she and her perennially unemployed husband opened Antiquity Recalled—the first of two antiques stores that Floyd managed while Rosemary continued working. By this point in her career, she had graduated to the position of associate administrative analyst for the state of California and was looking toward the kind of financial security that her parents never enjoyed. Never mind that Floyd had been everything from a truck driver to a property manager to a counter salesman, all with mixed results, throughout their marriage. Now that he was running their antiques business, Rosemary's plan for an early retirement with lots of life insurance and a healthy state pension to carry them through recessions looked like it was right on track. Still in her thirties, Rosemary had a new home in an exclusive wooded area east of Sacramento, a successful career, a thriving antiques business, two healthy teenage sons, and a husband to whom she had been married for nearly twenty years.

But she may as well have had no sister. She and Theresa never spoke to each other, and the only contact the two families had with each other was through their sons. Howard and Rosemary's older son, Joey, got to be friendly during high school. But the long-running rivalry between Theresa and Rosemary kept the rest of the families apart.

In November of 1979, tragedy finally reunited the two families.

Joseph Mansel Norris, born to Rosemary in 1962 exactly one day after Theresa gave birth to Howard Sanders, came home sick from Mesa Verde High School one morning. He lay down on his bed with heavy-metal music blasting from the stereo speakers in his room. And his heart stopped.

He was sixteen years old. The cause of death was given as acute myocarditis—an inflammation of the heart muscle. The doctors told Rosemary and Floyd that the condition is usually brought on by vigorous exercise coupled with a viral infection, but it could also be triggered by a couple of other things, including drug overdose.

The story Theresa told her children was that Joey had always had a heart condition. "When he went to sleep, sometimes his heart would literally stop, then start up again," Terry said. "This time he came home sick from school and he went to sleep and never woke up. His heart never did start again."

Joey was buried three days after his death, on November 19, 1979, at East Lawn Sierra Hills Memorial Park. Theresa's children noted the differences between their mother and her sister at graveside. At five-eight and 185 pounds, Rosemary towered over her short, stout sister. Theresa probably weighed the same—maybe more—but she was half a foot shorter. Rosemary dressed better, arrived in a nicer car, and was surrounded by dozens of coworkers, friends, and well-wishers.

Theresa was surrounded only by her children and her wheelchair-bound father, who had been released from the convalescent home for the day in order to attend his grandson's funeral.

There was one other difference Theresa's children noticed. Rosemary was inconsolable. She could not stop grieving as her son was laid to rest. Later on she refused to let Floyd sell Joey's gold Pontiac TransAm, according to Terry. For months afterward she refused to change a thing in his room.

But Theresa's eyes remained dry. She shared her sister's grief to the extent that she bowed her head in prayer for Joey and laid flowers at his grave. But secretly, she later revealed to her children, she couldn't help but gloat just a little.

After nearly twenty years of hard-earned good fortune, her sister finally had to face up to the same ugly whims of fate that seemed to have plagued Theresa from the day she first left home.

X

Theresa did not want to go on welfare. When she was growing up back in Rio Linda, her parents labeled those who lived off the state "bloodsuckers," and Theresa had always shared their contempt. It was a level to which she tried mightily never to stoop.

But with the approach of the 1980s, she had exhausted all of her other sources of revenue. Her hip and back still bothered her and convalescent homes balked at hiring her for fear she might be looking for workers' compensation or permanent disability instead of a forty-hour-a-week job. She was not the kind of prospect most other employers were looking to hire either. She had put on even more weight, the beginnings of jowls sagged from her rounded face, and her flirting glances no longer reeled in even a one-night stand at the bars. Long-range prospects were out of the question. Men as a source of revenue were history.

Her other schemes to raise cash likewise came to nought. Once, before they were divorced, she had hopes of opening a child-care center in Rio Linda with the help of Chester Harris. She dropped that plan when she found that Chester had his own hopes: indoctrinating preschoolers into his lurid voodoo practices. At least, that's what Theresa told her children.

After reestablishing relations with her sister, Rosemary, the two of them chatted a few times about buying a ranch together somewhere away from the city and turning it into a rehab center for young drug and alcohol offenders. But that plan was doomed, too. Theresa wound up borrowing some cash from Rosemary after Joey's funeral and found herself unable to pay the money back, so she began ducking her sister the way she avoided other creditors.

Her economic status sank so low that she became dependent on the meager earnings of her own kids: William's paper route, Howard's clandestine sales of substances that Theresa would just as soon know nothing about. Her children had even begun lying about their ages so that they could get hired at fast-food restaurants and help their mother out with mortgage payments.

One of Theresa's financial mainstays had always been Social Security. She still collected once a month on Howard and Sheila. It was the regularity and size of those government checks that got Theresa to thinking about Supplemental Security Income. Homeless crazies got SSI. Why not Sheila?

"Sheila wasn't mentally retarded or anything by any stretch of the meaning, but she did have learning problems. She was manic-depressive," said Robert. "Personally, I think she didn't learn because she didn't want to learn."

Sheila had dropped out of school in the ninth grade. In her eldest daughter's vacant stare and perennial sloth, Theresa began to sense a gold mine. She began coaching Sheila on what she was to say and how she was to present herself at the Social Security office. Then she dressed her in rags and told her not to put on makeup, do her hair, or even clean herself for a week.

"Sheila put shit in her hair before she went in for the interview," said Robert.

When she was given a mental competency test at the Social Security Administration offices in downtown Sacramento, Sheila "fucked off," according to Robert. She searched out the wrong answers on most of the test and didn't answer any questions she thought she might mistakenly answer correctly. Sheila had never been a threat to Einstein, but she played the part of a total moron for the benefit of the bureaucrats so convincingly that nobody raised an eyebrow about her right to collect permanent mental disability. Even if she had come up with a passing score, her appearance and smell apparently persuaded her examiners that she was not all there.

"She wasn't big on showers in the first place, but she made it even worse before she went in for the interview," said Robert. His sister had also developed a terrible athlete's-foot problem and added to her raving-maniac routine by showing up shoeless and itchy at the Social Security office. "So I'm sure that's why when she went in there, they said, 'Oh yeah, we'll go ahead and put *her* on SSI,' " said Robert.

Within weeks, she was getting her checks. They went to Theresa's post office box, and the payee was Theresa. Sheila, after all, had been found to be incompetent.

Theresa also found other ways for her children to earn money. She began sending the girls out to scout for odd jobs in the neighborhood and discovered an elderly man just a few houses away who needed help cleaning his house. His sister lived with him, but she was unable to stay at home twenty-four hours a day.

"He lived on Sutton Avenue, three houses down from us and he was on oxygen all the time," said Robert. "He was still ambulatory, but he was using one of those canes with the three prongs on it to get around."

He welcomed the girls who came knocking at his door, and soon Theresa, aided by her daughters, found herself back in the convalescent-care business. Suesan, Terry, and Sheila ran shifts, taking care of the old man—fixing his meals, washing his floors, disposing of his trash. Once, not long after they'd begun, Suesan came home laughing hysterically.

"I guess she was wearing a halter top over there when she was cleaning up and one of her breasts fell out," said Robert. "The guy almost had a stroke. I got the feeling that Suesan did it accidentally on purpose. She snickered about it at the time, but frankly, I think that may have been where my mother's little prostitution thing came from. Suesan was heavily breasted, and I think that gave my mom ideas."

Theresa urged her daughter to let the accidental breast revelation happen again and see whether the peep show got any further rise out of the old man.

"I can't imagine him being able to consummate an act like that, considering that he was on oxygen and almost infirm," said Robert. "But who knows? We did find out later he was one of those perverts who liked to take pictures of his granddaughters in the bathtub."

He also took to specifically requesting Suesan, and Suesan alone, whenever he needed something special done around the house—or help getting in or out of bed. The lesson was not lost on Theresa. Her own good looks may have faded into middle-age flab, but her daughters were just coming into full bloom.

"Mom did take her and Sheila out to a couple of bars so they could get experience," said Robert. "I don't know what happened on those outings. There were times when I'd wake up at home and everybody'd be gone but me."

But all of the money schemes Theresa came up with—from Social Security to pandering for her daughters—were only postponing the inevitable. She finally swallowed hard and went down to the Sacramento County Department of Public Social Services, filled out the applications, and went on the welfare rolls. She feared the inevitable snooping from social workers and compliance officials as much as she did the shame of having to accept government handouts. Her children were already on the free-lunch program at school and frequently came home with stories about how they were ridiculed for being welfare kids. Theresa figured she would also be fingered as a welfare mom and suffer the same public humiliation.

But nobody ever showed up to check on her or her children. "I never saw a social worker in my life," said Robert. "I was never interviewed by anybody."

"The truant officers never came," said Terry. "Nobody was doing their job."

The nearest any of the children came to revealing what went on at 5539 Bellingham was when Robert and Terry were cornered one day by the Palisades Elementary School nurse. By then, Theresa's two youngest had switched schools three times and chalked up more absences than any of their other classmates. The nurse wanted some answers and had not been able to get any from Theresa. Therefore, she demanded that Robert and Theresa remain after class until she and the principal and their teachers could find out why they were not coming to school regularly.

"So we escaped," said Robert.

Terry and Robert ducked out before school administrators could begin quizzing them. They hid for what seemed like hours in the bushes of a vacant lot, where their mother claimed devil worshipers left dead cats and dogs as sacrifices to their infernal master.

Before it got dark, and the demons came out of the weeds, Robert and Terry raced back home through the side streets "like commandos," and sneaked in through the back door. Out front, the school nurse was banging on the door, demanding that Mrs. Knorr open up and answer some questions about her truant children.

"We all huddled together in the living room, not breathing a word," recalled Robert. "It was pretty humorous. Pretty pathetic at the same time."

After keeping her children out of school for a few days, Theresa sent them back and it was business as usual at Palisades Elementary. Even the school nurse had given up on the Knorr family. "No one else ever tried to talk to us," said Robert. "Not Child Protective Services, not Social Security, not welfare or the Veterans Administration or anybody else. My mom just collected the checks and that was it."

Being at home all of the time did little to make Theresa a better parent, though she did occasionally make some effort to become more of a friend to her growing children, when she was in the right mood and when they were at home. Howard increasingly spent his free time living at his friend Bud Watson's house and William had gotten involved in track and other sports at school, but the girls and Robert still stayed close to home most of the time.

Theresa and Suesan became chummy again. They talked philosophy and argued over religion, and when the conversations didn't disintegrate into a shouting match, they actually seemed to have a genuine mother-daughter bond. There were times when Theresa and Suesan would stay up drinking nearly all night, listening to Rod Stewart or Gerry Rafferty on the stereo. Suesan was only about thirteen, but she and her mother got tipsy enough to dance together, and even invited the boys to join in if they happened to be around.

"At one time Theresa was dancing in her underwear and she was really starting to gain weight and I told her, 'You know, you look like a slut when you do that,' " said Robert. "I would have been all of eleven at that time. I still don't know why I said it."

Theresa grew very quiet after her youngest son's comment. She even unconsciously tried to cover herself with her hands. "She said she wasn't doing it to be a slut or anything like that," recalled Robert. "But she said after that, she'd never dance again—that I had taken away her one remaining joy in life: dancing."

Robert felt terrible. "But she wouldn't accept an apology," he said. "She'd still stay up at night and listen to music and drink, but from that time on, she wouldn't dance anymore. I think Mom could make Jesus Christ feel guilty."

Suesan quit school somewhere between the seventh and eighth grades, just as the real trouble began with her mother.

She did not drop out for want of intelligence.

"Suesan was nothing short of a genius," said Terry. "I was just an average student. Suesan was a straight-A student all her life. She went to Arcade Fundamental Middle School for gifted genius kids with brains. Computer-whiz kids. I couldn't produce the grades that Suesan did."

It wasn't because she was ashamed of her appearance.

"She looked a lot like me back then," remembered Bill. "Sandy-blond hair, blue eyes . . . maybe she weighed like 150 pounds. She was shorter than I was, so probably put her around five-eight."

Suesan quit school, her mother told her other children, because Suesan was a witch.

To Robert, his sister was "rambunctious." To Terry, she was "gutsy." Unlike Sheila, she stuck up for herself, even when she knew her reward would be the back of her mother's hand.

But her defiance cost her much more than a black eye when she began cutting classes to go to the mall with her friends. The school contacted Theresa about her daughter's excessive absences, and one day after school, Theresa confronted Suesan about it.

Suesan answered her mother's hands-on-hips stance with one of her own. She would not back down. Yes, she had cut classes. She taunted her mother further by telling her that she wasn't off at a videogame parlor somewhere playing Donkey Kong. She was actually having secret trysts with Chester Harris and his Rio Linda warlocks.

"The shit really hit the fan because my mom had forbidden Suesan to continue seeing Chester," said Robert.

Theresa made Suesan stay home from school because she no longer trusted her outside of the house at all. She began checking up on her daughter at all hours of the night, to make sure that she was asleep in her bedroom, not sneaking off to Rio Linda to dance by the light of the moon.

It was during one of those midnight checks that Theresa found strands of hair and some dried flakes of dead human skin tucked away in a cellophane bag beneath Suesan's pillow. After she had slapped Suesan awake and demanded to know the meaning of the contents of the cellophane bag, Suesan stuck her chin out and told Theresa that Chester needed it for one of his spells.

"Mom said she made a pact with the devil," said Terry. "She sold her soul, and she was no longer her daughter. She was a demon in Suesan's body. When Suesan ran away and went to the Receiving Home and told them about the abuse, my mom just totally chalked it up to the fact that she was a demon."

Exactly how Suesan arrived at the Children's Receiving Home of Sacramento is a matter of speculation among her brothers and sisters. Terry says she was taken there by her mother, because she had become too much for her to handle. Robert remembers Suesan running away from home, and the next time anyone heard from her, she had been arrested and was living at the Receiving Home.

"Basically it's like a child detention center," said Terry, who spent some time at the facility herself several years later. "Lock down, go to bed at a certain time, get up at a certain time. It's life in a dorm. They tell you when you can shower. They tell you when you can eat. You can only go out and play at certain times."

The county facility is located at the corner of Auburn Boulevard and Watt Avenue, on a large, beautifully landscaped patch of land adjacent to Interstate 80. For fifty years the Receiving Home has been the destination of last resort for unwanted, uncared-for, or unruly children. One recent study commissioned by the Sacramento County Board of Supervisors said that an average of 278 children each day have nowhere else to go and wind up in one county facility or another. Usually it's the Children's Receiving Home. Until a more permanent place can be found for them with a relative or in the care of a foster or group home, the incorrigibles, the molestation victims, and all the other underage wards of the court usually find themselves spending the night in one of the home's seventy beds.

On most days, automobiles pull up in the parking lot out front, loaded with suitcases, stuffed toys, and unwanted youngsters who will remain there for a few days, or a few weeks, until someone takes them off the county's hands. "These are children of abuse, or runaways," said Terry. "These are children that don't have a good life. The Receiving Home looks nice from outside, but it's hell on the inside."

At first, Suesan didn't see it that way. She saw it as a chance to escape. One of the first things she did was ask a counselor to locate her father and ask him if she could live with him.

At the time Bob Knorr had two other daughters he could barely care for, and he and his wife, Georgia, were increasingly quarreling over how they were going to make ends meet. Nevertheless, he said several years later, he would still have taken Suesan in, had he been contacted. But he never got the call. The way the message was related to Suesan, her father had been contacted and refused to accept her.

Her aunt Rosemary gave a similar answer. It wasn't that Suesan was not wanted. It was simply that nobody had a place for her in their lives.

So Suesan ran away.

For the next few weeks she lived on the mean streets of the Del Paso Heights or "North Town" section of Sacramento, ducking police cars and falling in with other runaways. She turned on to whatever street drugs she could find and turned tricks to earn money for food, using men the same way that she had seen her mother use them. She found a protector who was more than willing to initiate the blond and buxom young freelancer into the "life" in exchange for a percentage of her earnings. One of the first special requests that Suesan made of her new boyfriend was to pay a visit with her to her old neighborhood in suburban Orangevale.

"A car pulled up in front of our house and Suesan was with some guys who said they were going to kill everybody," remembered Robert. "I don't remember the exact context of the shouting, but basically they were going to sacrifice a couple of people."

The entire neighborhood emerged from houses up and down the block to see what was going on. The quiet home on the corner of Bellingham Way and Sutton Avenue had suddenly turned into a battleground, with mother and daughter hurling the foulest possible language at each other.

"I don't know exactly what was going on with Suesan at the time," recalled Chris Garrett, who lived next door. "She ran away and she came home to get some things or something, but her mom didn't want her to leave. Her mom was trying to get her to stay home and they were out in the front yard screaming. They got into a big confrontation while Suesan's friends were waiting for her up the street."

The slaps and kicks and rage that had gone on for years behind closed doors suddenly had a public arena and a public audience. When Theresa yelled for backup assistance, Howard and his friend Bud Watson entered the fray. But this time Suesan had her own reinforcements.

"Her pimp punched them out," recalled Terry. "Gave Howard a bloody nose."

Before anyone could call the police, it was over. Suesan and the young man Terry identified as her pimp retreated with a couple of other guys and girls to a car waiting for them half a block away.

"Afterward, nothing was ever said about it," said Chris Garrett. "Terry or Robert would come by every so often, but nothing was ever said about the incident."

Suesan's triumph over her mother was short-lived. Within a few days she was picked up by a truancy officer and sent back to the Receiving Home. This time county officials gave her behavior a much more serious assessment.

"After she ran away the first time, she spent some time at Sutter Memorial Psychiatric Ward downtown," said Bill. "I don't know if it was her evaluation or if it was . . . I don't know what that was about. But she did spend time there.

"I went down with my mom to visit her one time, and they wouldn't let me see her. I had to stay in their game room while my mom went in and talked to the doctors and Suesan, so I never actually saw the doctors and Suesan . . . I never actually saw her while I was there. . . ."

The reasons that Theresa relayed to her children for Suesan's detention at the hospital were as lurid and unbelievable as any Stephen King story.

"The Receiving Home supposedly told Mom—or at least this is what she said they told her—that Suesan was caught engaged in lesbian activity with one of the other children there," said Robert. "Actually, she said that what had happened was that Suesan had forced this other child to eat her pussy. According to Mom, they had also cut her hair and the next day it had grown halfway down her back, because she was a witch. At that point, they called Mom up and said, 'Take her back. We don't want her.' So Mom was more or less forced to bring her back home."

Terry remembers the day she and her mother went to fetch Suesan from the Receiving Home. Suesan had been pleading with her counselor not to send her back, claiming that her home was a concentration camp and that her mother was nothing short of Adolf Eichmann. When Theresa and her youngest daughter arrived, the counselor explained what Suesan had been alleging— that she had been a victim of the worst kind of abuse. Theresa looked the counselor squarely in the eye and told her it was not true. In addition to all of her other well-documented problems, Suesan was a pathological liar.

Then the counselor turned to Terry and asked her if she had ever been abused.

"I told her no. Never," said Terry.

On the drive home, Suesan was dumbstruck and despondent. Her mother snarled that none of the other children would back up her story of abuse either. Terry did not share her sister's silent, hopeless fear about what might happen once she got home. On the contrary, she shared her mother's outrage that her sister would dare break the family silence about what went on inside 5539 Bellingham Way. She remembered turning to her older sister and telling her as much.

"I could have helped her, but I was scared," said Terry. "You know, the only person I knew as loving me or taking care of me, as sick as her love was, was my mother."

Terry also remembered with chilling clarity the last

thing her mother snarled at Suesan before they pulled up in front of the house. "She said, 'If you think you were abused before, you just wait. I'll show you what abuse is.'"

Once inside, with the shades drawn, Theresa let loose her full fury. If Suesan flinched or showed the least defiance, she was walloped even harder. Theresa put leather gloves on before administering a beating, but she made no pretense about leaving her daughter without bruises. The gloves were strictly to protect Theresa from injuring her own hands while she worked Suesan over like a side of beef.

"Suesan tried to protect herself by hiding her stomach, but she never tried to hit my mom," said Terry. "None of us ever did."

The other children were not allowed to leave the room or even to sit silently by as reluctant observers. Led by Howard, Suesan's brothers and sisters were ordered to line up in order of size and age like the singing Von Trapp family and, one by one, don their mother's gloves in order to punch their sister in the abdomen.

"We had to pass gloves from one to the other and hit Suesan in the stomach for what she did to the family by running away and everything," recalled Robert. "And I had to hit her twice because I didn't hit her hard enough the first time."

That night, and every night thereafter, Theresa's children took turns standing watch over Suesan to make certain she would never flee the family again. To make doubly sure that the "witch" would not make her escape by casting a spell over one of her siblings in the blackest hours between midnight and dawn, Theresa acquired a pair of handcuffs and shackled her daughter to the headboard of her bed. Then she offered her a dire warning against running off to Rio Linda and joining Chester Harris and his coven. "'If you run away from home again, you will be separated from your siblings and you'll end up in a worse situation than you ever were with me,' " Robert recalled his mother telling Suesan.

"Suesan was yanked out of school by my mom and never permitted to go back, 'cause my mom didn't want her talking again," said Terry. "My mom got away with it because the truant officers never came to check or anything. Nobody was doing their job in this case. That's why my mom got away with it for ten years."

None of her brothers or her sister could explain why Suesan didn't try to run away again. She never left the house, but she wasn't always forced to wear the handcuffs. During the nightly watches, there was ample opportunity for her to slip out while Robert or Terry or Sheila napped. But she never did.

As time passed Suesan carried on as though nothing had ever happened. She helped her brothers with their homework, cooked dinner and breakfast for the family on occasion, teamed with Sheila to wash clothes and clean house, watched TV, continued to devour every book she could get her hands on, and even participated in family discussions. Her mother persisted in accusing her of witchcraft, however, and Suesan neither said nor did anything to dissuade her.

Terry speculated that her sister's spirit had finally been broken. Like a cruel boot-camp sergeant who uses the entire unit to bring a single insubordinate recruit to his knees, Theresa enlisted every member of the family to keep Suesan in check. Suesan had become a prisoner of war, broken and brainwashed, and she simply gave up.

But Robert thought Suesan's surrender went deeper. She and her mother were still on speaking terms much of the time, and an outsider—who did not know to what violent depths their debates could sink—might believe that their mother-daughter discussions of history, religion, psychology, music, movies, or family matters were perfectly normal. To Robert, that artificial normalcy was just one more paradoxical sign of Suesan's irrational submission to Theresa's brute force.

Suesan did not run, Robert said, because she could not. There was nowhere for her to run to. "Better the devil you know, than the one that you don't," he said.

XI

In the 1981 autumn semester at Casa Robles High, fourteen-year-old Bill Knorr "got the crap kicked out of him," his youngest sister said, describing the beating he took outside the gates of the school.

His karate lessons never paid off in a black belt, and his brothers and sisters doubted he would ever use martial arts against a bully even if he had to. Bill Knorr was not one to pick a fight, or even to defend himself. He might hold one of his sisters down when Theresa wanted to belt her, but Bill rarely hit them himself. It was not in his nature.

William Knorr had learned instead to channel his aggression into basketball, cross country, and the hundred-yard dash at school. And the girls noticed.

So when one began flirting with him in class and her jealous boyfriend challenged Bill to a fight, he declined. The boyfriend was not appeased. "One day at school, this guy jumped on William from behind and started hitting him in the back of the head with a padlock from his locker," Robert recalled.

School officials rushed Bill to the hospital where X rays revealed a mild concussion. After she picked her son up from the emergency room, Theresa told her other children that the doctors called their brother a very lucky young man. Bill had always had a bad sinus condition, and had he been hit in the wrong place with the lock, he might have died.

Bill came home bruised and bleeding, but very much alive, and another chapter in the family's ignominious history of getting even at any cost was about to unfold.

Howard, who didn't get along with his mother and was living more at his friend Bud Watson's house than at home, still fancied himself the father figure at 5539 Bellingham. If one of his brothers or sisters needed a defender, Howard was it. He was a senior at Casa Robles at the time Bill was attacked and he wanted revenge, even if Bill didn't. As the school's premier dope dealer, Howard had precisely the right pull to get it.

"Howard got the football team in full-dress football gear, and they went out and surrounded this guy so the teachers wouldn't be able to stop him," said Robert. "Then Howard beat the hell out of him for jumping William. There were even some pictures taken of it for the yearbook, but they never got put in."

At six feet and 195 pounds, Howard was no weakling, but his brother's attacker, though three years younger, was just as big.

"Howard was a little bit afraid of him, so he hit him with everything he had when he first landed on him and the kid didn't fall down, so Howard kept hitting him," said Robert. "Howard is what you call a scared fighter: he gets to hitting you and just keeps on doing it until you don't move anymore. What he didn't realize was the first punch had already put the kid out on his feet."

While Howard punched, the incident took on elements of slapstick. The girlfriend who had started the whole thing by flirting with William got into the act by shrieking and jumping on Howard's back like a scared monkey. When he drew back to slam her boyfriend once again, Howard accidently belted her. Then, in order to save Howard the dishonor of being accused of hitting a female, several of the other freshmen girls who admired the handsome young athlete William Knorr and his gallant older brother Howard Sanders, pounced on the girlfriend. They thrashed her in a separate battle while Howard finished beating her boyfriend to a pulp.

When it was over, and the boyfriend was sent to the hospital with a concussion, Howard was arrested for battery. As a minor, the court gave him three years informal probation, but it was a small price to pay. Howard had become a legend at Casa Robles High, and the family honor had been restored.

"There was a loyalty there, but in a screwed-up sense," said Robert.

Terry was more blunt about Howard's savage sense of discipline and family honor. Just as easily as his angry pride could avenge and protect a brother, it could be turned against a family member. "Howard's a control freak like his mother," said Terry. "If he can't control you, then he's gonna beat you up and make you do what he wants. I don't know what he's capable of, personally."

His girlfriend, Connie Butler, knew he was capable of manipulating and strong-arming others because he had manipulated and strong-armed her. But she also admired that strength and saw a sad and, she believed, more sensitive side to Howard as well.

"I met him in high school through my brother," she said. "When he first started coming around, he talked big words, sounded real smart and intelligent. He played little games, talking about auras. He could tell me what I was thinking. I felt like: 'This guy really knows me! He knows how I feel!'

"He'd come and cry on my mom's shoulder, saying how he loved me all the way. He convinced me to be with him. I'd have problems with my parents and go talk to him, and he'd make me feel like everything was okay."

Howard confided in her, dropping the machismo curtain he used to hide himself away from the rest of the world. He told her how he had to take full responsibility

for all the other kids in the family once his various step-
fathers were out of the picture. He told her how Bob
Knorr used to beat him when he was young—how his
stepfather entered his room when he was small, throwing toy soldiers at his chest, and calling him a dirty Indian. He spoke of the terror of watching his stepfather
rape his mother, right in front of him and his invalid
grandfather.

"He was so emotional about it," said Connie. "He'd
break down and cry that he never wanted to be that
way. He was afraid of hurting people."

Whatever else might be said about his brutal side,
Howard Sanders tried his best to fulfill the big-brother
role that he had inherited. "He was the oldest and the
biggest," said Connie. "He took on the father image in
that, you know, he disciplined the kids when the mother
couldn't do it physically. He set down the house rules.
You name it."

But Howard had, at times, odd ways of demonstrating
brotherly concern. "One time he beat the living shit out
of me because I got some dope from somebody else,"
said Robert. "He told me, 'You don't know *what* you're
getting from somebody else! You get your drugs from
me!' "

Howard' Sanders had developed a reputation as a
neighborhood character—both sinister and comical. He
was seen as a gruff, burly cross between a stand-up guy
and a junkyard dog. The Garretts, next door to the
Knorrs, and the Lane family across the street were all
certain that Howard ran a brisk drug business out of his
mother's house, but no one ever reported it.

Howard also tried to run with the toughest crowd he
could find. At one point, he and his pal Bud Watson
even became chummy with the Hell's Angels.

His brothers and sister don't remember him ever
holding a real job while he was in high school, though
he did go to work as a dishwasher at a restaurant not
long after graduation. He cut his hand on a knife during

that job and had to go on workmen's compensation. Howard was skilled at earning money in other ways, though.

Before his after-school showdown with Bill's attacker, he had an accident in the hallway at Casa Robles that turned out to be as lucrative as it was painful: he ran the palm of his hand through a piece of metal that stuck out of the lock mechanism on one of the student lockers.

"I guess he got pushed into the part that you pull up in order to open or lock the door," said Robert. "He impaled his hand, sued, and got a settlement."

The settlement was substantial enough that Howard was able to loan his mother about $2,000, according to Robert, and still live fairly well for quite some time afterward. He was not so disabled by the injury that he could not protect his family.

"Once I was getting some medication for his hand and I got hit by a car over there by the Capri Market," recalled Robert. "Some asshole was looking at the dress-shop window and rolled up on the sidewalk and hit me while I was on my bike." Not only had the driver wrapped the front of Robert's bicycle around his front axle, he had also pinned Robert beneath the tire and "tore just about every ligament in my left leg," Robert recalled.

While the absentminded driver was trying to pry the bike off of his car and figure out how he could avoid any liability, Howard and Bud Watson showed up. This time Howard limited his temper to merely screaming at the driver, an act of self-restraint considerably abetted by the fact that his hand was still bandaged. He got the driver's name and license number as well.

"Then Howard and Bud picked me up and carted me off," said Robert. "It was the only real big-brother scene I can remember with Howard. It made me feel like wow!"

Usually, Robert was as ambivalent toward his oldest

brother as every other member of the family. "Howard was one of the focal figures of my life," he said. "His idea of being in charge was being a complete ogre authoritarian. I guess that was the only experience at being a father figure he ever had. He liked to yell and intimidate a lot.

"One thing he didn't like was crying in front of him. That would really set him off. He didn't like cowardice, or maybe it reminded him of himself when he was younger."

Once, after eating a pile of magic mushrooms, Howard made a revealing confession to his friends gathered around the hookah in Howard's bedroom, and Robert overheard it from the hallway. "He said, 'It's terrible knowing that there's a world full of monsters and you hate the monsters. But then you wake up one day and you look in the mirror, you find out that you've become one of the monsters you hate.' I remember that," said Robert. "Howard has a lot self-hate concerning things that he did to his family."

Of all the children, Howard got along least well with Suesan. She hated him and the feeling was mutual. He had seen enough of her hocus-pocus and heard enough of her eerie incantations to believe what Theresa claimed: that Suesan was a bona fide witch. Suesan's disdain for Howard did not lessen after she was brought back from the Receiving Home. When she went into one of her demon-possessed trances, Howard would leave in disgust. Nevertheless, her predictions of doom began to scare Howard as much as they did Theresa.

"At one point Suesan said Howard was supposed to kill everybody in the whole family," Robert remembered. "Suesan said she would be gone, everybody was going to die, Howard was going to kill everybody and be left sitting in the middle of the living room with a gun. When my mom asked Suesan where she would be, she said she didn't know. She was just gone."

During her trances, Suesan saved her real venom for

her mother. While cuffed to her bed or strapped to a chair, she related to Theresa in her most demonic voice how her mother would continue to grow obese while Suesan was transformed into a living goddess.

"My mom said that Suesan was doing spells at night to get rid of her weight and put it onto Mom," said Terry. "Suesan did absolutely nothing! My mom was just a sick pup. In the worst clinical sense, a sick woman. She just went berserk. She wasn't pretty anymore. She was fat, she was ugly, she was getting old. She hated herself, and that's why she took it out on her daughters, because we were all growing up and growing out."

Howard's girlfriend, Connie Butler, heard the same story from Theresa that she planted in the minds of her children: that Suesan had some magical way of removing fat from her own young body and putting it onto her mother's.

Suesan managed to do this, according to Theresa, by slipping a sedative into Theresa's food. While she was asleep Suesan would snip off strands of her mother's hair and eyelashes and pieces of her fingernails. Like one of the hags in *Macbeth*, Suesan would put the hair and nails into some kind of supernatural concoction that allowed her to cast a spell over her mother.

The proof of her suspicions, Theresa told Connie, was that Theresa had contracted a bizarre disease that caused her to gain weight and no doctor understood why.

"She had intestinal problems, the weight gain, stomachaches, high blood pressure, headaches . . . you name it, she had it," said Connie. "She always told me that Suesan was the one that gave her the disease, that she had the power to do these things because she had signed her name in blood, sold her soul."

Robert heard another version of how his mother got her disease that didn't include Suesan or Chester Harris or the curse of the coven at all. In this version, Theresa was the victim of a government plot. "One night, she was out of the house and a black limousine pulled up," said Robert. "Someone kidnapped her, drugged her, and she heard a guy with a Russian accent refer to himself as 'Big Stuff.' Obviously that meant to her that he was into highly classified things.

"There was a scientist in a lab coat who came over to her bedside. There were several files, and one of them was open—her file. He injected her with something and they put a number on her file and said they would keep an eye on her and see what happened. She said the doctor's features changed into those of a demon and then back into the doctor. She was drugged again and then put back on the street."

Theresa was not so taken with her government conspiracy theory that she was ready to abandon her witch theory, however. She continued to speak to the fiend occupying Suesan's body for clues on how to lose weight. In her ongoing campaign to purge Satan from her daughter's soul, she chatted with the demon almost every day.

"Mom's conversations with Suesan became like a debate between her and the demon as to what was going on," said Robert. "It was a personal challenge to Mom's righteousness to get these things out of her: what she was promised for her soul, what exactly the coven was doing, what disease was put into her.

"It was her personal fight. It was her against hell, trying to save her daughter's soul. She put herself in the role of hero while at the same time destroying the very thing that she said she was going to save. And she counted it all as righteousness. It became gratifying for her in three ways: she got to destroy the person she wanted to destroy, she felt good about it afterward, and she would go to heaven for doing it. And no matter what anybody told her, she was a martyr.

"She was on the front lines of the war between good and evil and everybody was against her. She said she had dreams that all her kids were going to turn against her, so she was paranoid of all of us. Everybody. It just got progressively worse."

As the youngest Knorr, Terry tried desperately to play out her role as the baby of the family, even while events all around her conspired to make her grow up far more quickly than any child should ever be forced to. One of the ways she tried to make her own life more like *The Brady Bunch* than *The Addams Family* was to fantasize about her grandfather. "He was a good man. He was in the wheelchair most of the time I had known him and it got to a point where he couldn't communicate, but he was a good man," she said.

In earlier years Terry remembered sitting on his knee during a Fourth of July celebration, playing with sparklers while Jim Cross watched from his wheelchair. When he was still able to do so, he spoke in halting tones about his college days and the years he'd put in as a cheesemaker for the dairy. When his speech became indecipherable, Theresa filled in the details for her daughter. Jim Cross, an educated man who had lived through tragedy to a ripe old age, became a beacon of hope to Terry and to her brother Robert.

When she was in sixth grade, she finagled her teacher into taking her and other members of the class on a field trip to the nearby Orangevale Convalescent Home, where her grandfather lived. Her plan was to surprise him with her rendition of "Tomorrow" from the musical *Annie.* When she arrived, though, disappointment was waiting. "I remember going to my teacher crying because they wouldn't get my grandpa out of bed 'cause he had Parkinson's disease and he was bedridden," she said.

"By that time his speech was pretty well unintelligible," remembered Robert. "They were treating him like a child at the convalescent hospital, calling him Jimmy instead of James, talking to him like you would to a six-year-old. I felt badly that he was in there. Basically a convalescent home is a pretty depressing place for an eleven-year-old."

But Theresa managed to make it even more depressing for her children by telling them her own appalling fantasies about what the nursing-home personnel did to her father behind closed doors. "Mom said that Grandpa was raped by one of the nurses while he was in there," said Robert. "She said he was looking really yellow for a long time. Then, all of a sudden, he was back to normal. She was sure that it was because one of the doctors had forcibly taken a kidney away from Grandpa."

Theresa told her children that Rosemary had always been James Cross's favorite, but she herself remained the dutiful daughter. She had loyally stuck by her father even after Rosemary ran off with Floyd Norris, a man whom Jim Cross loathed. Theresa made it clear that she cared very much for her father, but she was not so positively committed to the memory of her mother.

"My grandma wasn't all that nice to my mom," said Terry. "I only knew of my mom going to visit my grandma's grave one time, and that was real late at night. She was intoxicated when she did it. Afterward, she told us that she was followed home by a man dressed in black. She was talking crazy."

The crazy talk both bewildered and angered Terry. Her mother's wild imagination plus her proclivity for finding the very worst in any situation made Terry retreat into her own imagination every time her mother opened her mouth. Terry created her own world, populated with dolls and dreams. Her persistent attempts to buck the odds and preserve some element of her childhood were finally halted when she was crossing the vacant lot near Skyridge Avenue one day after school and three boys blocked her way.

When she came home hours later with a tear-streaked face and torn and dirty clothes, and told Theresa her story of being dragged into a shack and held down by two of the boys while the third raped her, she got no sympathy. Terry was stunned. There was no outrage. There was no call to the police. There was only punishment for coming home late in dirty clothes.

In fact, the story she related to her mother was merely validation of Theresa's long-standing belief that her youngest daughter was a liar. And if it was true that she had been raped, then she must be a slut who brought it on herself by teasing the boys. Either way, she was no more or less than her mother had come to expect.

Besides, the last thing Theresa wanted to do was bring attention to herself and her family by calling the police. It was the same reason she did not call 911 the day that Suesan was shot.

William and Howard weren't at home at the time. It was just Robert, the girls, and their mother. As usual, the battle was between Suesan and Theresa. Theresa had her daughter cornered in the hallway, shouting at her for witching more pounds onto Theresa's already bloated body. She had already belted Suesan a couple of times when Sheila and Robert moved up behind their mother to see what was going on. Terry stood a few feet off, across the hall.

"Suesan was up against the wall between the bathroom door and my mother's bedroom," said Robert. "I was told to restrain Suesan. The next thing I know, there was a shot fired."

"There was a lot of screaming," Terry remembered. "I just remember that everything was in slow motion after I heard the pop of the gun, and I watched my sister grab her chest, gasp, grab onto the door frame of the bathroom, and fall into the tub."

"A bullet had entered under Suesan's left breast," said Robert. "She was bleeding profusely at that point, or at least there was a lot of blood on her shirt because she was wearing a halter top and there was a lot of blood on that."

They watched in horror as Suesan sank back into the empty bathtub and their mother underwent a near-miraculous transformation, switching instantly from a deranged aggressor bent on beating the devil out of her unrepentant daughter to a concerned practical nurse. She quickly pulled her daughter's clothes off, searching for the damage the bullet had done. She found the entrance wound beneath her daughter's heaving left breast, but there was no exit wound.

Much later, when Suesan allowed Terry to run her hand along the left side of her sister's back between her spine and armpit, Terry was able to feel the lump where the spent slug came to rest, deep inside Suesan's body.

At the time of the shooting, however, Theresa was too busy stanching the blood to worry about where the bullet was. As a nurse, she was in her element. Having pilfered from convalescent homes for most of the previous decade, she had all that she needed to treat her daughter: restraints, gauze, surgical bandages, syringes, disinfectants, gloves, drugs.

"We had a remarkably well-stocked first-aid kit," said Robert.

And yet she remained as leery of physicians and hospitals as she was of the police, or any other authority figure. She wouldn't go to doctors herself and only took her children if she absolutely had to. A gunshot wound would raise questions. She was not going to take her daughter to any emergency room.

Theresa had collected a large selection of pills over the years and came up with her own prescription for her daughter's needs. "She gave her antibiotics for infection, to keep infection from going in," said Terry. "I think she even gave her some ibuprofen and some Flexeril to kill the pain."

Theresa left her daughter in the tub for the next month, propping her up with pillows and covering her

with a blanket. When Suesan needed to use the bathroom, she did so where she lay and the family simply
washed her refuse down the drain. When it came to
changing the dressings on the wound, Theresa became
"Dr. Kildare" and wouldn't let anybody watch what she
was doing. The rest of the time, she left the convalescent duties to Suesan's brothers and sisters.

"My mom made us take care of her," said Terry. "As
far as changing the dressings on her wound and so
forth, she did that, but as far as meals and stuff like
that, we took 'em to her. I talked to her. My sister was
my best friend. My sister Suesan was my best friend."

Years later, when she first gave her version of the
long-suppressed details of that awful day, Terry was
very clear about who shot her sister. Her mother owned
a small two-shot derringer, and when the argument in
the hallway hit fever pitch, Theresa aimed the gun at
Suesan and shot her own daughter point-blank.

"I remember my mother saying she was sorry and
asking my sister to forgive her, and my sister looked at
my mother, and with all her heart, she said 'I forgive
you,'" said Terry. "You know, I love you, and they
cried and da, da, da, da, da, and so forth. . . ."

But Robert remembered events quite differently. He
recalled tempers flaring and shouting and slapping that
put everyone in the hallway that day into a state of hys-
teria, whipped to a frenzy by his mother's fury. He remembered hearing a loud pop come from behind him,
and he turned to see what it was.

"After I heard the shot, I looked over and I saw Terry
with the gun, crying. The gun was shaking," he said. "I
took the gun out of her hand, ran down the hall with it,
and for some stupid reason, wiped the fingerprints off.
I took the bullet out that had been spent and threw the
casing away, reloaded the gun, and put it away in its
customary spot. Then I came down the hall again.

"Terry was basically bawling. She was hysterical at
that point. Mother was mad. But she was more mad

that, if Suesan had died, how was she going to explain it? I was punished for wiping the prints off the gun because, had Mom wanted to tell the police what Terry had done if Suesan died, Mom wouldn't have been able to prove Terry did it, because I had wiped the prints off the gun."

Upon hearing her brother's account of the sequence of events—and who really fired the gun that day—Terry's certainty that her mother did it grew hazy.

"I don't remember," she said. "I really don't remember."

But the wound was not fatal. Even though the bullet remained lodged deep inside her rib cage, it had miraculously missed any major arteries or vital organs. For a few days Suesan seemed to worsen, and then she got better. Within a few weeks she was up and walking. She was moved from the bathtub back to her bed, where Theresa visited her in a redoubled effort to talk the demon into dropping the weight curse that it had put on her.

As she grew stronger Suesan also seemed to grow lovelier. Her wound had given her a pallor and an expression that was almost beatific, and her scant appetite during her convalescence resulted in a thin fashion-model look: still big-breasted, but slimmer in the waist and hips. Far from wasting away from the small sliver of lead she carried inside of her, Suesan made a full recovery.

She did not die. Yet.

XII

Theresa broke with her usual practice of isolation and answered the front door several weeks after Suesan had been shot. It was her old friend Cherise Kelly, who had commiserated with her after Theresa's breakup with Bob Knorr. As in the days when they first became friends, Cherise and Theresa still shared an interest in the supernatural. Only now, Cherise was proselytizing as well as schmoozing. And Theresa listened.

"She gave Mom this religious pamphlet which had a picture of Christ that Mom nailed to the wall in the living room," said Robert. "Then Mom began sprinkling holy water all over the place and trying to bless the room. She used to sprinkle holy water on Suesan all the time, I guess expecting it to burn or something. Basically she did the same thing to everybody. I was blessed two or three times a day."

Nothing helped, though. Theresa kept gaining weight and Suesan didn't, even if Theresa made her eat and hovered over her to make sure she finished every bite. And Theresa found other signs of demonic possession, too.

"My mom got a hole in her water bed and it mildewed the foam mattress," said Terry. "She said Suesan was evil because the hole was where Suesan had once slept. My mom said it was kinda like *The Amityville Horror*, one of the books she always read."

It wasn't long after Cherise's visit and the mysterious water-bed incident that Theresa decided to have Suesan exorcised.

"Mom took Suesan to see the pastor of the Hazel Avenue Baptist Church to try to have an exorcism performed," said Robert. "It was after she had healed up and everything."

Even before the shooting, Theresa had concluded that her daughter needed a cure for her soul a lot more desperately than she did for her body. Once she was out of the tub and able to walk, instead of taking her to a doctor, Theresa turned to the church.

"But the Baptist church wouldn't do it," said Robert. "I don't know if they suggested psychiatric help or what, but evidently they did not believe that Suesan was possessed."

Theresa pleaded with the pastor and Suesan's former Sunday-school teachers to reconsider, but their answers were unchanged: Baptists did not perform, or believe in, exorcisms. Exorcism was a seldom-used rite of the Roman Catholic church, based on medieval belief in demon possession and devil worship. Except in popular novels and films, like William Peter Blatty's *The Exorcist*—which Theresa had seen several times—the practice of exorcism was all but extinct. It had not been in wide use even by Roman Catholics since the days of the Spanish Inquisition.

"Shortly thereafter things started happening at the Baptist church," said Robert. "Their piano player's arm got busted and a couple other bad things began to befall the church."

The church leadership saw no correlation between its run of bad luck and Theresa's outlandish request for an exorcism, but several of the church's members did. They got together and delivered their own message to Theresa and her children.

"They said we were cursed of God. That what was happening to us was retribution, and as long as we were in the church, things would keep happening to them," said Robert. "So we were told not to come anymore. We were excommunicated from the Baptist church."

Theresa was undaunted. If she could not get help from the church, she'd try to perform the ritual herself, using the power of family. In the spring of 1983, she waited until after midnight and had her children hold a séance, although she didn't tell them what she was up to.

"One night Mom woke us all up except Howard, who was asleep in his room," said Robert. "She woke up Suesan, William, Sheila, myself, and Terry and had us go sit in a circle on the floor in the living room. Mom was on the sofa. She said, 'Don't say anything. Don't do anything. And stay awake.' If we went to sleep, we would be fucked over somehow."

In the darkened front room, Theresa's children did as they were told. They remained very still and quiet. They heard some vibrating coming from the water pipes under the house, but no other noises. Theresa told them the vibration was an overture for a spiritual visitation, and again ordered them to be still and listen.

The séance seemed to go on for hours without event. Robert believes he must have nodded off out of boredom.

"The next thing I remember, my mom slapped me in the face and told me to shut up," he said.

He shook the sleep off and started to ask what he'd done to deserve a slap, but his mother's attention had switched to the rest of the family members. Robert turned his own gaze to the opposite side of the room to see what his brothers and sisters were doing, and that's when things began to get strange.

"I was looking around, and Sheila was crying but not saying anything," said Robert. "Her hair was just hanging in her face and she was crying.

"William was picking at one of the bottom doors in the china hutch with his fingernails, and Terry was staring off into space. And as this continued William said, 'We like your book collection. We like your library.' Just really weird off-the-wall things like that." His brother seemed obsessed with a pair of red-and-blue insulated Löwenbräu beer-can holders in the china hutch, describing in minute detail how the colors seemed to be melting into one another.

"Sheila just continued to cry," Robert went on. "She never said anything. Terry mentioned seeing a guy in what I would have to describe as an eighteenth-century or Victorian-era costume. The man was wearing black with a white ruffled shirt. He was approximately seven feet tall.

"And she said there was a party going on in the dining room. Of course I looked. There was no party. There was no seven-foot-tall guy wearing anything. But Terry said she could see it all when she looked at the TV, which wasn't on.

"I wasn't saying anything, but everybody else was weirded out," said Robert.

"Then Mom asked something about Bob [Knorr]," he continued, "and Terry said, 'Bob's had it long enough. We don't need him anymore.' And there was a bag lying on its side on the floor, which contained Bob's Purple Heart and his picture and other things that belonged to him that Mother had kept, and all of a sudden it crumpled into itself, all by itself."

They stayed up all night, but Robert never got an answer from his mother about why she had slapped him.

The next day, Theresa had her own vision. She told her children that she had seen Howard hiding in a closet with her .22 six-shot revolver and she believed he was planning to kill her.

"So she took off," said Robert. "She went to north Sacramento and rented a hotel room. She ran away from home."

The children were both relieved and panic-stricken. Her absence meant that nobody would get beaten or scolded, but she had left no note and told nobody where she was going. She hadn't even packed, which is why the children thought she'd simply gone off on a binge somewhere and would return soon, hungover but safe.

But she did not come home after two days and nights, and their concern mounted. They went looking for her, without success. Then, on the third day, she walked through the front door. She had stories to tell.

While she was gone, she said, she had been stalked. They did not catch her, and she checked into a hotel. In her room, she saw red eyes peering in at her through a vent. When she rode the bus to get around downtown, people she'd never seen before approached her and, for no apparent reason, told her to read her Bible because Jesus saves. She was still afraid, but she finally decided it was safe to come home.

Afraid? Afraid of what? Robert wanted to know. Which led to Theresa's explanation for slapping Robert's face and telling him to shut up on the night of the séance. "She told me that I had been telling her how she was going to die of a brain aneurysm," said Robert. "Describing how it was going to be so great to watch the blood drip out of her eyes and nose and ears. How I was going to dance and piss upon her grave. That was when she slapped me.

"I don't remember saying any of that," he added.

Theresa also explained to her son what she had seen happen on the night of the séance after he and his brother and sisters lapsed into their trances.

Theresa did not go to sleep. She remained alert and, after a time, began to see red beams of lights flashing through the front windows. The lights pierced the backs of each of her children's heads, signaling their possession by something or someone from another dimension. Then she heard a voice.

"She said she was offered a cure for her disease if

she would have the rest of the family follow the coven," said Robert.

But the voice threw in one more catch, Theresa told her son. Without explanation, the voice had told her that she and her children were all descended from the tribe of David, through the Cross bloodline. She could have her youthful slimness and health back, she was told. But in exchange for curing her of her weight disease, the voice demanded that the Cross line be wiped off the face of the earth.

And Theresa refused.

In June of 1983, right after his high-school sweetheart graduated from Casa Robles, Howard brought her home, not to meet his mother, but to move in. They were going to get married, but for the moment they just wanted to live together.

Connie Sue Butler remembers that Theresa was pleasant to her at first. "She claimed she liked me when I lived with her and I was the daughter she never had and all this stuff," she recalled. As soon as her prospective daughter-in-law was out of earshot, however, she denigrated the eighteen-year-old brunette to anyone who would listen.

To Connie's face, however, Theresa was all peaches and cream. "She showed me a picture of her from her younger years and she had bleached her hair blond," said Connie. "And she used to not demand, but insist that I try on the clothes she wore when she was younger so she could see herself again."

Theresa welcomed Connie to her house with open arms. She was so happy to have Howard home again that she gave up the master bedroom to the young couple, and began to sleep on the living-room couch. Nevertheless, Connie was intimidated by the sheer size of her fiancé's mother and kept to herself a great deal of the time during those first few weeks.

"When I moved in, I was ten pounds overweight, but

she was huge," said Connie. "Being so uncomfortable around her, I stayed in the master bedroom a lot. I was eighteen, had just graduated from high school, and Howard had me controlled like a little puppet. I was told what to say to who, and anybody I talked to I had to report back on exactly what was said."

Howard warned Connie about his mother before they moved in. She would talk one way but act another. And his brothers and sisters might seem to be normal enough kids, but they did exactly what their mother told them to do and they were all spies. And Suesan, of course, was possessed. He cautioned Connie not to believe everything she saw or heard.

"While Howard and Connie were living with us, a lot of the punishment sessions were curtailed for a while," said Robert. "But we still had to watch Suesan all the time, so I know Connie had to see all that."

She had heard about Suesan from Howard all the way through high school—how they had to tie her up and make her take drugs to control her psychosis. Once Howard had even asked Connie's stepfather to come by his house, sneak up to the back door, and eavesdrop on one of Suesan's rants. The idea, he told him, was to get an outside witness to verify that Suesan was nuts so that Howard and his mother could commit her to an insane asylum.

"He used to come over and tell me and my parents the stories of her and her being in the cult and the cult members trying to pull her away from the house," said Connie.

After she first moved in, Connie rarely saw Suesan at all. And when she did see her, what she saw seemed normal enough.

"Suesan never put up a fight," said Robert. "By that time she was pretty much docile. I think she was convinced that what was happening was for her own good. . . . She never told Connie anything and never tried to get away."

The Suesan that Connie saw had become a slightly heavyset strawberry blonde of average height, with an ample bosom. bright blue eyes, and stooped shoulders. She wore thick glasses and skimpy clothes, but she was not the fire-breathing monster that Howard had described. Instead, Suesan struck her future sister-in-law as quiet and meekly submissive to virtually every other family member. "I'd only seen her come out to eat twice in, like, two weeks," said Connie. "The rest of the time, they took food into her. They only gave her beans and rice."

Over time, as Connie became a regular member of the family, she gradually got to see firsthand what it meant to live in the same house with a witch. "Theresa handcuffed Suesan every night to her bed, especially on full moons," said Connie. "And she would feed her Mellaril, which Howard got through a friend of his in the Hell's Angels. Supposedly the Mellaril made her normal, because at night she would freak out. Voices would come out of her, different voices. She was always trying to kill Sheila because Sheila was still a virgin and she was gonna use her for a human sacrifice.

"Living with her for the time that I did, I thought that Suesan was really nice. She was intelligent, if she was allowed to show it. But she kept her intelligence hidden. She played stupid to please her mother."

Connie remained only half-convinced that Suesan was the psychotic her family said she was. It seemed to her that her future mother-in-law behaved in a far more deranged way than her daughter. "She was like a hermit," said Connie. "She went to the store twice in the six months I was living there."

Theresa was also a cleaning fanatic. She had her children clean house often and thoroughly, making them put on rubber gloves and use toothbrushes and ammonia so that the floors and walls shone immaculately. Like some gargantuan inspector general, she waddled through the kitchen rubbing her fingertips over shelves and counters, checking for specks of dust.

"Theresa would have these kids up at the oddest hours," said Connie. "They'd be up all night long scrubbing the floor, getting it ready to wax. Theresa'd tell Howard and me, 'You can't come through the front door. We're waxing the floor.' So we'd have to climb through the bedroom window just to get into the house."

Howard was around to protect his fiancée most of the time, but he did leave Connie with his mother once while he was away on business. Before he left, he stood Connie in front of his mother with this admonition: She doesn't know how to clean the proper way. Teach her.

For the next three days Theresa gave Connie a boot-camp course in the "proper way" to clean. She learned to scrub the kitchen floor with a toothbrush, to wash clothes with ammonia so that they were absolutely antiseptic, and the correct way to do dishes: run them through the dishwasher and then boil them in vats on the stove to kill all bacteria before letting them drip dry.

"It was so clean it was like being in a hospital," said Connie.

She was glad to see Howard return, although she was seeing some changes in his behavior that made her uncomfortable, too. The tender, vulnerable guy beneath the macho swagger whom she had first fallen for had all but vanished. All that was left was the macho swagger. When one of his younger brothers or sisters got out of line, he didn't waste words. He boxed them into submission.

"Howard beat 'em up while I was living there," said Connie. "And Howard beat up his own mother one time 'cause she got in his face. He pushed her head through a wall."

He slapped Connie around, too, when he discovered that she was reading his mother's religious tracts. "He said his mom was trying to control my mind," she said.

While Howard was gone Connie was lectured often about the tribe of David and Theresa's direct line to God. She heard about Chester Harris and how he had turned Suesan into a monster, and how Theresa had grown to the size of a sperm whale as a direct result of Suesan's sorcery. Connie also learned little-known facts about witchcraft from her fiancé's mother, such as the precept that coal must be used to burn a witch, and that a witch can only be exterminated if she has been burned to death. She was also told that unless Theresa could somehow reverse the process that Chester Harris had set in motion years earlier, Suesan was damned to be a witch. She had swapped her soul for a promise to grow up to be famous and beautiful. And look where that evil past had gotten her.

Despite all Connie had heard from Howard before she moved in and all that she was told by Theresa afterward, the Suesan she came to know did not seem demented at all. She seemed tortured.

One night, when the moon was full and Theresa had forgotten to give Suesan her pills, Connie passed by her room. Suesan motioned for her to come in and talk. She wanted to show her that she was not crazy.

Connie could see that she was sitting in a chair, her arms handcuffed behind her. The room was dark, but Connie came in, sat down opposite Suesan, and listened. What she heard was the pitiful pleas of a sad teenage girl who felt trapped, without friends, without hope. But Connie didn't stay long. When she got close enough to see Suesan's face, she gasped.

"I don't know if it was because of all the things they told me and the movies I've watched in the past, but I swore there was little knobs coming out of her forehead," said Connie. "Looked like horns."

Since then, she has explained away that moment to herself as the direct result of Theresa's harangues. When she came face-to-face with the young woman everyone around her had described in diabolic terms for weeks, she simply saw what she had been conditioned to see, believing she was sitting in front of a creature from Hades. Connie cut the conversation short and left.

Ducking bill collectors and process servers had become a daily ritual, so Connie was not surprised one afternoon when Theresa came bustling into her room in a panic, asking her to go to the front door and fend off yet another guy with yet another sheaf of papers in his hand. All Connie had to do, she said, was tell him that Theresa Knorr didn't live there, that she had moved and Connie was the new tenant.

But the man she greeted on the front porch was not interested in collecting money. The man with the wavy, graying hair and the bulldog jaw demanded instead to see his children. As a stranger to the war between Theresa and Bob Knorr, Connie only learned for sure who he was after she'd sent him away.

Bob had tried off and on for months to track Theresa down. When he attempted to locate his children through their schools, he was told by bureaucrat after bureaucrat that "the mother would not allow me to see the children because it wasn't convenient for me to see them at this time," Knorr recalled.

It was roughly the same answer he'd been given for years by the Veterans Administration, the Social Security Administration, and the county department of public social services. They'd get a message to her, but they wouldn't reveal to him where she lived. Theresa's right to privacy was more important than Bob's right as a parent to see his own children, despite a divorce settlement that clearly stated that he was to be allowed reasonable visitation. Tired of bureaucrats, Bob wheedled Theresa's address from a school secretary and went to the house himself.

So when Connie came to the door, he was both suspicious and disappointed. "This girl said she was renting from Theresa, that she wasn't any relation to her," said Bob. "I talked to her, gave her my home phone, and asked her if she could get hold of Theresa to tell her I wanted to see my kids."

Years later he discovered Connie's real identity and that his children had all been there that day, peeking at him from behind the living-room curtains.

Connie didn't understand all the subterfuge, so Theresa explained in detail what an ogre Bob Knorr had been and why it was so necessary to hide from him. After hearing all the allegations of his terrible abuse when Theresa had been married to him, Connie was baffled. Somehow the brutality she witnessed on a daily basis at 5539 Bellingham Way seemed no worse than the kind that Theresa claimed the crippled Bob Knorr used to inflict upon her or her children.

In the meantime the bill collectors kept coming and Connie kept going to the door to tell them that Theresa didn't live there anymore. Theresa's bad credit was climbing to critical mass. In order to keep the gas and lights from being turned off, she had even put the utilities in her children's names because her own credit was destroyed. She borrowed from everyone.

The only time Connie met Theresa's sister, Rosemary, was when she showed up at the front door wondering where the money was that Theresa owed her. "She was very nice, well-off, the complete opposite of Howard's mother," said Connie. "Her manners showed she came from a very well-to-do family. Howard's mom was really jealous of her sister. She claimed her sister's nose was so high in the air that she pitied us and looked down on us. But she still wanted us to act perfect around her, to be as polite as possible."

Besides owing her sister, Theresa also continued to borrow heavily from Howard, who no longer made any pretense about dealing drugs out of his mother's house.

One morning, strangers showed up at the front door, but they weren't bill collectors and they weren't relatives. "They were plainclothes and they came to the door without a warrant," said Connie. "Howard's mom and the kids kept them from getting in the house until Howard jumped out the bedroom window and ran over to my mom's house.

"We had just gotten up, I was in my robe, there were two policemen, and one pulled me into the living room, asking me questions. The other policeman took the rest of the family into another part of the house for questioning."

Connie gave the officer her name and told him she was Howard's fiancée, but didn't reveal Howard's whereabouts. His partner got even less information out of Theresa and her children.

Theresa selected an ID from her pocketbook that gave her name as Knorr, but she professed to know nobody named Sanders. She had just bought the house, she said, and the former owner must have been the mother of Howard Sanders.

But the two cops were not fooled.

"When they brought us all together, they had a whole binder full of pictures showing Howard in front of his dealer's house. They'd had their eye on him for a long time," Connie said.

They had apparently followed Howard to his mother's house and decided it was a good place to try to nail him with the goods, said Connie.

Howard had always boasted to Connie that he would never be caught because he never sold anything to anyone he didn't know personally. In fact, she said, it was Howard's very good connections in the netherworld of drug dealing that kept him out of harm's way on the day the two plainclothes cops busted in. He had heard several days earlier from a friend of his who was wired into the Sacramento County Sheriff's Office that he might be targeted.

"So one night Howard and I took a little walk," said Connie. "We buried a coffee can full of mushrooms, the scale, everything. It was all set up to where they wouldn't find anything."

And they didn't. Following a cursory and unsuccessful search for drugs in the house, the cops sat everyone down in one room to deliver a stern warning. "You tell him to knock it off," Connie remembered being told. "Once a drug dealer, always a drug dealer. We know what he's doing."

Connie began shaking. She looked around the room at Howard's brothers and sisters and his mother, and saw that they were not going to volunteer anything. Their stoicism was absolute and impregnable. Suesan even sided with the family.

"I wasn't gonna lie to these guys 'cause you get caught in your lies eventually," said Connie. "It always comes back around. So I told them: that's Howard's mom and brothers and sisters."

And with that, she was excommunicated before she had even married into the family. The cops left and did not return, but that made little difference in the eyes of Connie's future in-laws. She instantly became persona non grata.

In later years Connie compared the whole experience on Bellingham Way to that of becoming a Mafia wife. By violating the code of *Omerta* of the Knorrs, she had not signed her own death sentence, but she had guaranteed that she would forever after be shunned by the family.

But it wasn't drugs or cops or bill collectors who finally ran the Knorrs out of the neighborhood. "We got to be one of the few families ever run out by the Hell's Angels," said Robert.

A few members of the outlaw motorcycle club lived in the neighborhood, and Howard knew them all, but they had never bothered Theresa or her younger children. In the autumn of 1981, however, a small group of angry bikers congregated on Theresa's front lawn with an edict: sell and get out of the neighborhood, or else.

The incident that sparked this final confrontation began innocently enough.

According to Robert, Howard owned a BB gun that he used for target practice in the backyard. Unfortunately, the family that had moved into the house behind the Knorrs had two small twin daughters who were afraid of Howard and his gun. When the twins' mother asked Howard to stop, he refused. So she turned to a family friend for help—a friend who turned out to be a member of the Hell's Angels.

"Everybody and their brother who was a Hell's Angel ended up coming to the neighborhood," recalled Robert.

Theresa knew a biker herself—a friend from high school named Marvin who lived up the street. When the Hell's Angels showed up on her doorstep, she sent for Marvin.

"So we had this little showdown, and shortly after that, we ended up leaving," said Robert.

The compromise hammered out by the rival bikers was simple, direct, and to the point: if Theresa sold the house, fast, and moved out of the neighborhood, the Hell's Angels would not trash her home and beat her and her entire family into a pulp.

Theresa put her house up for sale that same week.

According to Sacramento County real-estate records, Theresa wound up selling 5539 Bellingham Way to Connie's mother Diana M. Butler on November 10, 1983. Howard and Connie moved out the same week.

"She sold that house right about the time I turned fifteen and she got a $35,000 check out of the house, and that's when we moved into Auburn Boulevard," remembered Bill.

The apartment they moved to was a good ten miles away, in a run-down section of north Sacramento, but certainly not the worst neighborhood in the city. Up and down the block were pickup bars and motels that charged by the hour, mixed in with mobile-home parks and seedy but semirespectable housing. Their new home was sandwiched between a trailer park and Eddie's Hofbrau, a venerable tavern and family restaurant. Theresa's was the largest of six units in the big pink apartment house at 2410 Auburn Boulevard, just off the Interstate 80 freeway.

As it turned out, selling her house became a temporary solution to many of Theresa's mounting money problems. The family was able to afford some new furniture, buy a car, and put in a telephone. Theresa was also able to pay Howard what she owed him, plus interest, and she finally repaid her sister, too.

"After the escrow closed, there was like four or five months of normalcy," said Robert. "Mom went through the money quick. For some reason she thought she had to pay everybody double what they had loaned her. I guess there was an old loan her sister had made her, and I guess she paid twice the amount of what she got on that, too."

Theresa and Rosemary resumed real sister-to-sister dialogue for the first time in more than a decade. Terry remembers her mother telling her about Rosemary's domestic problems after one such conversation. Her life was not the nirvana that Theresa had always believed it to be.

Since her son Joey's tragedy, Rosemary had been heartbroken. Her apparently rock-solid marriage turned out not to be so terrific either. Uncle Floyd had been carrying on with someone—perhaps more than one someone. And when Rosemary found out about it, she had gotten even by carrying on her own affair with another man. And there was more.

"She'd had a miscarriage, and she was crying because she wanted another baby 'cause she missed Joey," said Terry.

Despite Rosemary's shocking news, Theresa did not confront her brother-in-law about his affair. In fact, she still felt free to call upon Floyd Norris to help her and her children move out of Bellingham Way. He never let on that anything unusual was going on between himself and Rosemary, and Theresa didn't quiz him on his marriage. Floyd gladly made the round trips from Orangevale to the Auburn Boulevard apartment in his GMC truck. Robert met his uncle Floyd for the first and last time when the two of them unloaded a washer and dryer together.

Three weeks later, while Theresa and her children were still settling in at the new place, the phone rang. It was the police. "I'll never forget," remembered Terry. "My mom was standing in the back bedroom of the apartment, and she had her back toward the window, her hand over her face. All of a sudden I hear this bloodcurdling 'Noooo! Fuck you, son of a bitch, nooo!' That's when they told her."

The Placer County Sheriff's Office informed Theresa that a man who was out walking his dog just after nine P.M. on the last day of November 1983 had found the body of a woman. It had been identified the following morning by Floyd Norris as his wife of nineteen years: Mrs. Rosemary Norris. Floyd said that he had been out of the state on business when she died.

Rosemary's body, it seemed, had been tossed next to a ditch at the dead end of a service road in an industrial park near the Sacramento suburb of Roseville. She was wearing blue jeans, wire-rim glasses, a sweater, jacket, and boots, but her purse was missing, along with the truck she had been driving just a few hours earlier. Less than five hours before her body was found, she had called a friend from her home phone, but the Norris residence showed no signs of having been broken into, nor were there any signs of struggle. In addition, the coroner found no evidence that she had been sexually assaulted.

Cause of death: manual strangulation.

On the night that she died, Rosemary Norris was exactly six months shy of her fortieth birthday.

XIII

"When they had the viewing of my aunt Rosemary, my mother wouldn't let anybody go because she was in a closed casket," said Terry.

Nevertheless, when Theresa returned from the funeral home, she told Suesan tales of how Rosemary's mouth had been sliced into the cheek on either side and had then been sewn up crisscross style, like a football. Later that same night, Suesan gave her little sister more strange descriptions of the way their aunt's body appeared in its coffin. "My sister Suesan told me that my aunt Rosemary had gone from having permed, shoulder-length hair to hair that was straight and gray," said Terry. "We're talking about a woman with beautiful chestnut-brown hair. Like my mom's."

Both the sewing of the mouth and the graying of the hair were the devil's work, Terry was told. Her mother and sister were certain that some cult had ritualistically murdered Rosemary—perhaps Chet Harris's Rio Linda witches' coven.

The autopsy report did not reflect any of these shocking details, but the report was not available to an impressionable and superstitious thirteen-year-old girl. In the world in which Terry had grown up, the conviction that Satan had somehow had a hand in her aunt's murder was inescapable. The police had other ideas. Rosemary's body was barely in the ground before her husband, Floyd, began inquiring about payment on four separate life-insurance policies, totaling more than $250,000.

"When I went to my aunt Rosemary's funeral, Floyd didn't cry," said Terry. "Not one tear did that man cry. Danny was basically like his dad: very cold. Didn't want nothing to do with the family. He didn't cry either. Danny was very reserved."

Within weeks of Rosemary's death, the homicide investigator assigned to the case told life-insurance claims adjusters to hold off on paying on Rosemary's policies. There were a lot of inconsistencies in the statement Floyd Norris had given police, said Placer County Sheriff inspector Johnnie Smith. When Smith and his partner sought to reinterview Floyd, he referred them to his attorney, Clyde Blackman, who told the police to stay away from his client.

For the next month or so Inspector Smith's investigation focused on two suspects: Floyd Norris and his eighteen-year-old son, Daniel. Then Daniel was ruled out and the investigation narrowed to one. *Floyd Norris is the prime and only suspect in this case*, Inspector Smith wrote in a memorandum filed in Sacramento County Superior Court.

But Floyd Norris never spent one night in jail. By March of 1984, less than four months after the murder, Inspector Smith's investigation had hit a dead end. He had interviewed hookers who admitted that the balding, heavyset Norris had been a customer long before Rosemary's death. He had found the missing truck that Rosemary drove the night she died, and went over it with a fine-tooth comb, turning up lots of questions but few answers. He had done a thorough background check of Floyd and traced his movements before and after his wife was murdered. But he still did not have enough to formally charge him with manslaughter, let alone first-degree homicide.

It took another year and a series of lawsuits against the insurance companies, but Floyd Norris finally prevailed. He collected on his wife's policies, sold the family home, closed his antiques business, and moved to Reno. Officially, the Rosemary Norris murder case was never solved.

Rosemary's murder had cast a temporary pall over Theresa's family, but it disappeared by the new year. Theresa and the five children who still lived with her were in a new home, far from the trouble and dark memories of Bellingham Way. Theresa was still spooked by the murder, but she had money in the bank and money went a long way toward brightening her spirits. She kicked off 1984 with a spending spree unlike any she'd been able to have since her marriage to Ron Pulliam.

"Mom decided to spend money on everything," said Robert. "That was her way of showing caring."

She donated cash to a church, got Terry new clothes, and bought three cars—two of them for William, even though he was barely sixteen and had no driver's license.

"She ended up buying a Karmen Ghia for William, but it had an electrical problem and he couldn't drive a stick very well, so she traded it in and bought him what we called the 'Pimp Mobile,' " said Robert.

Bill's second car was a 1978 caramel-colored Mercury Cougar with a vinyl top, sunroof, power windows, and a yellow interior. His mother told him it was his, but she wouldn't let him drive it.

"It was like one of her little toy games," said Bill. "She'd buy stuff and let it sit out in front of everybody and say that it was mine. If I came in, she'd say it was somebody else's. It was a little head-trip thing she had."

For herself, Theresa bought a maroon '79 LTD Brougham with a white vinyl top, wire spoke wheels, and whitewall tires.

She indulged her children, but only if it meant that

she remained in control. When Bill decided he wanted to start his own rock band, Theresa bought him a bass and an amplifier, knowing he would have to stay home to practice. She did the same with Robert, buying him an electric guitar.

"We ended up giving it to my sister because the members of the band decided they didn't need another guitarist," said Robert. "What they needed was a keyboardist. So she bought me a keyboard."

For the first time in their lives Robert and William got to go to a rock concert, courtesy of their mother. The Scorpions were in town, and Theresa bought them the best seats available.

But Theresa's free-spending ways didn't end there.

Robert had racked up so many school absences by 1984 that he was suspended from the public schools. It might not have mattered so much if he had been born a girl. Suesan and Sheila both dropped out while they were still in junior high school. But Theresa's boys, on the other hand, *had* to have a proper education.

"The only way Mom could get me back into school was to send me to Victory Christian, which is a private school," said Robert. "The tuition was something like $2,000."

Money was no object for a while, but the money didn't last, and neither did Theresa's upbeat mood.

"As soon as the money ran out, the old patterns started again, even worse," said Robert. "It was weird: when she had money, she was almost normal."

It was after they had lived at the Auburn address for a while and the money began to run out that Theresa's anger resurfaced. She began using handcuffs for the first time on the other children as well as Suesan. Whenever she wanted to beat them, she got the boys to hold the girls down, according to Bill. "When she would whip one of the kids, she would make the other ones hold that one down," he said. "And if we couldn't hold them, then we would get a whipping ourselves.

"She never beat me as bad as the other kids," he said. "I don't know why."

But even Bill caught a right hook now and then.

Just as it had been at Bellingham, none of this torture was ever detected outside the apartment. To the neighbors, life appeared normal. Suesan almost never left the premises, so nobody outside the family even knew she lived there.

"They were quiet," said Susan Sullivan, who lived in one of the upstairs apartments during the entire period that the Knorr family lived there. "I didn't see much of them. Terry and William came up occasionally and visited and talked, but other than that, I very rarely saw or heard any of them."

In school, Robert and Bill continued doing fairly well. Victory Christian seemed to turn Robert around. For the first time in his life he was getting good grades and enjoying going to class.

Bill had transferred to Mira Loma High, where the ugly memories of the Casa Robles schoolyard melee did not follow him. He made the track and basketball teams and spent hours away from home at varsity practices.

When he turned sixteen, he'd gotten an after-school job at Taco Bell. Within a couple months he'd graduated to an even better job, working for Agency Rent-A-Car. By the time the family moved to Auburn, Bill had taken yet another job, working at a book warehouse. At night, he also worked as an usher at Century Theaters. There he met Emily Lewis, a secretary three years his senior, and he took her to the company Christmas party. She became his steady.

Except for band practice, Bill rarely came home. He still turned over most of his paychecks to his mother, but that was a small enough price to pay for the freedom of being able to stay away from home, sometimes for days.

Terry, Sheila, and Suesan might not have been pampered as much as their brothers during the brief time that Theresa had money, but their mother's reduced delusions did ease the pressure on them. "Even the nightly watches on Suesan were relaxed," said Robert. "Granted, she was still chained to the dining-room table, but the watches were relaxed. Suesan was actually given some stuff. Sweaters, makeup. For a while we were really happy."

Suesan even gave up witchcraft and claimed to have found God shortly after they moved to Auburn. "She was telling my mother she was convinced that she was possessed," said Robert. "She was convinced that the demon came in and out."

One day Suesan stood in the kitchen and asked Christ for forgiveness. Then she collapsed. "Like when someone cuts the strings from a puppet," said Robert. "She just fell on the floor. I had seen that sort of thing at certain religious revivals, but for all I know, it could have been the effect of exhaustion. It could have been the effect of infection. I don't know."

Suesan's act of contrition did little to pacify Theresa, though. In a daily ritual that no one was allowed to witness but Terry, Theresa weighed in on the bathroom scales and determined that Suesan was still secretly casting spells. Terry was called in to read the numbers because her mother could not bend over to see the scales herself. On hands and knees, Terry swallowed hard and revealed the unflattering truth. Theresa was past the 240-pound mark and climbing.

And she was not eating. At least that's what she told her children. She was *not* eating!

Suesan was eating—whether she liked it or not—but she wasn't gaining an ounce. In fact, she seemed to grow thinner as Theresa expanded. Theresa tried to make up for it by force-feeding her daughter.

"Suesan would throw up, so Mom started cooking a concoction of flour and mineral oil to bind her up, to make her keep things down," said Robert. "A lot of the food that Suesan was getting was grease-laden. If I were to see it done today, I'd think Mom was trying to kill her by giving her a coronary. Things like big bowls of really greasy potatoes.

"Some of the food that Suesan was forced to eat was really unappetizing, to say the least, and it seemed like that was how it was supposed to be. There were times when Suesan would puke back into the bowl and she was forced to eat it."

Sheila remained in the background during these dramas. Her role at Auburn was little different from her role back on Bellingham Way. "Sheila was the slave," said Connie Butler, who officially became Mrs. Connie Sanders on June 1, 1984, when she and Howard eloped to Nevada. "Her mom would work her fingers to the bone. You'd actually see the girl falling asleep standing up. Sheila did all the cleaning, scrubbing, washing. She was the one sent to the store most of the time."

When Sheila or Terry or Suesan got too far out of line, Theresa would still call on Howard to drive over and beat them into submission. The only pleasant aspect to Howard's visits was that he frequently brought along pills or weed. Unlike the boys, Theresa's girls were not adjusting quite so well to their new home. Their only means of escape were drugs.

"When I was in seventh grade, I got straight F's because I'd started smoking pot," said Terry. "I was being very abused at home and I didn't know how to tell anybody. I was always afraid."

She got no support from her fellow victims either—even Bill.

"They called me from high school to come pick her up on a couple of occasions," said Bill. "Terry was having a fit in the classroom. Throwing books and cursing out the teachers and such. They asked if she had behavioral problems before, and I told them no."

Bill had no problems telling such lies to Terry's teachers. His sister backed him 100 percent: she had never been abused and she wasn't acting out of emotional turmoil. She just happened to be in a bitchy mood, she said.

"We just got used to living with the abuse," said Bill. "[Mom] said it was all our faults. I mean, if we hadn't been such rotten kids, she wouldn't't've had to resort to such measures to keep us in line."

By the spring of 1984, Theresa's bank account was exhausted. She was back to scratching for dollars anywhere she could find them. One of the ways she decided to boost her cash flow was to put her daughters to work.

"Suesan was turning tricks on Auburn Boulevard at some car lots," said Bill. "She was going from car lot to car lot turning tricks. I don't know if my mom put her up to it or not. I don't know that. I don't."

But Robert knew.

"She sent all three of my sisters down there," he said. "Terry went along to keep an eye on them, but Sheila and Suesan were both doing guys."

Terry was upset by her sisters' actions, but not so much because it was prostitution. What unnerved the youngest of Theresa's daughters was the gutter level to which Sheila and Suesan had been reduced by their own mother . . . and how neither of them fought back.

"My mom told Suesan to go up the street, on Fulton Avenue, and get $250 from this car-lot guy and screw him," said Terry. "So she did and brought the money home. Now me, myself, personally, I would've said, 'Hell, if I'm getting $250 for doing some guy up the street, I would've taken the money and I would've left home.' But Suesan didn't."

Theresa did not reward Suesan for prostituting herself and bringing the booty home to mother. She began thinking that it must be part of Suesan's master plan, along with the weight spell. Instead of thanking her for having sex with a stranger so that the family could buy food and pay the gas bill, Theresa began to suspect that her daughter's "born again" religious experience of a few months earlier had been an elaborate con.

"My mom got it in her head that she was screwing these guys not for money, but for leverage to get out of the house," said Bill. "She saw this as a control play and that's [when] she really started beating Suesan. I mean hard."

It was the worst that it had been since the Receiving Home episode. Suesan had to kneel for hours with her eyes aimed toward the floor. Whenever her mother passed her, she'd kick her or try knocking her down with her fists, like a bowling pin. She no longer slept in a bed, handcuffed to the headboard. She slept on a blanket and pillow on the dining-room floor, eyes closed most of the time. If she had to go to the bathroom, she had to raise her hand and wait for Theresa to nod that it was okay. She had to address her as "Mrs. Knorr" because Theresa refused to allow a demon to call her "Mother." The rest of the children were forbidden to speak to, look at, or go near her, and if any of them gave Theresa a glance after she had beaten Suesan, they, too, were beaten.

"I remember my mom standing on Suesan's throat till she was literally convulsing on the floor," said Terry. "Then I watched my mom pound her in the chest and shake her. I knew my sister was doing the guppy on the floor, but I didn't know she was convulsing."

Suesan's sin this time was unforgivable. At seventeen, she had hinted to her brothers and sisters that she liked getting out and meeting people again, even if it was for a quickie in a used-car lot. She implied that she might actually like to leave home.

"What was happening was when Suesan was going out and doing what she was doing and then coming home, she would talk to the other kids about it—Sheila, Terry, Robert, me when I was there," said Bill. "And my mom saw this as a control play: teaching the kids how to get out of the house basically. And she didn't like it at all.

"So when she saw it was getting too much in the head of the other kids, that's when she started beating the shit out of Suesan. I mean, beat her constantly."

When her mother gave her food, Suesan would now simply not eat at all. Theresa left the food in front of her, sometimes for days. Since the children were little, she had made a practice of having them clean their plates. If they failed to do so, she would make them remain at the table until they did. Though Suesan grew more pale and sick with each passing day, Theresa stuck to her forced-eating edict like a drill sergeant.

"If she wasn't eating the food constantly, my mom would come over and crack her on the head, back, whatever, and make her continue eating," said Bill.

From her spot on the dining-room floor, Suesan would pass out rather than finish the food her mother put in front of her.

"It got to a point where she wouldn't wake up at all," said Bill. "I mean, she was breathing, but she wouldn't wake up. She wasn't conscious.

"And my mom said, 'Oh, she's just faking it,' and would kick her."

In June, after Howard and Connie were married, Howard all but quit responding to his mother's demands to come whip the kids into shape. As a couple, they saw even less of Theresa and Howard's brothers and sisters. When they did see her, it was only when Theresa drove over to Orangevale and parked outside Connie's mother's house. She refused to come inside.

By then, the accounts Theresa delivered about Suesan's transformation into a full-fledged witch kept Connie rapt, if dubious. Suesan's "born again" experience was now a full-fledged fraud, in Theresa's estimation. It was clear to her that her daughter had, in fact, signed a blood oath to do Satan's bidding in exchange for a knockout figure and a future of fame and fortune.

Her blue eyes were turning green. Her strawberry-blond hair was now honey blond. Her body was downright devilish. A witch achieves her full powers when she turns eighteen, Theresa told her daughter-in-law. "So her mom said, 'She's getting what she wants. She will get it by her eighteenth birthday. Something has to be done about it,' " Connie remembered.

Shortly after the first of July, Theresa and Suesan called a temporary truce.

Following a pattern that was now very familiar to all of the children, their mother had lapsed into a psychotic fury one night and thrown a pair of scissors at Suesan when she had her back turned.

"My sister didn't die from it, but they had stuck in her back," Terry said.

Theresa blamed Suesan for provoking her to throw the scissors, but even Theresa knew she had crossed over a line. She stopped abusing and berating her daughter long enough to dress the wound and talk with her a little. Soon they were carrying on a conversation just like old times. "Her and my mother sat and smoked pot together and got drunk and they started talking, you know," said Terry. "I guess my mom still had some sense of reality left in her mind. They started talking like a mother and daughter would."

Suesan took a chance and asked permission to leave. She would never reveal anything to anyone, she promised. Not the beatings, not the shooting, not even the fresh scissors wound in her back. All she asked for was a plane ticket to Alaska, where she could begin a new life. She'd become a hooker for the men who worked the Alaska oil pipeline. One thing she knew she could do to earn a living was deliver up sex for the right price. She'd disappear and never be a bother to her mother ever again.

Theresa thought about it and agreed. She would buy Suesan a one-way ticket to Alaska on one condition:

that she let Theresa remove the bullet that remained lodged inside her body. Her reasoning was logical, in a paranoid way. If she were to let Suesan leave with the bullet still in her, and Suesan had it removed at a later date, the police would be able to trace it back to Theresa's derringer. Theresa had been in jail once before for shooting a husband. She wasn't going back because she was accused of shooting her own daughter.

So Suesan agreed to the operation.

Theresa's preparations for surgery began with anesthesia. She ordered Suesan to swallow a handful of green Mellaril capsules and what seemed like a quart of hard liquor. Terry remembered it as Old Crow. Robert said his sister's last cocktail was half a bottle of Southern Comfort. Regardless of the brand, the result was the same. Suesan passed out on the pillow and blanket where she had been sleeping for several months.

"She was knocked out cold by this point," remembered Terry.

Robert recalls her lying flat on her belly on the dining-room floor as their mother ordered him and Terry to fetch the surgical tools that Theresa had filched from various nursing homes over the years. "Mother got an X-Acto knife, peroxide, gauze, a few other things. We had butterfly bandages that she made herself by cutting down bandages with scissors. Then I was told to cut into Suesan's back and take the bullet out."

In the more than two years since she had been shot, the bullet had traveled in Suesan's body. It was now nearly visible—a dark swelling just beneath the shoulder blade on the left side of her back.

"It wasn't in very deep," Robert recalled. "I only had to cut one layer of muscle to get to it. After the first couple of layers of skin, you could see the black mark on her back where the bullet was, and feel the lump. So I cut, maybe two to three quarters of an inch and spread that apart with my fingers. And I could actually feel the bullet. I had to cut some of the muscle there, which was kind of stringy. It was hard to cut that with an X-Acto knife, but I was really surprised because there really was not too much blood."

The reason, Theresa explained to her son, was that Suesan had actually not been alive for some time. She was among the undead, animated by a demon, but essentially bloodless.

The next day, when Suesan came to, she was groggy and in pain. "She really never came out of the grogginess," said Terry. "She just kept getting worse."

For the next week Theresa fed her daughter antibiotics, anti-inflammatories, and painkillers, all from her own private pharmacy. She tried different combinations, tossing in a Mellaril from time to time to subdue Suesan's demons.

"And my sister just kept getting worse," said Terry. "She started hallucinating. At one point she called my brother William 'Grandpa.' She thought he was my Grandpa Cross."

When she passed into a feverish babble, she described her life as a movie passing before her eyes. She could not eat and only drank when someone held her head up and poured liquids down her throat. Each day she grew thinner and weaker.

"At one point I even exhibited the same symptoms to where I couldn't hold down water or anything like that," said Robert. "Mom slapped me around and told me not to do it. She said that I was doing it on purpose. To my knowledge, I wasn't. All I know is that I went through the same thing and came out of it. Suesan kept going downhill until she was in a state of delirium."

Finally, Sheila went to her mother and begged for the unthinkable. Her sister was dying. They had to get her to a doctor.

" 'Well, what do you want me to do about it?' " Terry remembers her mother saying. " 'I tried to help her, to let her go. There's nothing more I can do. She's got lockjaw. If I take her to the doctor, I'm gonna go to jail because she's been beaten so badly.' " If Sheila was so concerned about her, Theresa suggested, then Sheila could sit up all night with her, feed her, and make sure that she stopped vomiting.

So she did, but the all-night vigils didn't help. By then, Suesan's eyes had turned a yellowish green, as if she were suffering from jaundice. She could no longer control her bowels. Sheila and Terry took turns changing makeshift diapers that they pinned on their sister. During one of these changings, Terry noticed black marks on Suesan's back opposite the wound that had been left by Robert's amateur surgery. It looked almost like a rib was poking through, said Terry. She concluded that it was the result of internal bleeding and that her sister had been busted up inside far worse from her mother's last beating than anyone had imagined.

Suesan's condition deteriorated to a point where she could no longer even take liquids. She seemed to have slipped into a coma. By the evening of July 15, Theresa had made her decision.

"I came home from work on this fateful evening, and my mom had packed all [Suesan's] stuff up into plastic bags," said Bill. "[She] said, 'We're going on a car ride right now.' "

Theresa set two Hefty trash bags containing all of Suesan's personal belongings, including clothes and books, next to her weakening daughter. When Bill asked where she was taking everyone, Theresa remained cryptic. "She goes, 'We're taking care of something,' " Bill recalled.

She ordered Bill and Robert to pick Suesan up off the dining-room floor and carry her out to the car.

"I didn't have a thought to say no," said Bill. "I mean, 'no' was not in my vocabulary at all. It wasn't in Robert's. It wasn't in Terry's either, or Sheila's. And so I picked her up, and we take her outside and put her in the backseat of the Cougar. And we started driving off."

Robert and Bill propped Suesan up as best they could

and had Terry sit on top of her to hold her in place. Sheila sat on one side, and Robert sat on the other. Bill sat up front with his mother.

And Theresa drove. She drove east, past their old neighborhood, past the foothills and into the mountains along State Highway 50. After a short time on the road Bill told his mother that he smelled gasoline.

"She goes, 'It's gasoline in the back,' " said Bill. He started to ask her what it was for when the engine began making a terrible racket.

"She goes, 'Ah shit. Rods knocking.' Without another word said, she turns around, comes back [home]," said Bill. "We unload everything, pick Suesan up, put her back on the floor where she was."

Terry was assigned to watch her. The rest of the night and most of the next day, she sat in her mother's champagne velour rocker and stared at her sister's frail, still form lying like a rag doll on the dining-room floor.

"I thought she had died at one point in the night," said Terry. "I thought she quit breathing. But then I got down on the floor with her, and I sat next to her and I shook her, you know, and I talked to her. . . . She started babbling at me again. So, yeah, she was still alive."

The following night, July 16, the family got a later start in a different car. It was near midnight when Theresa told her brood to load up the Ford and get ready to go for another ride. "This time we put her in the LTD. Same seating arrangement," said Bill. The one difference was, this time Terry was told to stay home.

Suesan remained mute and apparently unconscious, but would not have been able to speak even if she had wanted, or been able, to. Her mother had bound her wrists and covered her mouth with duct tape. She was as limp as a scarecrow. Her two brothers had to hoist her up, drape each of her arms over their shoulders, and drag her to the car fireman-style with her feet scraping the ground.

Instead of Highway 50, Theresa drove up Interstate

80 this time, and the engine gave her no trouble at all. They drove for the better part of an hour in heavy silence.

"I remember Sheila talking to Suesan just before the end and I thought I heard Suesan whisper back," said Robert. "Then Mom told her to shut up. That was the last thing I heard her say and I wasn't even sure what they were saying, if anything. And Sheila never revealed it."

Just a mile or two before they would have passed through the Donner Pass town of Truckee, on their way toward the Nevada border, Theresa turned off the interstate. She headed south on Highway 89, weaving over the forested ridge that led down toward Lake Tahoe. She pulled to the side of the road, next to the Squaw Creek Bridge. There were no headlights or taillights visible anywhere on the highway. Outside, it was cold and dark.

" 'Okay, get her out,' " Bill remembered his mother telling him.

He and Robert unloaded their sister on the ground next to the LTD and got back into the car. Theresa turned to her two boys and told them that they were not finished.

"No, no, no. You get out, get the gas out of the trunk."

"Why?" Bill asked.

" 'Cause we've got to get rid of all this stuff," his mother told him.

Robert and William unloaded the two Hefty bags out of the back of the LTD and set them on a sandbank, down near the creek bed. Then they picked up their sister one last time.

It was summer in the Sierras and the smell of pine tar was in the air. The place where they lay Suesan down was green and grassy, and the only sounds that could be heard were crickets and the cascade of spring snowmelt rolling over the rocks of Squaw Creek. It was pitch-black outside, but up above, a million stars twinkled and a new moon shone on Suesan's ghostly face. Her brothers tucked the bags that contained all her worldly treasures beneath her and zipped up her yellow parka to keep her from the cold. Then Bill handed the gas can to his mother.

"And she threw this all over the place, the gasoline," said Bill. "Threw the gasoline all over the place, and then she started dousing Suesan. And then the shrubs and a bunch of grass and stuff around.

"And I go, I said, 'What are you doing?'

"And she goes, 'Shut up or else the other kids are gonna hear and I'm gonna have to beat the shit out of you.'

"And then she finished dousing everything down and she goes, 'I'm going to run back and start the car. You light a match, and you just drop it and run.'

"And I did."

The night sky erupted in a flame as Bill leaped in the front seat and shut the door behind him. Robert was already in the backseat, unable to turn his eyes away from his sister's funeral pyre as his mother pulled away. He shuddered.

Sheila, who had never left the car, sat next to him. She was shaking and saucer-eyed, but did not dare cry. The inside of the LTD was silent as a tomb as Theresa sped off into the night.

She drove south, along the edge of Lake Tahoe, for what seemed like hours, until she came to Highway 50, which led back over the Sierras toward Sacramento. Along the way she broke the deadly silence by speaking hopefully of Suesan's soul and how she was certain she saw it leave her collapsing body and fly toward heaven while she and Bill were still splashing gasoline over her.

"We hit a bird on the way and my mom said, 'See, that was a sacrifice. God thinks we did a good thing,'" said Bill.

"The rest of the way, not even a single word out of anybody. All the way back."

Detective John FitzGerald was only one of the legion of deputies, paramedics, medical examiners, and other officials who showed up at the Highway 89 roadside next to Squaw Creek the morning after Jane Doe #4858-84 was discovered lying there, smoldering atop a pile of half-burned clothes and ashen memories.

FitzGerald was new to the Placer County Sheriff's Department. He'd worked in other cop shops over the years and was now pushing fifty. The hair was going silver and the waistline was expanding. He walked to places where he used to run.

He had begun thinking about retirement prospects when he began looking for a new position in the early 1980s—somewhere that appreciated a man with more than twenty years' experience in police work but that wasn't overrun with cement overpasses, stucco subdivisions, and all-night convenience stores.

FitzGerald picked Tahoe, in part because he liked the great outdoors and in part because he and his new wife had a young daughter. There might be drunken tourists and holiday traffic jams and rowdy ski bums to contend with, but basically Tahoe seemed like a good, safe place to commune with nature and raise a kid.

FitzGerald was among the last of the Placer County sheriff's deputies to see Jane Doe #4858-84, but he got a good look at her.

Only half of her face remained, but it radiated such a deep, rich ivory sheen that it could have been Dresden porcelain. The long, blond lashes of her eyelid were the same golden color as her hair. She wore a melted yellow nylon windbreaker that was almost useless against the overnight temperatures in the Sierras. It was as if she had put it on at the last minute because she misjudged and thought it might keep her from getting cold up in the mountains. Bits of the charred yellow nylon matted her skin and hair.

The eye on the side of her face that remained un-burned was closed, as if she were sleeping.

FitzGerald felt a wave of bitter sorrow clutch at his belly that would not let go. He hoped to God that she was dead before the fire had started.

XIV

It was nearly daybreak when Theresa and her children returned to the apartment at 2410 Auburn Boulevard. Bill went straight to bed.

Four hours later Theresa grabbed him by the ears like a bloodhound, the way she did when he was still a toddler. She shook him awake.

"When I call you, you better wake up," he remembered her saying.

"What did I do? What did I do?" Bill asked in a panicky voice. Theresa jabbed her finger in his face and warned:

"If you ever tell anybody about this, you're gonna be next."

But her rage suddenly melted into the deepest and most bleak form of melancholy. She backed off and stared at her blond and blue-eyed athlete of a son, now the same age that his father had been when she had first met him. The moment did not last long. In a split second, she transformed from wistful to menacing again. Bill was never to leave her—or else, she warned.

"You ever try to leave here and I'll just kill you 'cause I can't take not having my kids," Bill remembered her saying.

* * *

A few days later Theresa pulled up in front of Connie's mother's house.

She ordered Howard and Connie to climb in the LTD. Connie rolled her eyes at Howard, but they both complied. The two of them listened agreeably while Theresa told them how she and the children had taken Suesan to the mountains because "she was rotting from the inside out and she was losing control of everything," Connie recalled.

She told them how they'd dressed her in diapers and a yellow windbreaker and set her afire to free her soul from the devil's grip. But just before she died, Theresa said, Suesan had revealed a secret: Connie and Howard were going to become parents.

The child would be a boy, he would have a heart defect, and he would be born on Valentine's Day. As a witch, Suesan was obligated to steal the child and sacrifice it to Satan, Theresa said. The reason Suesan had to do this, she went on, was that Connie and Howard's son would be the next descendant of James Cross, who traced his ancestry to the tribe of David, and the demons that haunted Suesan were obligated to wipe the tribe of David from the face of the earth.

"So she said we didn't have to worry about our son anymore," said Connie.

Suesan was no longer a threat. Suesan was gone. Their unborn child had been spared.

Connie and Howard traded knowing looks. Connie wasn't pregnant to their knowledge. Theresa was ranting. They humored Howard's mother a little while longer, and got out of the car. They would all visit longer when they had more time.

The next morning, Connie cracked the newspaper and read an article about a charred body found in the woods near Lake Tahoe. It was clad in diapers and a yellow windbreaker. It had been burned beyond recognition and there was no ID. She called Howard to the breakfast table and stabbed at the article with her index finger.

"We read it and Howard got real upset," said Connie. "He was crying and everything. Howard told me never to speak of it."

On the first of August, Robert was taking the rent check to the landlord when he was stopped by his next-door neighbor. The man asked where he was going, and when Robert told him he was paying the rent, he joked that he was under the impression his brother Bill was the one who worked in the family and it was he who paid the bills.

"My brother goes back, tells my mom that I'm spreading all these rumors about her," said Bill.

When Bill got home from work that day, his mother was waiting for him. She was angry.

"So you're telling everybody you're paying our bills. You go out and pay your own. Get the fuck out," she snarled.

He wasn't allowed to get his clothes, his bass guitar, or even a toothbrush.

"When I was thrown out, I was flat thrown out," said Bill. Nevertheless, he calls his expulsion from his mother's apartment "the best thing that ever happened to me."

He moved into his girlfriend Emily's apartment a couple miles away on Fulton Avenue. They lived together for the next year and a half. Bill was now far enough from the nightmare on Auburn Boulevard to begin a refresher course in how to live as a normal human being, but he remained close enough to return to do his mother's bidding if she commanded him to do so.

In the summer of 1984, Robert got a real job and lost his virginity. Theresa wasn't very happy about either development.

Her youngest son had been folding burritos for a couple of months at Taco Bell, until he found a job at the Red Lion Inn, where he was working at the time his mother took the family on its midnight drive to Tahoe. Unlike his older brother, who stopped turning his weekly paycheck over to his mother after he got kicked out of the house, Robert still had to give everything that he earned to Theresa. His social life, therefore, was confined to the apartment building and the trailer court next door.

"At that time I was really socially inept," said Robert.

He did manage to befriend an older guy named Mike who lived upstairs. He offered Robert his first beer away from the stifling presence of his mother and the two of them got to be drinking buddies.

At about that time a woman in her late twenties moved into the apartment next to Mike's. Her name was Connie. She was smart, she was attractive, and she was partial to halter tops, just the way his sister Suesan once had been.

"I was trying to look underneath it and see if she was really wearing a bra, which I didn't think she was," said Robert. "I must have succeeded with all the stealth and slyness of a fifteen-year-old because I guess she decided she wanted to teach me."

Connie contrived an excuse to get Robert into her apartment, hit the lights, and locked the door. For the next two months they were lovers.

"At the time my brother and his friend Willy were making fun of me, saying I was a little effeminate, maybe even homosexual," said Robert. "And here I was, you know, Connie wanting me to live with her. I was going to move out, and she was going to support me while I went through school."

And it might have happened, if it hadn't been for Robert's passion for Doritos. "I had this thing for [them]," he said. "If there's an open bag of Doritos, especially ranch style, it's not 'take a little and have a little later.' It's—the bag is gone. I used to do that over at Connie's house."

Since his sympathetic illness during Suesan's final days, Robert's appetite had returned with a vengeance. His sister Terry, who also went upstairs to talk with Connie now and then, took note of the fact that Connie did not have a Dorito in the house, thanks to her brother.

"Terry mentioned to Mom that Connie said, 'Doesn't he get enough to eat at home? He wolfed down like two bags of chips over here!' " said Robert. "An innocent enough comment. But my mom went ballistic."

Robert came home one day from Connie's apartment, and Theresa laid into her son with a haymaker. She was at least as angry that he was acting like he didn't get enough to eat at home as she was that he was sleeping with a woman almost twice his age. She forbade him to ever see Connie again. Robert complied.

"Connie actually wrote me a note wanting me to explain why I was dumping her, and I ended up throwing that note away," said Robert. "Strangely enough, later on when I told my mom about it, she said, 'Oh, you could have kept the letter.'

"I could have kept the letter, but not the girl."

Terry still played halfheartedly at the game of trying to please her mother and win her approval, but it was clear to her after Suesan that it was a loser's game—especially if you were a girl.

"To me, my mom died when my sister Suesan died," said Terry.

Howard had been able to get away, as had Bill. The odds for Theresa's daughters leaving home, on the other hand, had suddenly plummeted. At thirteen, Terry watched her remaining sister become little more than a zombie.

As she was ordered, Sheila cleaned up the mess in the dining room where Suesan had spent her final days. She scrubbed down the apartment with a mop and toothbrush and disinfected with ammonia, but she did this without saying a word, without even humming a song. She fell into a "concentration camp" hush while dutifully sterilizing away the last remaining traces of her sister.

Terry was determined not to let Sheila's defeat become her own. Despite her mother's efforts to keep her indoors like her sisters, she stayed in contact with the outside world.

"My mom was never *not* in a rage!" she said. "She got angrier at certain times, but she was just always an angry person inside. She was never bubbly and happy. She's nothing like me at all." Theresa's anger made her a recluse—a quality she pretty much succeeded in passing on to Sheila.

But Terry was anything but a recluse.

When her brothers Robert or William went out visiting the neighbors, she tagged along. As the two youngest Knorrs, Robert and Terry became recognized around the apartment complex and trailer court as a team. "If you saw one, the other'd be right nearby," said Lucian King, one of the trailer court's oldest residents. "They were always together."

But Theresa even used this closeness of her two youngest children as a weapon against them.

Whenever Robert and Terry went anywhere, Theresa would quiz them separately upon their return, like a cop trying to get two suspects to trip one another up. Nothing her children ever said or did fell into the category of "innocent fun." Everything was unruly mischief at best, deceitful evil at worst. If her cross-examinations revealed that one of them was hiding something, as in the Doritos incident, she punished the transgressor and rewarded the snitch.

"Me and her went to one of her school friends' birthday parties and we forgot the presents," said Robert, recalling one such incident. "My mother thought for sure that we weren't at a birthday party, that we were probably engaged in some kind of sexual activity, especially Terry.

"And the more I denied it, the more my mother assumed I was lying for her. So my mom decided to give her a haircut to make her a little less popular in school. And she ended up shaving her head—something she said was a punishment for sluts in the old days."

The head shaving was something that the boys had gotten used to early. Both William and Robert had their heads shaved while they were in elementary school. Theresa told them that it would make their hair grow back thicker. But the effect at school was devastating. The Knorr boys were treated like pariahs by their classmates. William came home crying, and his mother relented. She stopped cutting his hair. Robert was not so lucky. His tears seemed to mean less to his mother. She kept sending him to school, bald as a cue ball, for years.

"It made me *real* popular in school," Robert said.

Terry cried, too, but her mother told her to hold still or she would slice her head open.

The shameful shearing had its desired effect. Terry's hair grew back, perhaps even thicker than it was before. But it didn't matter. When the school year came around again, rather than submit to the merciless gibes of junior high classmates, she simply didn't go.

That winter, Sheila was hit by a hearse.

"She was on a bicycle, and this guy pulling out of Lombard and Company Mortuary on Olive Boulevard at about twenty miles an hour knocks her off her bike," said Terry.

Sheila almost never left the apartment except to run an errand for her mother, so when she came back to report what had happened, her brother and sister found the whole thing both funny and sad at the same time: during one of the few times their sister had gotten out of the house, she wound up flattened by a funeral procession.

Theresa saw nothing funny about it at all. From that point on, she began wondering what her daughter was doing near a mortuary in the first place, and what might have *really* happened to her as she lay there, while mortuary officials scrambled around her in a desperate effort to revive her and discourage her from filing an accident report or a lawsuit.

"Mom was convinced that Sheila's soul was knocked out of her body for a split second and something jumped in," said Terry. "And you know what my mother said about that? That my sis had actually died when he hit her. And she was just a demon in my sister's body. That's when she started beating my sister."

Connie Sanders's first child wasn't born on Valentine's Day as Suesan had allegedly predicted. His birth date was February 1, 1985. But he *was* a boy, and the obstetrician *did* say that he had a heart murmur. Two out of three correct prognostications by Howard's deceased "witch" of a sister, as related to them months earlier by Theresa, planted more than a few doubts in both parents about the future of Howard Clyde Sanders Jr.

Thus, when they began getting heavy-breathing hang-up calls a short time after the baby's birth, neither Connie nor Howard ascribed them to pranksters or one of Howard's disgruntled drug customers. Howard was certain that the voice he heard on the other end of the line belonged to a sinister figure from his past. He was certain Howard Jr. was not out of danger, as his mother had reassured them the previous summer, because he was certain that the caller was Chester Harris.

"It was always Howard who answered the phone," said Connie. "He'd get really paranoid, get out the gun, and say, 'He knows where we are! He's gonna come and get me!'

"I said, 'We've got a newborn baby here. I'm not

gonna live like this, wondering if some maniac's gonna come in and kick the door down.' "

Howard and Connie had friends in Rio Linda and decided one weekend that they would pay them a visit to show off the new baby. While they were there Howard got tanked and conceived the idea of going looking for Chester Harris.

"He went out to that American Legion hall with his friend, and he came back white as a ghost," said Connie. " 'I seen Chester,' he told me. 'I sat right next to him and told him not to bother my family.' "

For the rest of the evening Howard continued to drink and tell his friends the tales his mother had told him about the fat, sick old beer addict who sat at the end of the bar in the American Legion hall and who lived off the blood of babies, sacrificed virgins, disemboweled animals and humans, and chanted in ancient tongues to pagan spirits during the full moon. With enough alcohol, those stories grew more and more vivid. By midnight, Howard's wide-eyed tales of terror had the skin crawling on everyone in the room.

And Chester lived just a few blocks away.

"Our friends we were staying with got so scared, we all left," said Connie. "We came back to our house, and we didn't sleep that night. I kept getting the willies."

"Lucian King had a little trailer at Eddie's Hofbrau, next door to the apartments on Auburn," said Terry. "Originally it started out that my mom was cleaning his camper, then Sheila, and then it ended up that I was doing it."

King was in his seventies and had been a gold-nugget dealer most of his life. He was something of an intellectual oddity at 2410 Auburn Boulevard. He spoke Spanish fluently, read the classics, had lived with a mistress for many years in Europe, but finally retired to the hills of California's gold country, where he envisioned himself as a modern-day forty-niner. In his motor home and trailer, he lived like a happy hermit, free to pull up stakes at a moment's notice and travel to any corner of the Sierras. He did most of his business in Nevada City, a gold-rush town on State Highway 49 in the heart of gold-rush country, but he lived fifty miles to the southwest, in the Sacramento flatlands, in a trailer right next door to the Knorr family. He didn't like long-term relationships, but he did like to live in a tidy place. So when Theresa offered to clean his trailer for him, he didn't think twice.

Almost immediately, items began disappearing from his trailer and turning up in the medicine cabinet at Theresa's apartment. She pilfered a bottle of pills that King used to treat a thyroid condition, believing that they might correct her own perceived thyroid condition and reverse her weight gain. One thing that had not seemed to change following the ritual burning of Suesan by the light of the summer's first moon was Theresa's obesity. Instead of reversing the problem that had caused much of Suesan's abuse in the first place, Theresa continued to balloon ever larger, according to Robert. At one point, his mother tipped the scales at nearly 270 pounds.

"My mom very rarely went out of the house when she started gaining weight," said Terry. "The only time she'd shower was when she had to leave the house, and the only time she'd leave the house was when she had to go get a check."

The thyroid pills didn't help her, so Theresa made off with a container of protein powder that Lucian kept in the kitchen for quick breakfasts. This, too, she regarded as a means of taking off pounds and returning to a smaller dress size. It had no effect whatever.

Theresa found something more in King's trailer while she was supposedly cleaning for him. It was his stock-in-trade: gold nuggets. He kept most of his inventory under lock and key, but there was enough evidence of his gold dealings lying around to give the wrong idea to someone with a weakness for free money.

"Eventually, he didn't let my mom clean anymore because she kept flaking out, and his gold nuggets would turn up missing," said Terry.

It was just as well that she had been caught. Theresa was so heavy that she got exhausted easily and did not do the crack cleaning job she had been capable of back in her convalescent-hospital days. She offered King a compromise. She would no longer come over herself to clean. She would make Sheila do it.

"Sheila, I think, was looking for a way out of the house," said Bill, who had resumed coming aound to the apartment again by this time, even though he was living with Emily Lewis. On his irregular visits, the only real change that he witnessed in the family's routine was a curious restlessness he'd never seen before in his docile older sister. She was not yet ready to confront her mother about leaving, but when she talked with her brothers or sister, Sheila made no bones about wanting to escape from beneath Theresa's thumb.

Theresa noticed the difference in her daughter's behavior, too. Even though Sheila dutifully brought home the money that King paid her each week, Theresa was convinced that her daughter was earning a little extra on the side and squirreling it away so that she could pursue Suesan's dream of running off to Alaska to become a hooker.

"She did not want the kids to leave at any cost," said Bill. "And that's why when I was working before I got thrown out, I had to turn my paycheck over to her every Friday. And when Sheila got paid for doing this cleaning of this guy's trailer, she gave my mom all the money from that. [But] my mom accused her of prostituting to this guy to get more money that she wouldn't know about."

To Theresa's children, Lucian King seemed like an odd old bird, but not one inclined to carry on an affair

with a teenager. Unlike Chester Harris, King's interest
in sex began to decline by the time he hit his sixties. He
was more interested in good conversation than he was a
roll in the hay.

But Theresa was blind to this fact, just as she was
blind to the far more obvious object of Sheila's fancy:
a handsome young British Columbian Indian who lived
in a trailer by himself near the back of the trailer court.
He had an unpronounceable traditional Indian name and
was known around the trailer court only as Chief.

"Sheila liked Chief," said Robert. "But Mom never
really stated any overt fear of Sheila leaving with him.
I think Mom was convinced that Sheila would disgust
the Chief sooner or later and nothing would ever come
of it."

Chief adhered to the native ways in which he had
been raised on a Canadian Indian reservation. He wore
his hair in braids, kept himself in good physical condition, and lived very simply. The walls of his mobile
home were lined with hundreds of volumes about Native Americans: their religion, their relationship with
their environment, their betrayal by the white man,
and their inviolable inner strength. He trusted in nature and the stars. One of the few things he shared with
visitors was his regret about what modern America had
done and was continuing to do to the essential harmony
between his people and the land.

Chief earned his living by turning out handmade golf
clubs, prized by a wide-ranging clientele for their sym-
metry and style. He never wanted for work. It was one
of the many ironies of his peculiarly spiritual lifestyle
that he had never played golf and never had any desire
to do so.

For all of his idiosyncrasies, Chief displayed a Zen-
like patience with his neighbors. He was never without
a smile and never spoke a cross word to anyone, if he
left his spiritual plane long enough to break his silence
at all.

Sheila saw all of this, and she fell in love.

Unlike Lucian King, Chief was still in his twenties and young enough to appreciate a beautiful young woman. But he did not believe in sex for the sake of sex. In accordance with his worldview, he believed that an invisible bond was created when a man and a woman joined in the act of procreation. It was not something to be taken lightly, and it was not something that a man could ever pay for. It was a gift. It had to be given.

Chief was as different from the johns down at the car lots on Fulton Avenue, who paid $250 to go around the world, as night was from day. Sheila understood this and, with virtually no social skills to call upon at all, tried her very best to flirt.

"Sheila was slow, but she was not retarded," said Terry. "Sheila was different. She had a beautiful voice, beautiful hair, beautiful skin. She was very petite, tiny. Nothing like the Knorrs. Sheila was tiny, like my mom when she was eighteen. Me and Suesan were always big girls, but Sheila was always small, thin, pretty."

She and her brother Howard had so often heard themselves called "dirty Indians" as they were growing up that they both believed themselves to be more Indian than English or French or Irish or any of the other nationalities that were part of their heritage. Sheila saw Chief as her one true destiny. She began wearing her hair in braids when she did the laundry, hoping he would notice. Once, when she carried a basket of laundry past his trailer, she even wore a leather headband with a feather in it.

But before Sheila could catch Chief's eye, Theresa confronted her about Lucian King. When Sheila denied that anything was going on with the old man, her mother slapped her allegedly lying mouth and called her the same names she once used for Suesan: a whoring, demon-infested slut.

"And my mom just started beating her, really bad," said Bill.

Theresa had Terry take over Sheila's cleaning chores at Lucian King's trailer. King liked her well enough and even gave her the nickname "Burrhead" because her hair was just starting to grow back in. But he still wanted to know what had happened to Sheila.

Terry told him what her mother had instructed her to tell him: Sheila was sick and couldn't work for him anymore.

"And he started asking all kinds of questions about her, and Terry came back and told my mom the guy was asking about Sheila," said Bill. "And that made my mom more suspicious, and [she] beat her even harder."

Theresa made Sheila sit on her knees with her hands in her lap and stare for hours at the edge of the carpet next to the kitchen. "And that's where she had to stay, looking down," said Bill. "She wasn't able to look at anybody or talk to anybody."

When Sheila moved, to scratch or adjust her weight from one knee to another, Theresa beat her with fists and feet. She tied her up with strips of sheets that she made Terry tear up for restraints. Terry also wound up having to feed Sheila because her mother refused to untie her.

Besides the possibility that she might escape with Lucian King or Chief, Theresa found yet another reason to persecute Sheila. She concluded that her own health problems, including the ever-increasing weight gain, might be attributable to venereal disease. It was a disease she was sure she had contracted from sitting on the same toilet seat that her eldest daughter used.

"My mom said Sheila had given her VD," said Terry. "But my mom didn't have any venereal disease."

Theresa, however, was certain she had chlamydia, or worse, and was certain Sheila had gotten it first from Lucian King or Chief or some stranger she'd met while Theresa had her back turned. When she demanded answers from Sheila, her daughter told her she didn't know what she was talking about and wound up with blackened eyes for her supposed insolence.

One of the items that Theresa had lifted from King's trailer when she had been doing the cleaning was his telephone credit card. Once she was sure she had a venereal disease, she started using the card to call various doctors and clinics outside of the Sacramento area. She didn't want to go to anyone nearby for treatment. The shame of having caught VD was not something she wanted bandied about the neighborhood. She called doctors as far away as Nevada to find out about the transmission and treatment of VD, according to Terry. She suspected that her youngest daughter had gotten it, too.

"One time my mom drove up to Carson City, Nevada, and she made me go have a pelvic exam," said Terry. "She thought I had a venereal disease at age thirteen. She didn't want the doctors here to know about it, so she took me up there, and made an appointment for me under some bogus name."

Theresa watched to see how the examination was done so that when she got back home, she could do her own pelvic exams on her daughters.

By this time the question of whether Sheila did or did not have a venereal disease had become moot. She never left the apartment, was punished every day, and had no appetite. In the spring of 1985, she had fallen into the same anorectic pattern as her sister had done just one year earlier. Her mother saw her refusal to eat as yet another act of defiance and took to force-feeding her. During one feeding session, she rammed a spoon in her mouth and broke off one of her daughter's front teeth.

But Sheila was not Suesan. She continued to remain defiant. If she ever got away, she could run off with Chief. She had something to live for.

"Sheila was the only one with the nerve to talk back to her mother," remembered Connie Sanders.

One day in June, just about a year after Suesan's death, Sheila pushed her scorn one step too far.

"Sheila kicked her," said Robert. "There was an argument because Sheila had stopped eating and she was going through similar symptoms the same as Suesan was for a while, and Mom was extensively arguing with her to 'save her life.'

"I was told to grab hold of Sheila while Mom was arguing with her. Mom slapped her a couple of times, and Sheila kicked her in the shins. Mom said that Sheila had broken her shin."

Later that night Robert called on his older brother Bill. Their mother had ordered the two of them to wrestle their sister down and shut her in the linen closet in the hallway of the apartment. She screamed and fought. Unlike Suesan, Sheila would not be brought down like a steer and sent to slaughter.

But she was no match for Theresa's two boys. They finally got her inside the closet and shut the door.

"The only thing Sheila did while she was in the closet was beg to get out," said Terry. "My mom would stuff towels underneath the door so we couldn't hear."

It was hot in June, and the apartment had no air-conditioning. Sheila's prison was a two-by-two-foot space that was four or five feet deep at most. After a few days she stopped yelling and pleading and scratching at the wood to get out. Terry and Robert did not remember their mother opening the door to feed her. If she was allowed to leave long enough to go to the bathroom, neither of them ever saw it.

One particularly warm summer day, Robert and Bill were both at work and Theresa left the apartment to go to the store.

"It was the only time I was left alone with Sheila," said Terry. "Very seldom did [my mom] go to the store. She always made us bring the groceries back in a shopping cart, and then walk the cart back up to the store."

On this day Theresa drove off in the LTD and Terry tempted fate. When she was sure she was alone, she opened the door to the linen closet. Sheila's hands were tied, and she was half-naked.

"I was only there for like half an hour in the house by myself, and I knew she was coming right back," she said. "My sister Sheila was twenty, and I was like fourteen. Her body was so sweaty and hot. And Sheila was such a tiny little thing. She looked really bad. I didn't realize she was dying at the time, but she was drenched with sweat.

"And she just fell out onto the floor when I opened the door. I cried, I felt so bad. I had opened the closet because my sister was crying that she was hot, wanted something to drink. I took her a beer. That's all my mom wanted her to drink. That's all my mom would give her."

Terry started to talk with Sheila, but the conversation died before it began because Terry heard her mother's LTD pull up and park outside the apartment. In a panic, she shut the door on Sheila. Her sister was too weak to push it back open.

"I shut it because it was either shut the door or me end up in there with her," said Terry. "Basically I was putting my life above hers, and I shouldn't have done that. That's why I'm having a hard time, because I did shut that closet. My mother was coming into the apartment. She had pulled up outside, slammed the car door, and she was coming into the apartment."

Robert doesn't remember exactly how long his sister remained in the closet. It might have been a week. It might have been two weeks. Maybe longer. But he does remember the smell.

"I don't know if you've ever left a chicken to defrost in your sink, where it bleeds a lot and you get a little water in there," said Robert. "If you leave it in there for a few days, you get that smell. The smell of rotted flesh and blood."

Theresa didn't open the closet herself to find her dead daughter. She called on Bill.

"Mom and Terry were asleep in the bedroom together," said Robert. "Terry was sleeping on the floor, and Mom was sleeping on one of the bunk beds. Their room was right across the hall from the closet. As I remember it, William was in the shower. He was supposedly leaving for work when they heard the noise in the closet."

The noise, Robert later speculated, was probably his sister's corpse falling over.

Theresa got out of bed and knocked on the bathroom door. Instead of going to work, Bill followed his mother's instructions. He went down the hallway and opened the door to the linen closet to see where the stench was coming from. Bill peered inside and saw his half sister, naked except for a pair of underwear. Her hands remained tied behind her back, and her knees were pulled into her chest, in a fetal position.

Theresa told Bill to remove the closet door and set it against a wall heater in the hallway so that he and his brother could get their sister out.

"And there was a sort of pine-cone-looking pattern that started halfway down her legs, and then it got darker and darker and got sort of almost purple at the bottom," said Bill.

"It looked like what they show in the movies . . . like, blood settles and stuff. And I was like, I was completely in shock. I'd never seen anything like that before. . . . My mom hit me in the back of the head and says, 'Pick her up.' And me and Robert grabbed her out of the closet."

The horror was far from over. When the two boys tried hefting their sister's corpse out of her prison, her rotting flesh stuck to the floor of the closet.

"William said that she had no nose when he first looked at her inside the closet," said Robert. "He wouldn't go into any other detail on it."

As they pulled her out of the closet the sounds and smells seared themselves into the two boys' memories.

"She made, like, a pulling sound, like sweat off of a car seat," said Bill.

Years later the two brothers remained at odds over the amount of blood they found on the linen-closet floor.

"It wasn't like when you cut your finger really bad and it bleeds like all over the place," said Bill. "But there was some blood. Just a little bit toward the face and maybe on the neck side of her shoulder, you know. But it wasn't like a puddle or anything like that."

Not so, said Robert.

"There was a lot of blood on the closet floor and on the walls of the closet," he said. "When she was carried out, there was a gurgling sound and her neck was really wet and she was obviously dead. She was really limp. I think it was possible she was killed. I think it was possible she had her throat cut."

Regardless of how their sister died, it was evident that she had been dead for days. While Terry shrank back into a corner, watching her worst nightmare repeat itself in stinking, horrifying color, her mother began calling out orders to her paralyzed sons.

"And she brought out this sort of large ... moving box," said Bill. "She said, 'Put her in here.' So we went to put her in, and she says, 'Stop, stop, stop, stop!' Okay, and we held her over the box for a minute or two."

Theresa lined the box with a pair of pillowcases, but not until she had carefully examined them both for hairs that might be traceable to the family. When she was satisfied, she had the boys lower their sister's corpse into the box. They taped the box shut with silver duct tape and carried it out to the trunk of the LTD.

"One of the things my mom asked while this was going on was what we were thinking at the time," said Robert. "William said that it was like a Stephen King movie. You know: special effects. It wasn't real.

"For some reason, I told her that some words from a Kool and the Gang song kept running through my head. The song was 'She's Fresh.' I guess it was a kind of reaction to what was going on. I think the smell was one of the things that affected me the most. I guess it was my mind trying to compensate, although at the time I thought it was pretty morbid. But I couldn't get the damn song out of my head."

The nightmare ride from a year earlier repeated itself, only this time Sheila was in the trunk of the LTD. Again, Terry remained at home alone. Bill sat in the front seat with his mother driving while Robert sat in the backseat, and they drove "straight away up Highway 80," according to Bill. This time he was not so silent as the car crawled through the dark over the Donner Pass and down into the Tahoe basin.

"I'm like, 'Well, what the hell happened here?' And my mom goes, 'I don't know,' " said Bill. "I went, 'What are you talking about, you don't know? She's *laying* here.' She's like, 'Well, she was in the closet and she started moaning and then I heard a crash and there she was.' I go, 'What was she doing in the closet?' 'Well, you just never mind . . .' "

Theresa missed the Highway 89 turnoff and drove on toward Nevada, but when she saw a suitable place by the side of the road and not much traffic she pulled over. Bill and Robert had shovels out and were starting to dig a hole to bury the box when a squad car pulled up behind them.

"I think it was Nevada police that came over and asked why the car was off the side of the road," said Bill.

Robert nearly dropped his shovel as one of the police officers snapped on his flashlight and began crunching through the gravel toward the driver's side of the LTD.

Bill and his brother hustled back to the car where they set the shovels inside the trunk before the second cop meandered over to see what they were up to. Bill figured the stench from Sheila's cardboard crypt would surely give them away.

"I just remember just kinda stopping and freezing 'cause it was stinking," said Bill. "It was smelling. I didn't notice in the house, but I was noticing it when the police pulled up. You know, it smelled really bad."

Theresa handled the situation calmly, explaining that she had to pull to the side of the road because the boys needed to take a leak. Bill was certain the cops would get a whiff of the box before he got the trunk shut, but the clear mountain air and the midnight temperatures were enough of a cover. By the time the officer got to the boys, they had already closed the trunk and were scrambling to get back inside the car. When their mother had finished her explanation and the patrolman questioning Theresa finally opened his mouth, Bill and Robert held their breath.

"He goes, 'Okay. You're not allowed to be out here. I need you to turn back around, get back on the highway, and go where you're going,' " Bill remembered. "And she goes, 'Okay.' And we turn around, got back on the highway, and continued on."

Theresa drove back through Truckee and headed south, toward Tahoe, as she had done the year before. This time she took a road that wound through a mountain meadow where Martis Creek forms a shallow lake before it feeds into the Truckee River. She made a left turn onto a gravel road and drove down to the edge of the lake, near a campground. She stopped when she came to the end of the road.

"I don't even know where we'd gone to," said Bill. "And she says, 'Okay, get her out.' And she popped the trunk from the inside and me and Robert got out, dropped off the box probably ten feet from the car, jumped back in the car, and drove off again."

Theresa had no idea where she was either. It took them three hours to get back to the apartment.

XV

"He went down to the lake first thing in the morning, like he always did, and saw this box," recalled Hazel Barber, remembering daybreak of June 21, 1985, when her husband, Elmer, made his early-morning rounds at the Martis Creek Campground.

As the camp's official caretakers, the Barbers were used to people dumping their trash on their grounds. Martis Creek was close enough to the main highway to be convenient, but far enough removed to be a free county dump for people who were too cheap to pay a few bucks to get rid of their garbage and didn't give a damn about messing up the environment for everyone else. One of the Barbers' less pleasant duties was getting rid of other people's trash. When Elmer came across the box down by the lake, he figured it was one more dump job he'd have to clean up before that day's quota of fishermen, hikers, and campers rolled in.

"Cardboard box, about the size of a TV set," said Hazel Barber. "Maybe three feet by two. And he walked over into the bush and he opened it up.

"And arms just flew out at him! That's stuffing somebody, really stuffing 'em in tight. That was one stinky mess, and that's an understatement."

Elmer and Hazel should have been enjoying breakfast two hours later, but instead they found themselves guiding a half-dozen Nevada County sheriff's deputies around the spot where the decomposing body had been found.

There was almost no way to make a positive identification of the young woman found in the box. It was even hard to tell how long the box had been there. It had been sitting in the sun long enough for the flies to get to her. Maggots up to six millimeters long crawled in and out of the crevices of her five-foot-four-inch frame.

When she had been alive, Jane Doe #6607-85 had probably weighed between 105 and 120 pounds, the police concluded. She had dark hair and pierced ears and must have been right around twenty years old, according to the coroner. She was wearing only hip-hugger panties and a pair of white athletic socks when she'd been hog-tied with Ace-bandage material and stuffed inside the box. There were a couple of pillowcases inside the box with her, but nothing else.

It appeared as though she might have been hit in the head and suffered a possible slash of two to four inches in length across the center of her chest, but Jane Doe #6607-85 was in such an advanced state of decomposition that it was impossible to say with any certainty that either of those wounds caused her death. After examination and reexamination, Dr. A. V. Cunha had to write *undetermined* under the heading CAUSE OF DEATH in his final autopsy report.

Dr. Cunha, who acted as medical examiner for Nevada County where the body was found, as well as for neighboring Placer County, saw nothing to connect Jane Doe #6607-85 with a young woman still known as Jane Doe #4858-84, who had been found a few miles away just one year earlier in Placer County. Cunha had conducted the autopsy on that corpse, too. But the Placer County woman had been blond, big-boned, and large-breasted, and had died of flash burns. The Nevada County Jane Doe was brunette, tiny, with small breasts, and could have died from any of a half-dozen causes, burning not being among them.

At first, Nevada County Sheriff's Deputy Elizabeth Rehkop had little to go on with Jane Doe #6607-85. Nothing showed up on missing-persons reports over the next few weeks that could be positively matched with the body. The autopsy didn't yield much. There had been some dental work done on the young woman's teeth that might be used to identify her if the department were ever fortunate enough to narrow her identity down to a handful of possible victims. But that possibility was a long way off. The teeth and jaws were packaged and sent off to a forensic dentist for safekeeping until detectives could come up with dental X rays of someone—anyone—who might match their victim.

Meanwhile Jane Doe #6607-85 was so decomposed that it didn't look like the detectives would even be able to get a usable set of fingerprints from the body. When Dr. Cunha tried to take prints from the corpse, the skin slipped off the bones of the hand, like plastic gloves. Nevertheless, Detective Rehkop kept the fingers and palm skin following the autopsy, along with samples of the woman's hair and her clothing. Like her teeth, they might be used in the future for identification purposes.

Despite the doubtful findings, officials remained optimistic. Through the FBI, Nevada County was tied in via computer to a national network that kept tabs on suspects and their possible victims. By feeding in raw data about a victim, the FBI was often able to help local authorities track down a killer hundreds, even thousands, of miles away.

And so it happened with Jane Doe #6607-85.

"The sheriff's office sent us a letter about six months later saying they caught the murderer," said Hazel Barber. "But we were surprised that they never did say why the girl was murdered and what became of the body afterward. They had it in a mortuary in Truckee for a long time waiting for somebody to claim it. No one did while we were there."

Even though they'd found the killer, the authorities were never able to identify the girl, said Mrs. Barber. "They had an idea that she was picked up—that she was one of those streetwalkers who got into an argument with some guy. They seemed to think it was just this one fellow—broke her arms and legs and stuffed her in this box and sealed it."

The one fellow the Nevada County Sheriff's Office believed was responsible for the murder was a forty-two-year-old long-distance Texas truck driver named Benjamin Herbert Boyle.

Boyle had been arrested and charged with the rape and murder of a twenty-year-old Amarillo woman on October 17, 1985, just four months after Jane Doe's body had been found near Truckee.

Boyle, a philanderer with a bad temper from Canute, Oklahoma, had a long-standing reputation of using his truck routes to pick up young women and cheat on his wife. He had a sleeper cab built into his cherry-red Peterbilt, ostensibly for catching a little shut-eye whenever he was on a desolate stretch of highway, or needed to stay overnight at a truck stop.

But Boyle, who used the handle Mr. Whipple, found that the compartment could accommodate two people just as easily as one, and he began using it for purposes other than taking a nap. In the case of Gail Lenore Smith, who caught a ride with him on Interstate 287 from Fort Worth on her way to Amarillo, Boyle's purpose was kidnapping, rape, and murder. Her naked body was found north of the Canadian River, just fourteen miles outside of Amarillo, trussed up and taped into a fetal position, not unlike that of Jane Doe #6607-85.

Boyle had also been accused of the abduction and rape of another woman several months earlier during one of his trucking runs through Missouri. And as far back as 1979, Boyle had been convicted of attempting to kidnap a Colorado Springs woman who managed to stab him and get away.

At his trial in Amarillo a year after Jane Doe's body was found, no one spoke in Boyle's defense except his mother. She tearfully praised him for helping her raise his younger siblings after Boyle's father died, and pointed out that he had once been a volunteer for the Boy Scouts.

Everyone else who knew him, from his wife and daughter to his employer and a wide array of acquaintances, agreed that "Mr. Whipple" was mean, deceitful, perverted, and predatory.

"I'm very scared of the man right now, and I have been for quite some time," testified his daughter, Mrs. Connie Smith.

So when FBI Special Agent Michael Malone flew in from Washington, D.C., was sworn in, and testified that a fiber found on the body of Truckee's Jane Doe #6607-85 matched fibers from a blanket found in Boyle's house in Canute, Oklahoma, nobody said or did much to refute him. Tests also revealed that rope fibers found near Jane Doe matched rope fibers in Boyle's truck.

Detective Elizabeth Rehkop flew in, too, from Truckee, California. She explained to the court that Jane Doe had been found in a box five miles south of Truckee at about the same time that Boyle had been driving through the area. An Amarillo police detective followed Detective Rehkop to the stand and confirmed that long-distance phone records and receipts showed that Boyle had indeed been in or near Truckee at the time Jane Doe's body was dumped.

Though Judge Don Emerson listened closely to the evidence, he did not allow the jury into the courtroom during the Jane Doe testimony. The jurors already had plenty of damning evidence to consider with just the Gail Lenore Smith murder, including two eyewitnesses who watched the woman climb into his cab and drive off to her death down Interstate 287.

Boyle was subsequently convicted and sentenced to die in Texas State Prison at Huntsville for the murder of Gail Smith, but not for the murder of Jane Doe #6607-85.

Nevertheless, the crime had been solved in the view of the Nevada County Sheriff's Department. There was no further need to pour investigators' time or resources into it. They might not know the identity of the victim, but they knew who the killer was, and that was all that really mattered now.

The day after Theresa and her sons returned from Truckee, they washed all of Sheila's clothes and gave them to Good Will.

"Her cowboy hat was black, like velour or velvet, and it had a big feather decoration on the front," Terry recalled. "And she loved that hat, and it was a personal belonging. I mean really personal.

"So my mother got rid of that hat. She thought that as long as my sister's belongings were there, that my sister's spirit would still be there. So she had to get rid of the belongings."

All of Sheila's treasures went to Dumpsters at Winchell's Donuts, Raley's Supermarket, or the Red Lion Inn on Fulton Avenue where Robert worked as a busboy.

And then, there was the matter of the linen closet to consider.

"In the closet itself, there was a lot of blood, which is why I don't go along with the presumption that she died of starvation," said Robert. Though the decomposing body authorities found showed no sign of a slashed throat, there was evidence of a four-inch stab wound to her right breast as well as a bloody wound on the left side of her scalp.

"Mom believed later on that Sheila had tried to stand

up and get out of the closet," he said. "The shelves were stacked on little wooden runners ... and the shelves were relatively heavy. So she thought that maybe Sheila had stood up and knocked the shelves down on top of herself."

It fell to Terry to clean the closet. There she found chunks of her sister's flesh sticking to the floor.

"She made me scrub the floor, clean the blood and everything out of it," said Terry. "I remember we were trying to drink grape Crush sodas 'cause it was hot. And I was trying to drink a soda and all I could smell was the decomposing smell ... the soda tasted like that because it had permeated."

Her mother didn't talk about the ride up the mountain much, but she did seem to remain fixated on Sheila even longer than she had on Suesan. She stayed up nights brooding. She read the Bible.

Down the hall from the linen closet, next to the bathroom, was the room where Robert and William slept. From the doorway, the linen closet could be seen easily, even in the dark. The door that Bill had removed from the closet in order to get Sheila's body out had been cut up and tossed in a Dumpster. With its door off the hinges, the closet now resembled the square entrance to a cave set deep in the apartment's shadows. It was eerie. Bill didn't want to look at it ever again.

"William never came back to the house after that night," said Robert.

After his brother left home, Robert had their room to himself for a while. But then his mother's back went out not too long after Sheila died. She ordered Robert to move out so she could sleep in his room. It was closer to the bathroom.

"When my mom's back went out, she slept and sat in the room that me and William used to share," said Robert. "She'd sit there the whole day and watch the closet."

Robert did not put up a fight. He had not the least desire to look at the closet either. Ever.

He moved to a storage area next to the living room, down the hall. It was a perfectly good place to sleep and well out of sight of his sister's solitary death cell.

"I was standing outside the hospital room, when he screamed out of a coma, *'Theresa'* " said Terry.

After cheating death since the day he was diagnosed with Parkinson's disease in the late 1950s, James Cross had fallen into a coma late in October 1985. Cross spent his final days in a bed at Mercy San Juan Hospital—the same hospital where Theresa had given birth to Howard Sanders more than twenty years earlier. With Terry as her only companion, Theresa was there at his bedside throughout the ordeal.

Until he shouted out his youngest daughter's name the day after Halloween, Cross had been oblivious to his visitors and the tubes and monitors measuring his heartbeat and temperature. The sepsis pneumonia from which he suffered had put him into the coma, and his nurses said he probably could neither see nor hear his daughter or granddaughter sitting nearby.

But Theresa didn't believe it. She waited patiently for a signal indicating that he knew she was there and that he was getting ready to breathe his last breath. When he shouted her name out loud, she knew he had given that signal.

"And my mom says, 'We're gonna go home so that my dad can pass,' " said Terry. "Knowing how crazed my mom was about death and life, I knew what she meant. He wasn't gonna let go until she was gone.

"We left that hospital at seven A.M., took the bus home, and I went to sleep on the floor at the foot of my mother's bunk bed soon as we got back home.

"I saw my grandfather's face in my sleep, and that's all I saw. And he looked happy. At one o'clock that afternoon, I woke out of a sound sleep. Ruth, the lady that lived in a trailer across from the apartment, pounded on the door.

" 'I've got a very important phone call for your mother,' she said. 'Her father died.' "

James Cross's death had occurred at 1:42 P.M. on November 2, 1985. He was eighty years old.

On the way back to the hospital, Theresa told Terry about her grandfather—how he had always cared more for Rosemary than he did for his younger daughter, but how Theresa stood by him when Rosemary would not because she had gone off and married the awful Floyd Norris against her father's wishes. She told Terry about her grandmother and how she and Jim Cross used to fight, but how they stayed together no matter what because that's what men and women were supposed to do when they got married and had children. Good men didn't leave, the way Terry's father had. Good men stayed no matter what, like Jim Cross had done.

She talked about the Parkinson's disease and how he shook so badly that Swannie Gay had to sleep in a separate bed during the last few years of her life. When they were on good terms, Swannie called Jim "Black Dutch" and Jim called her his Shanty Irish, because those names represented the black sheep of the two cultures they each came from, according to Theresa.

She told her daughter that staying together as a family was the most important thing on earth. Her father taught her that. That was why she could not bear to lose any of her children. She could not allow them to abandon her.

"When we got there, the doctor had to pronounce him dead in front of family," Terry said. "I had never seen my grandfather look so goddamn happy in all my life. That man looked like he was just breathing away. He looked happy, at peace. He was glowing, and he was dead.

"And I looked at this doctor and said, 'My grandpa's not dead.' And he whips up his hand that's all purple because of the blood settling. And he goes, 'Is this proof enough for you?' And my mother went off. 'You don't do that to my daughter, you son of a bitch!' In this hospital, right in front of the nurses, my mother went off.

"I looked at my grandpa's hand and my heart sank. I thought, 'Damn, my grandpa was a good man, and he's dead. My sisters were both good persons. They're dead.' "

She looked at her mother, then back at her grandfather, and she tried to make sense of the contradictions: family is all-important, yet children can be beaten until they die. Family. Staying together, and family. The sentiment was fine, but that was all that it was: sentiment.

"That's probably when I got my hard-core attitude," said Terry. "Fuck it. Just screw everything. I've got shit for family. I've got shit for brains. And that's when I started surviving."

Theresa spared no expense for her father's funeral. Jim Cross was buried in a casket that was lowered into a cement vault for which Theresa continued to make monthly payments for nearly a year afterward. When the graveside service was over, Theresa held her head high and left for Howard's house with Robert and Terry sitting next to her in the car and Bill following close behind in his own car. The short funeral procession ended at Howard's house, where they all posed for pictures.

Throughout the ordeal, Terry can't remember observing her mother shedding a single tear.

"Terry never really gave in," said Robert. "She continually would do stuff to get punished. She went out of her way to make sure she got in trouble, and every time she did, it invariably wound up involving somebody else. But she was the only one of my sisters who went up against [my mother]. The other ones, you know, they tried, but eventually I guess they got tired of fighting."

By the time her grandfather died, Terry was fifteen.

She had given up on school and worked part-time at Del Taco. Eventually, she got her mother to help her forge a birth certificate so that she could pass for eighteen and work full-time without a work permit. Usually, that degree of cooperation between mother and daughter was rare. If Theresa helped Terry, it was because she saw a benefit—like Terry's weekly paycheck. Most of the time Theresa did nothing to help her daughter. She disgusted her daughter, and gradually, Terry let her mother know just how much.

"She got to the point where she wouldn't take a shower but every two weeks, sometimes longer than that," said Terry. "She'd sit on the couch all day combing that fuckin' hair. That's all she'd do all day, was comb it. It could be greasy as a motherfucker, look like she just dumped her head in a fry vat, and she'd be combing it."

Terry stopped short of name-calling because she still lived at the Auburn apartment, under her mother's roof, and because she knew better than anyone what cruelty her mother was capable of.

"After my sisters died, she tried putting me in a closet and I went berserk, screaming 'Nooooo!' " said Terry. "She said I was screwing somebody in the car outside Del Taco 'cause I was two minutes late coming home from work."

Terry successfully fought off that attempt, but her mother outweighed her and she knew that another confrontation was just a matter of time. Following the closet incident, Terry tried to steer clear of her mother altogether. When she saw Theresa lumbering toward her, she found an excuse—any excuse—to do an about-face and walk in the other direction.

"I was just trying to do whatever I had to do to stay out of her way," she said. "I had it set it my mind: there was no way I was gonna die. I don't wanna die. I wanna live!"

But she could not duck her mother twenty-four hours

a day. Sometimes she would wake up and find her mother towering over her, the doorway blocked and no escape route in sight.

"That's when my beatings started," said Terry. "She beat me and started handcuffing me. When you're controlled that much and you've got this big ol' mama hopping on top of you, just manhandling you, it's real hard to fight back to survive.

"My beatings stopped while Howard moved back in. My mom wouldn't dare beat me in front of Howard. When I was a kid, I was Howard's little baby. After Connie and him had their first child-abuse thing, he moved back to my mom's house temporarily."

And she was safe.

Getting Howard back amounted to a major triumph for Theresa, even if the circumstances of his return were not the best. He had been arrested for beating Howard Jr. within an inch of his life.

"He'd been beating me from the time we first got together," said Connie. "He said, 'You ever leave me, I will hunt you down and kill you.' To this day, when I sleep at night I have a flashlight and a knife right next to me. Every time I hear a noise I get up."

Connie's paranoia began shortly after the birth of Howard Jr. Connie and Howard rarely saw Howard's family in those times, but Theresa still came around on occasion, honking her horn out front of their newly rented home a few blocks away from Connie's mother's house. "She never came up to the door," said Connie. "She would have him come out to the car, and they would drive around the corner or something."

She had grown larger and spookier than even Connie remembered, and Howard was afraid of her, too, given his suspicions about what she had done to Suesan.

"He said one time—it was right around Christmas— that he was really afraid she was gonna kill him," said Connie. "He said that she wore these real tight leather driving gloves all the time, and she'd never take them off so she wouldn't get her fingerprints on anything. And he said the way she was acting and everything, he didn't trust her."

When Howard asked her about Sheila, Theresa told him that she had run off with an Indian named Chief. Howard accepted her story, but that didn't make him any less jittery when she dropped by for a visit.

Keeping Theresa out of his life didn't make him any more pleasant to live with, according to Connie. His lack of exercise, combined with drinking and drug use, had turned much of his high-school muscle into flab by the time he was twenty-three. He was beginning to resemble his mother in terms of sheer girth. Howard worked as a dishwasher and, later on, as a cook at a nearby restaurant, but he never seemed to find or hold on to a job much better than that. He tried joining the military once and had actually passed the recruiting tests with flying colors. He was "a stallion when it came to math," according to Terry. But his hopes of getting on a career path with Uncle Sam were ultimately dashed because he was overweight and far from the acceptable physical shape the Marine Corps or the Army demanded of their recruits.

Connie was into recreational drugs herself, but still considered herself to be a good wife and mother. Howard, on the other hand, seemed to regard himself as a failure and underwent a complete personality change whenever he escaped into alcohol or marijuana. Instead of anesthetizing his pain, the drugs turned him from husband and father into a drunken monster.

On March 25, 1986, Connie gave birth to a second son: Miles James Sanders. No sooner had she brought him home than the trouble started.

Howard Jr. was just one year old and barely weaned, but Connie did her best to care for both babies. She got little help from her husband. On the evening of April 2, she gave Junior to his father to watch while she fed

Miles in the bedroom. No sooner had she returned to her newborn than Junior began throwing a temper tantrum. Howard, who had been drinking, told his son to shut up. When he didn't, Howard smacked him.

"Howard never used an open hand on anybody except for Junior," said Connie.

Connie heard the slaps and rescued Junior, carrying him back into the safety of the bedroom, where he began to calm down. But Howard was angrier now. He came through the door, pumped up over the baby's impudence. Junior began howling again the moment he saw his father.

Howard told the boy to be quiet, that he had no reason to cry. Over Connie's objections, he took the boy out into the living room, telling him to quit screaming. Howard hated the screaming. If someone cried, they had to have a reason to cry, and Junior did not have a reason, according to his father. Then, his temper boiling over into rage, Howard held the boy upside down by his heels and began striking him in the face, like a punching bag.

"He hit him on his face, back and forth, until he had a concussion and eye-retina damage," said Connie. "The court said it was the worst abuse they had seen in years."

As Connie shrieked, trying to plant herself between her husband and her son, Howard yelled that Junior was just being a brat. When Connie wrestled the boy away from his father and put him in his playpen, Howard began hitting her—a half-dozen rabbit punches to the face.

Connie grabbed Junior from the playpen, retreated to the bedroom, and Howard followed. Once she got her husband to stop shrieking long enough to see the damage that he had inflicted on his own child, Howard quit advancing. He stared at his hands, then at the red and swollen head and shoulders of his son, and muttered that he could not understand why he had done it.

Howard left.

A half hour later a friend who was also a nurse stopped by to visit Connie and, when she saw what had happened, made Connie take the boys to a nearby police station. It was not the first time that Howard had beaten his wife and belted his baby, the friend told police.

The police report said Connie suffered a black eye, but Junior was lucky to be alive. *The entire facial area, from the child's forehead down to his chin and back towards his ears, were reddened and purple,* wrote the investigating officer.

Howard would eventually wind up with a sentence of three years formal probation, ninety days in jail, and enrollment in a mandatory drug-abuse program after being formally charged with spousal and child abuse.

But in the spring of 1986, after police had picked him up for questioning and placed his children in protective custody, Howard asked only that he be allowed to go home to live with his mother until his case came to court. And the request was granted.

Bill never came by to visit after his grandfather's funeral, and both Robert and Terry were under strict orders never to speak of Suesan or Sheila. So when Howard returned home for his brief sojourn, the subject of the two missing sisters simply never came up. It was as if neither of them had ever existed.

Except for one small problem.

"Basically, after the disposal, Mom tried to clean out the closet," said Robert. "I guess she was afraid some of the blood had soaked through the floor because we had a wooden floor and we had cement pylons. It wasn't a complete solid cement foundation underneath the apartment, and she was afraid that some of the blood had soaked through the wood and seeped under.

So she decided that it needed to be burned in order to destroy that."

Theresa had always been meticulous about how she broke the law. From the shooting of Clifford Sanders to the shooting of Suesan to the careful removal of any identifying materials in the cardboard box that became Sheila's casket, her crimes were always well hidden or easily explained away. Thus, the lingering odor and unsightly bloodstains on the floor of the linen closet continued to haunt her the way the telltale heart haunted the protagonist in Edgar Allan Poe's classic short story. She could not help but believe that the stains would connect her to Sheila's murder someday, especially if and when the family moved out of the Auburn Boulevard apartment and some other curious tenant moved in.

"Mom had tried to put a new floor into the closet and later on decided that would not be good enough," said Robert.

By September of 1986, Theresa's paranoia had gotten the best of her. She concocted a plan to wipe out the offending linen closet and, with it, all trace of any connection she might still have with the death of her eldest daughter. She began by moving family furniture, her wardrobe, and all the rest of her personal belongings to a cheap motel a few blocks away. She got Robert to do the same. The going was slow because Theresa had traded the LTD in for a Honda and the smaller car didn't have the same trunk space as the Ford.

The next part of her plan involved Terry. While Howard had been living with them confrontations between Theresa and her one remaining daughter had cooled, but Howard's stay was short. The court saw to that. At the time Theresa put her "erase Sheila" plan into action, Howard's residence was the Sacramento County Jail. With no referee to keep them apart, Theresa and Terry were constantly fighting once again, particularly over Terry's interest in young men.

"I remember the first time I stayed the night at a

boy's house, right before I left home," said Terry. "I stayed the night with John Pief Jr., and we went fishing up in Auburn. Next day, my mom made a big ol' scene and got me fired from Burger King."

When she discovered that Terry had spent the night with a male, Theresa went into her usual tirade against her daughter's whoring ways. When Terry ignored her, Theresa played the role of the distressed mother and stormed down to the Burger King, where she informed the manager that her daughter was underage and could get the restaurant in trouble if they kept her on the payroll. Terry had just turned sixteen, but she had faked her way into the job at Burger King, using the birth certificate her mother had helped her forge.

"So I got fired," said Terry. "Yet she was the one who had done the forging in the first place! My mom had a history of doing that. Same thing happened at Del Taco. She gets pissed at me and goes down and gets me fired."

Terry wanted to leave home. She'd seen Bill and Howard do it, but she'd also seen what happened to her sisters when they insisted on going, and they were both older than Terry was when they made their ill-fated attempts.

Now Theresa was offering her daughter a compromise: if Terry would set the apartment on fire after Theresa and Robert were completely moved out, she was free to go. No strings attached.

On September 29, 1986, Terry accepted her mother's offer.

"She had me torch the apartment," said Terry. "With Gulf Charcoal Lighter Fluid. I believe I used three bottles."

Following her mother's instructions, Terry wore gloves so that she would leave no fingerprints. Then she sprayed the charcoal lighter all around the apartment. Backing to a side window so that she could leave undetected, she threw a match on the floor, climbed out the window, and ran down the street to the Las Robles Motel, where Theresa and Robert were waiting for her.

"I saw the fire trucks going up to the apartment as I was running down the street," said Terry.

The American River Fire Protection District turned out to be quicker on the response than Theresa had figured. Within minutes of the burst of flames, sirens were squealing through the neighborhood.

Bill had a friend who still lived in the apartment next door to the Knorr family. He called Bill at work not long after the fire trucks showed up.

"He was extremely pissed because he had a newborn baby sleeping against the common wall," said Bill. "And he called me up and said, 'Better get down here! Your mom's place is on fire.' And I came down and everything was over with."

Despite her best efforts to have the place burned to the ground, Theresa's empty apartment suffered only minor damage. Among other things, the linen closet was barely touched by the fire.

She could not escape the inevitable. The fire department knew right away that the fire had probably been set, and they wanted some answers. Investigators managed to track down Theresa and her two remaining children to the Las Robles Motel. When they did, she was ready with her version of events. "Apparently she came up with some story that I guess they didn't believe was true or something, to the effect she blamed my brother Howard for burning it down," said Bill. "He had a very good alibi."

It took a day or two, but the arson investigators were able to confirm that Howard was in jail for beating his infant son. There was no way that he could have set the place on fire.

"So they went back to find her to ask her more questions," said Bill, "and she had dropped off the face of the earth. . . ."

* * *

Actually, she and Robert had simply moved down the street to another cheap motel, but not before Theresa and Terry had their final showdown.

Terry had blown her end of the bargain, according to Theresa. She had not set the apartment on fire correctly—if she had, arson investigators wouldn't be snooping around, trying to find out who started the fire.

"She started beating me, and I yelled at her," said Terry. "I started putting my foot down. Made a big ol' scene."

The scene was so loud and the managers of the motel were so used to putting down melees in their establishment that they had police on the scene in minutes.

"They asked my mom, 'Was there a problem?' " said Terry. "She said, 'Oh, she's outta control.' Then the cops asked me if there was a problem and I said no, because I knew better. I just wanted to get outta there, go away, never see her again."

The police saw the incident as typical white-trash domestic violence: a grotesque, obese welfare mother mixing it up with her young tramp of a daughter, probably over a boyfriend who didn't pay enough for services rendered before he'd left that morning. They saw the same thing in motels in this section of town all the time. Usually it was a pimp disciplining one of his hookers. In this case, it just happened to be a mother disciplining her daughter.

They told Terry and her mother that they were causing a commotion and that they had to stop. They didn't say what the consequences would be if they didn't. Then they left.

"As soon as the cops left, she put a knife to me," said Terry.

Terry stared at the blade and visions of her sisters' dying faces whipped through her mind. It was then that Terry had her flash of illumination. "And I grabbed her arm and I flipped her around and I looked her square in the face and said: 'You're never gonna fucking touch me again. *Get your fucking hands off of me!*' First and only time I ever cursed at my mom."

Theresa kept coming, but Terry was too quick. She dodged her every lunge. Theresa called on Robert to come hold his sister down so that she could give her the thrashing she needed.

"And I said, 'Yeah Robert! Come on in!' " said Terry.

Robert, however, didn't even try to stop his sister. He'd been told to hold her down before, and she had more or less let him. But he'd never seen her this angry or defiant. Restraining her, especially while his mother tried to hit her, would be an exercise in futility, if not a very real danger to himself. While his mother seethed, Robert did nothing.

Terry backed out the front door in triumph without taking her eyes off of her mother. Theresa had beaten her for the last time. Once outside, she turned her back on her mother and walked away, free.

"She seemed to focus her anger on one daughter at a time," said Terry. "And by the time it got to me, Suesan and Sheila were dead. I was ready to boogie! She'd already done enough damage to me."

The same week that Theresa's apartment burned, the phone rang at the upper-middle-class home of the former Miss Clara Tapp.

Theresa's half sister had gotten married back in the 1950s and had stayed married to the same man. She and her husband raised three children and both held steady jobs for the better part of a generation. Only once did they ever leave California, when her husband's job forced them to move to Missouri for three years in the 1970s. The rest of the time they lived in the San Francisco Bay area, steadily building a life together and seeing to it that their children got both a good education and a decent chance at starting a life of their own.

Now, as Clara reached for the phone, she and her

husband were living in a comfortable two-story house on a hillside, overlooking San Francisco Bay. They were about to retire with a lifetime of savings and investments to cushion them.

Clara had maintained no contact with her family over the years. She had no idea what had happened to her stepfather or his spoiled younger daughter, Theresa Jimmie Cross. After Theresa's acquittal for the murder of her first husband, Clara had only heard about the family once: when the newspapers reported Rosemary's murder. Clara wept over Rosemary. She remembered her as a good woman.

But when she picked up the receiver and the caller identified himself as the chaplain at San Quentin State Prison, Clara listened with dry eyes.

Her brother, William Hart Tapp, was dead at the age of fifty-eight. William had made peace with himself and his God while he was in prison, the chaplain said. He had even become an assistant to the chaplain, helping him perform services. He died of natural causes—a heart attack apparently. The chaplain asked Clara what she wanted done with his remains.

Clara cleared her throat. Then, in a steady voice, she told him as politely as she could that she did not care what was done with her brother's remains.

She reminded the chaplain that before he had found God, her brother had been a cold-blooded, sadistic murderer and, before that, a selfish, conniving, mean-spirited bastard who would say or do anything to get his way. Perhaps he had made peace with himself and his God, and that was good. But he had not made peace with all those he had hurt and maimed and murdered during his miserable life. He had never apologized to her or to his own children or to any of the other survivors of his mayhem.

She spoke for them as well as for herself when she instructed the chaplain to do with his remains whatever the state does when a prisoner dies without friends or family. Because, in Clara's estimation, that's exactly how William Hart Tapp died.

XVI

By the autumn of 1986, Robert was the only child Theresa had left.

"My mom was even more demanding on me," said Robert. "Everyone else had flown the coop. She was paranoid that at any second the cops were going to bust in and arrest her."

The paranoia didn't come from feeling guilty about anything that she had done, according to Robert. In Theresa's estimation, she had been a good mother who had done the best she could with impossible children. Her fear was simply that her wicked children would turn on her, turn her in to the authorities, and concoct stories about how evil she was.

After Terry's dramatic departure, Robert and his mother moved from hotel to hotel for the next few weeks and finally wound up taking an apartment near the Red Lion Inn, where Robert was still working. "I kept my job at the Red Lion Inn for a while, but she wanted me to quit that," he said.

He had met a girl on the job, dated her a couple of times, and even went home to meet her parents. Then his mother found out. Naturally, she disapproved and put a stop to it. "I guess she thought I was getting too friendly with Mary Evans," said Robert. "I was even more constrained. I couldn't go out anymore. I had to come home directly from work. She would call work to make sure I was there. And she would be up at night waiting for me to come home."

Their relationship deteriorated into one based on guilt. Theresa claimed that she was suffering from the debilitating chronic disease that Suesan and Sheila had given her and that she was eventually going to die from it. Apart from Robert's income from bussing tables and washing dishes, she had no means of support except Sheila's monthly checks from Social Security, for which Theresa remained the payee. At sixteen, Robert had become his mother's sole caretaker, and she was his sole taskmaster.

Theresa, however, did not give up on the idea of luring her other children back She contacted Bill one last time in the hope of obtaining a free U-Haul truck so that she and Robert could move to their new apartment, but following this call, he essentially disappeared from his mother and brother's lives. He was working two jobs, finishing high school, and living with Emily Lewis. He had no time for his mother, even if he wanted to share a moment with her—which he did not.

Terry moved in for about three months with John Pief after she left her mother and brother. To save face, Theresa called Pief on the phone to tell him that he had her blessing. She was happy to be rid of her unruly delinquent of a daughter.

Pief, who was several years older and already had a male roommate, was little more responsible than Terry. For three months "we partied like dogs," said Terry. The rent money went for booze and drugs. After several warnings, the landlord kicked them out.

For the next year or two Terry's life fell into a general pattern: she stayed with acquaintances whom she ran into at work or at night on the party circuit. After a few weeks or months—sometimes after just a few days—she would wear out her welcome and have to move on to the next open door.

Once, a well-meaning older friend who saw what the drugs and alcohol were doing to her turned her in to Sacramento County's Child Protective Services. But the authorities took her to the Receiving Home, which only resurrected angry memories about Suesan's experiences there.

She moved through the county's runaway system, from the Receiving Home to foster care to group homes, where troubled teens were supposed to receive counseling and education as well as a fresh start. All these homes did for Terry was remove her access to men, drugs, and alcohol and make her even angrier.

Once, through the help of one of her foster families, she contacted Bob Knorr. "She was sixteen," he said. "She was very streetwise."

Bob had divorced Georgia, his second wife, in July of 1985 and was married a third time to a woman with children of her own, including a daughter about Terry's age. They lived in Citrus Heights, east of Sacramento, and did not have a lot of room, but Bob welcomed Terry home, if she wanted to stay. With hopes high, he picked his daughter up and tried to reestablish a bond that had really never been forged in the first place. There was trouble immediately.

"She was kind of mature," said Bob's stepdaughter. "She used to tell me how to have sex with guys and all that stuff. She has big boobs and she used to say, 'That'll get anybody for you.' She thought she could get any man she wanted. She was real smartmouthed— always lied. She'd say something to my mom, then turn around and tell Bob something else. She told so many lies, you couldn't really determine what was the truth and what was not."

The homecoming Bob had imagined for his and Theresa's youngest daughter did not materialize as he had hoped. She was evasive when he asked about his other children. The only thing Terry knew for sure was that Robert was living with Theresa and Howard was probably in jail. Bill was living with some slut and would no longer have anything to do with the family. He acted as though he was too good for his brothers and sisters, Terry told her father.

When he asked about Suesan, Terry told him she had run off to Alaska and no one had heard from her for years. Same with Sheila. She had eloped with an Indian somewhere to the north, maybe Canada. It wasn't until after Terry was gone that Bob's stepdaughter revealed to him that Terry had tried to get her to go to a liquor store to buy some booze with a false ID—a driver's license in the name of Suesan Marline Knorr.

While Bob was hungry for any kind of news about his children, he was not so desperate that he let his newfound daughter walk all over him. For all of his own foolishness and youthful excesses, the adult Bob Knorr had assumed his role as a parent more fully than he had during his marriage to Theresa. He'd learned something from his own sorry experiences. Bob knew how to set limits for his children and he was relatively adept at detecting a teenager's bullshit.

"She told the kids so many things that it was unreal," said Bob. "After a while you just tuned her out. Oh, man, the language! A real little trucker. I told her, 'Don't come into the house and talk like that! You gotta live under the same rules everybody else does: go to school, don't smoke, don't go out on school nights, be in by twelve on weekends.' About two days later she was gone."

Once again, Terry escaped. With the help of Gary, a new boyfriend and a well-known north Sacramento pot dealer, she found her way back to the street life. Her father had tried to force her to give him a blow job, she told Gary. "My social worker said Gary was nothing more than an overgrown child molester because I was seventeen and he was twenty-five," she said.

But Gary would become the typical man in her life: at least five to ten years older, stout, at least half a foot taller, and prone to getting his way through liberal use of his fists. Despite the obvious hazard of getting involved in a losing bout, Terry repeated this pattern again and again, taunting a man into an argument with little or no provocation. "When I got pissed at Gary, I threw his glass bongs off the balcony. Broke every one of them," said Terry. "I robbed this man of all his profits. He used to beat me up, and I used to get even by taking his pot."

One day, after she'd left Gary and was bunking temporarily with yet another set of her street pals, Terry was driving down a street near her old neighborhood with a girlfriend when she spotted a couple of familiar figures on the sidewalk.

"I saw my mom walking with Robert and I shouted 'Mom!' from the car window," said Terry. "And my mom turned around and looked square at me and turned around and kept walking."

Terry told her girlfriend to pull over. She got out and chased her mother down. "She started moving real quick," she said. "She and Robert were trying to run. But I caught up with them, and she acted as though she hadn't heard me when I was calling at her. So then it was all hunky-dory. Like, 'What are you doing?' and all that."

Theresa offered to take her daughter out to eat, so she and Robert and Terry met with a couple of Terry's roommates at a restaurant and made an evening of it.

"Mom proceeded to get drunk, tried to act the 'Oh-I'm-your-friend' bit, and told Terry, 'Let's go out and pick up on guys together,' " said Robert. "That kind of shocked me because I never saw her do that before."

Robert recalled his mother suddenly transforming herself from a strict disciplinarian who was too sick most days to get out of the house to a wanton trollop who propositioned the waiters. "I felt bad for this busboy because my mom was trying to pick up on him and she was being pretty lewd about it," he said. "Basically, she offered him sex right there on the table."

Later on they all wound up back at the apartment where Terry was living with two older guys, one of whom was pushing forty and just a few years younger than Theresa. They all drank more—Tom Collinses, Scotch, bourbon, and gin. They even smoked a little pot, including Theresa, and she began babbling about the supernatural.

"Terry's roommate friend called her evil," said Robert. "He looked like he was going to hit her, but he didn't."

Eventually everyone crashed, including Robert. Sometime in the middle of the night, while the inside of the apartment was a symphony of snores and wheezes, Theresa shook her son out of his drunken stupor.

"Mom woke me up and hissed at me that we could have gotten killed. We didn't know who these people were. Basically she wound up putting all the blame on me for us being there," said Robert.

She continued to berate Robert as they sneaked out of Terry's crash pad and returned to their own apartment, several blocks away.

The next morning, Theresa and Robert were gone, but Terry's roommates weren't. Through headaches and hangovers, they reviewed as best they could what had happened the night before, when alcohol and cannibis turned Theresa's bizarre stories of the occult into a soporific haze. Terry's reunion with her mother hadn't turned out the way she had hoped. The only positive thing she remembered from the evening was that Theresa had not tried to take a swing at her. Otherwise, she had been an embarrassment in public and a raving religious nut when they got back to the apartment.

Ken, the older of Terry's two roommates, had a helluva breakfast story to tell her about her mother's behavior once everybody else in the apartment had passed out. "They ended up screwing that night on the couch," said Terry. "That's all right. They were close to the same age. But I still felt quite betrayed by my mother that she was fucking my roommate."

It would be the last time Terry saw her mother.

The last time Connie saw her mother-in-law, Theresa appeared to have bleached her hair. "She'd cut her hair real short, 'cause normally it was down past her waist and it was dark brown," Connie said.

Theresa was wearing a wig—one of the habits she had developed since Sheila's "disappearance." But the wig was convincing. Connie didn't know it was not real and almost didn't recognize her.

Connie and Howard were still married, but separated. She was living off and on with Howard's best friend, Robert Watson, when Theresa came by to see Robert's dad. Over the years Theresa had become friendly with Robert and his parents, Bud and Helga Watson. Helga had worked at a convalescent home with her during the 1970s, and Bud shared Theresa's interest in the supernatural. Whenever they got together, Theresa abandoned her hypochondria and the two of them talked for what seemed like hours about the coming Apocalypse.

"He was into fortune-telling or something like that because he claimed to have predicted an earthquake in California," said Robert. "He was convinced that when the big earthquake hit, which could be anytime now, the California shelf was going to sink, we were going to see a very large tidal wave, and eventually parts around Nevada would become beachfront property.

"She believed it. I guess there were passages in the Bible that refer to this sort of thing, and she was afraid that, should we stay in California, we were going to have to learn how to swim really well."

Pack up, she told Robert after she'd spoken with Bud Watson. They weren't going to stay in Sacramento. Watson himself was planning to escape with his family to Ohio. Theresa wanted to leave before the deluge, too.

By this time she had made her son quit his job at the Red Lion Inn. She suggested Robert tell his boss that he'd gotten food poisoning and threaten to sue. That way, she reasoned, they might be persuaded to pay him off just to avoid going to court. It didn't work out that way, but Robert was still out of a job.

So when his mother told him they were moving to Reno, he put up little resistance. "I also believe she wanted to get me away from Howard, William, and any friends that I had," he said. "I think she was afraid I was going to pull up and leave like everybody else did."

In Reno, Theresa and Robert moved into a rooming house with no name over a mom-and-pop grocery store run by a Korean couple on Second Street near downtown. They had no money and Theresa said she was too sick to work.

"I had a job within a week at Circus Circus," said Robert. "My mom threw a fit. She didn't want me working at Circus Circus because evidently Terry's boyfriend had family who worked there at one time and Mom was afraid I would tie right back into Terry. She was afraid I would betray her at any moment and that I had purposely gone to work at that particular casino just so I could maintain contact with Terry.

"She got so paranoid in Reno that she wouldn't drink water. She said it was poisoning her. I had to lug bottled water up to her or she wouldn't drink at all. She would accuse me of going to a hose and filling up the jugs with tap water instead of going to buy it at the store and then she wouldn't drink. She got sores on her tongue from dehydration."

Between tending to his mother and escaping into what was fast becoming an addiction to marijuana and other drugs, Robert soon lost his dishwashing job at Circus Circus. Trying to work while on an LSD trip turned out not to be such a terrific idea, although it did not deter him from repeating the maneuver several times. There were plenty of other casinos and Robert had no problem getting hired, even if he was only seventeen. "I was passing myself off as a thirty-nine-year-old man," he said. "I had a Nevada state ID with the name Ron E. Bullington on it."

Theresa had saved at least one useful artifact from her relationship with Ron Bullington back in the early 1970s. She kept his military discharge papers. "I used those to apply for a missing Social Security card because I told Social Security I got robbed," said Robert. "After I got the Social Security card, I went down to the department of motor vehicles, showed them two pieces of ID, and got a state ID card."

With three pieces of official identification, Robert followed his mother's instructions and sent off to Albuquerque for a copy of Bullington's birth certificate. Robert Knorr had effectively become Ronald E. Bullington.

"I worked all up and down the strip," he said. "I went in under Ron E. Bullington's name. I was born in Albuquerque, New Mexico. My father's name was Robert Q. Bullington. I had been an accountant when I was in the service at Mather Air Force Base in California, where I was discharged. I memorized all this."

He hadn't gotten past the eighth grade, but Robert was a seasoned con man before he had turned eighteen, thanks to the survival skills his mother taught him.

"Working bureaucracy is the same thing as working a con," he said, recalling his mother's sage advice. "If you know enough information about a given subject, people will see what they expect to see.

"If you go in with the right bearing, and act like you know what you're doing, they usually have so many customers that they don't want to mess with you. Unless they have a really concrete reason to hold you up, they won't because they want to get to their next coffee break."

But Robert didn't always get away with things. Each time he mixed it up with the police, Theresa grew a little more paranoid. He and his mother had lived in Reno less than three months when Robert's drug habit and druggie pals began getting him into trouble.

"I was arrested the first time for vagrancy and prowling," he said. "I was on acid at the time, and me and a guy named Sean Dixon went looking for a gun that he 'shoved up a bush's ass,' as he put it. He had broken into a car and gotten the gun, a ring, and some methamphetamines. Basically, he got this guy's little drug pouch and a found a nine-millimeter to boot.

"So when the cops found us, we were looking for where he'd stashed it all and the cops got us for prowling. I spent five days in the Reno County Jail. I believe that was sometime around December of 1987."

A few months later Robert and a friend were arrested for breaking into a school and trashing it. Later that same year he and two others were busted for attempting to break into a car.

His trouble with police wasn't the only thing that disturbed Theresa. Robert's income from the minimum-wage jobs that he kept losing weren't paying the rent. Most of the time they had no car. When Theresa got a little money from Social Security or Robert worked some overtime, they would get a clunker by the week from Rent-A-Duck auto.

After stiffing the landlord at their first place, he and his mother kept moving from apartment to apartment in Reno's shabby downtown area. Theresa took to visiting soup kitchens and homeless shelters, like the one operated out of the parish hall at St. Thomas Aquinas Catholic Cathedral, catty-corner from the El Cortez Hotel and Casino in the heart of Reno. But she finally had to face the inevitable. In order to eat, Theresa finally had to go to work.

"Mom was cooking at John Ascuaga's Nugget in Sparks near the end," said Robert.

As Ron Bullington, Robert had found a job as a dishwasher at Harrah's. Not only did he not get fired this time, he seemed to do well enough and made enough friends that he and another guy who worked in the kitchen decided to get an apartment together. His mother took the news badly. She demanded to see the head of personnel at Harrah's. Robert was summoned from the kitchen to join Theresa, who was seated across the desk from an employee representative. Theresa revealed that her son was not Ron Bullington.

"She told them I was an ex-felon, which at the time wasn't true," he said. "She said that I was working under a false name, I was a drug addict, and a big-time criminal. The lady in the personnel office looked over at me and said, 'Well, do you still want to work here?' And I said, 'Yeah.' And she said, 'Well, we can just go ahead and change this over to your legal name, and you can continue working.'

"And Mom went off. 'Oh, no! That's falsification of his application! He can't work here! It's right there in your rules. You've *got* to fire him.' "

Robert kept his job at Harrah's, but even his mother's treachery did not drive him away from her after his plans to move out and live with friends fell through. He continued to help with the rent and the groceries and take care of his mother as best he could.

"We were like two weeks behind in our rent at the Virginia Street Hotel, and one day she comes home from work with a bruise on the inside of her arm," Robert recalled. "She said that I had someone kidnap her. They injected her with some kind of drug and threatened to kill her, so she no longer wanted to live there with me.

"So she left and came back the next day with the cops. She tried to antagonize a fight out of me while she was taking what she wanted to take from the place while the cops were watching.

"The next day she left a couple bags of groceries for me, and that was the last I ever heard from her."

* * *

"When I lost my sisters at that age, it didn't set in like it has now, if you can understand that," said Terry. "It didn't sink in that they were actually dead and how much I really loved them, until now. In my adult years I [understand] how much they really meant to me."

Most of the time Terry tore through her adolescence either high and dreamy or sober and angry. There was hardly time for her to be introspective because she was too busy fighting with ham-fisted boyfriends, scrounging up enough money to buy food and shelter, or looking for a drug and alcohol escape from the horrors of her past. When she'd had enough to drink, the memories from which she was trying to flee often played tricks on her. Instead of staying hidden away in pickled silence, they dredged themselves up and out of her subconscious, often leaving her huddled in a corner of the room sobbing uncontrollably.

"Lena[1] [a friend] heard me once—I guess I got good and slobbery—and I told her what happened to my sisters," said Terry.

Lena Jackson was a shrewd, stiletto-thin blonde from Sacramento's rural outskirts who had figured out early how to overcome her hick roots by using male ego and lust to her advantage. Even in high school, she vied to become a beauty queen with a difference.

She had her share of physical flaws, but she learned how to whisk them away by spending a little extra time on a diet and a little more time in front of the vanity each day before she stepped out into the world. Before she was eighteen, Lena learned through trial and error how to be a knockout.

By the time Terry met her, she owned her own lingerie boutique—Trashy Fashions. She was a fox in her early thirties, and she wasn't married. She was too smart to turn over what she had going for her to any

[1]Not her real name

man. Instead, she dated the men of her choosing—those with extra cash to spend on her often getting the edge.

The rest of the time she built her business with regular businessmen's luncheon "fashion" shows that featured scantily clad young women wearing the kind of lingerie first made famous by Frederick's of Hollywood. The men who attended her shows ran the gamut from attorneys to bus drivers. They usually said they were coming to watch young women walk down the runway in their underwear because they wanted to get a little something for their wives and needed to know how it would look on them before buying.

Lena was more than willing to accommodate their wishes. For a short time Terry became one of her models and came to live with her and another of her models, but not before Lena did a makeover and taught her what her mother never did. "When Terry first came to me, she had her hair hacked short, wore no makeup, and had on layered clothes," recalled Lena. "She had no self-esteem. She was crying all the time. I fixed her up, showed her how to use makeup. She was really a very pretty girl."

But Terry's makeover was only a partial success. She still cried herself to sleep at night. When Lena demanded to know the problem, Terry told her.

"She didn't believe it," said Terry. "At that point, I thought I was an accessory. I thought I'd get in trouble if I went to the police. Lena said she really didn't know if that was true, but she knew a lawyer who would."

Lena did not dismiss Terry's story out of hand because she dimly recalled the news reports about a burning body in the Sierras back in 1984. The following day Lena gave Terry half a Valium to calm her down and drove her to the law offices of John Virga.

"He told me that legally I was a minor, there was nothing they could do to me, I had done nothing wrong, and that he would check it out for me," said Terry.

Virga taped Terry's statement and promised to get back to her once he'd talked with the authorities.

Before he could do so, Terry cracked up Lena's car.

"I'd never driven before, and she asked me to pull her Cadillac out of the garage for her," said Terry. "Instead of putting it into reverse, I put it in drive and ran it right into the garage wall."

Terry was convinced that Lena's business involved more than lingerie sales. Lena herself never said that her Trashy Fashion runway shows were designed to encourage prostitution, but Terry believed that to be the case. So, when one of the other girls heard that she'd cracked up Lena's car, Terry was told she'd probably wind up in white slavery at a brothel in Vallejo, or perhaps the Mustang Ranch in Nevada, in order to pay off her debt.

Terry did what she had learned to do so well when trouble stalked her in the past. She ran, and left no forwarding address.

Robert had no idea where his mother had gone, so he stole a car and drove back to Sacramento in the spring or early summer of 1988, as near as he could recall. He was drifting and felt very alone, even though his mother's sudden disappearance had given him a curiously pleasant, if somewhat frightening, taste of genuine freedom. He wasn't headed back to Sacramento to find Theresa necessarily. He thought he might be able to find Howard or Terry or Bill, though, and figure out what he should do with his life, as well as with his nagging nightmares.

Cruising the streets of the old neighborhood turned up nothing. Howard was out of jail, but unreachable because he was still in a work furlough program. Robert couldn't find Bill and Emily either. And Terry had simply disappeared. No matter which old haunts he visited or which mutual acquaintances he questioned, he could find no trace of his little sister.

Finally he showed up at the front door of Connie's mother's house. "When I went up to the door, I was dressed in army camouflage, I had my head shaved, my eyebrows were gone, and I was wearing a boot knife," said Robert. "That's just the way I was at the time, so I'm sure I struck a handsome figure. They couldn't get me out of the house quick enough, but they were really polite to me."

Before they hustled him away, Connie and her mother brought him up to date on his brother's life.

Howard had been in trouble with the police almost nonstop since the child-beating conviction. He'd been arrested for trespassing with intent to commit larceny, driving under the influence, and most recently, wife beating.

Connie explained that she and Howard had reconciled once again following her tryst with Bud Watson. It was a mistake. Howard got drunk and tried to stab her while she was in the shower, she told Robert. They were legally separated on November 19, 1987, but Howard returned and beat her. On November 29, he was taken into custody and wound up spending Christmas and New Year's in the Sacramento County Jail.

Once he was out, Bud Watson and several of his friends exacted Connie's revenge by cornering him one night and pounding him as badly as Howard had once pounded the Casa Robles High student who jumped his little brother Bill. Howard spent several days in the hospital, according to Connie.

Robert returned to Nevada uninspired and unenlightened.

One person who might have had some answers for him, had Robert bothered to track him down during his Sacramento sojourn, was Chester Harris. He could not have told the boy where his mother had fled to, but he probably would have been able to explain why. There had been witchcraft in his short marriage to Theresa, but—as Chet was quick to explain to anyone who might have asked him at his beloved American Legion hall—*he* was not the practitioner.

The retired newspaperman still got to the American Legion when he could and still put down as much beer as his failing health would allow, even though cancer had taken his tongue, jaw, and most of his throat. In his waning years, he could not speak, but he could still drink and communicate with notes and nods.

His daughter, Terry Smith, flew from New York to California for a visit a few years before his bout with cancer. She walked into the American Legion hall much the same way as Mrs. Theresa Pulliam once did, asked the bartender which one was Chet Harris, and then sidled up to the man with the two beers at the end of the bar.

"Dad and I never got along when I was younger, and I hadn't seen him in more than twenty years," she said. "I sat down, put my purse on the bar, and asked, 'How about buying a girl a drink?' "

Now pushing seventy and totally retired from the *Union* except for a coin column that he wrote for the Sunday hobby pages, the portly Chet Harris thought he was being hit on. He perked up, smoothed back a make-believe wisp of hair, and growled; "I'd like to, but you've got to tell me your name first."

Before he embarrassed himself any further, Terry extended her hand and shook her head. Some things never seemed to change. "Dad," she said, "it's been a long time."

Chet finished his beer and took his daughter to his house. He introduced her to his collies and had her stay over a few days. It was a bachelor's place—cluttered, not particularly tidy, even downright dirty in spots—but there was nothing in the way of witchcraft or black robes or satanic literature lying around. From all that Terry could see, her father had simply become a lonely old man whose life revolved around his dogs and his pals at the Legion hall.

On the wall, he did have portraits of all five of his wives, neatly framed and smiling down on him as he shuffled in from the bar each afternoon. There was no doubt that he appreciated women, even if he never learned how to live with them. It also looked like he had developed a kind of respect for his wives, now that it was too late. If he had pornographic photos of any of the ex–Mrs. Chester Harrises, they were not out for company to ogle.

Chester Leroy Harris died on June 12, 1989. A year earlier he had declared bankruptcy after his medical bills ate up whatever liquid assets he had left. It was an aneurysm that killed him, not the cancer. A blood vessel exploded deep inside his alcohol-weakened body.

When paramedics showed up to remove his remains, they found transients living in his house. The young strangers claimed to have been taking care of him, but his sheets hadn't been changed for weeks and he had died lying in puddles of his own waste.

"My dad had always been one to take people in," said Terry Smith. "And while my husband and I can't prove it, we think he took people in who had threatened him at the time."

When Terry Smith and her husband flew out to attend his funeral and take care of probate, they found that there was no estate to speak of. The strangers who had been living in Chester's house were gone, and so was everything of value, including the portraits of the five ex–Mrs. Harrises.

"Everything in the house was stolen or destroyed, and we didn't get anything, including the pictures of my mom or any of the other things my sister and I wanted," she said. "The people who had been living in the house with Dad disappeared just after he died, along with the air conditioner and everything else in the house."

In his will, Chester divided his estate evenly between

his two daughters, his sister, his third wife, Dona, and his dogs. He also left a provision that drinks at the American Legion hall were to be on him on the day that he was buried.

"It was a very crowded place that day," said his ex-boss Robert Carney. "Chet would have been pleased."

When Robert Knorr Jr. was not in jail, he spent the next three years getting high—a practice in which he had developed his own personal expertise, almost from the cradle. "My mom said I wouldn't make it past eighteen, and I tried to prove her right," he said.

Once, he drained an entire quart of Jack Daniel's by himself. He'd seen his sister Suesan put down a quart of whiskey the night he had cut the bullet out of her back, so he knew it could be done. "I blacked out and the next day my friends said I was doing all kinds of crazy shit," said Robert. "I got into two fights, fucked about three or four women. I had a real good time, but I didn't remember any of it."

He tried cocaine for the first time, liked it, and stopped using it. He was afraid he might get addicted. "It's probably the only advice I ever took from my mother," he explained. "She said in social situations, never drink what you like or do any drugs that you like."

The reason to abstain, she had explained to her son, was so that one always remained in control. Staying in control was more important than anything else. Losing control spelled disaster. He might have believed in her advice, but he didn't always follow it, as, for example, the time he lost his eyebrows.

His friends talked him into taking "power hits of crack" until he passed out, he recalled. Then, as a practical joke, someone shaved off an eyebrow—a definite sign that Robert had taken too much dope and lost control.

"I woke up when he was halfway through and hit

him," said Robert. "When I went into the bathroom, I decided to shave both eyebrows to make it even."

But lack of control could result in losses far more serious than eyebrows. Robert was chalking up even more arrests as he floated through life. Each time he got high enough to be stupid, he found himself in police custody.

In 1989, he picked up a burglary conviction and spent several months at a minimum-security facility in northern Nevada. During the short time he was there he took and passed a standardized general education test and earned his high-school equivalency diploma.

But the positive was balanced out with the negative. He also met an influential new friend in prison: a Las Vegas native named Brian McNary. McNary had three felony convictions and a misdemeanor, and he was no older than Robert. McNary reminded him of his brother Howard. Like Howard, McNary had a tendency to knock down those who crossed him and protect those who did his bidding. Robert never saw himself as a fighter—a classic passive-aggressive male who might not like violence himself, but admired those who could use brute force to get their way. He and McNary became best friends.

Robert also tended to be a follower, not a leader. Later on, when his probation officer had him tested at the New Frontier Drug Rehabilitation Center in Fallon, Nevada, he was found to be above average in intelligence. And yet Robert Knorr Jr., a twenty-year-old legal adult, had the social skills and emotional development of a fifteen-year-old boy.

The following year Robert was busted for felony possession of a firearm and for possessing methamphetamine. This time when he was convicted, he graduated to a regular state prison. He was shipped to the southern part of the state and did eighteen months in a correctional facility. When he was released, he was within a few miles of Las Vegas and Brian McNary.

By now, the pattern was deeply ingrained. Robert was

back into trouble within weeks. This time McNary offered to show him the fast, loose town of Las Vegas, give his buddy a place to stay, and teach him how to make money breaking into cars.

Just before midnight on February 4, 1991, a security guard spotted Robert and McNary loitering near a 1987 Ford Taurus in the Circus Circus Hotel parking structure. They were both wearing trench coats. When the guard stopped the pair as they were trying to leave, he found McNary packing a .38 revolver and Knorr carrying a mechanism used by locksmiths to pop the lock of a car door.

Robert spent a week in the Clark County Jail until police discovered he had violated his northern Nevada prison parole. He was transferred to the Southern Desert Correctional Center for most of the rest of 1991, but was out and back prowling the Vegas strip by the first week of November. His old pal Brian McNary invited him to crash at his friend Bobby Coyle's trailer on the northeast side of town until Robert could get back on his feet.

Sometime after two A.M. on November 7, 1991, a thirty-six-year-old bartender named Robert Arthur Ward was executed at Redd's Place cocktail lounge, about two and a half miles from the trailer park where Robert and McNary were living. Ward's killer fired a .25-caliber pistol three times into his skull and took about a hundred dollars from the cash register and another eight hundred in coins from the slot machines.

Investigators found a witness who described three men who had fled the bar sometime after two A.M. From his description, police artists developed a pair of sketches that were published in local newspapers. Though cartoonish, the sketches resembled Brian McNary before he shaved his mustache and Robert Knorr before he had a barber lop off his ponytail. In addition, forensics specialists dusted Redd's Place from top to bottom and found both men's fingerprints on drinking glasses and pool cues.

Within a week Las Vegas police found Bobby Coyle's trailer and surrounded it with a half-dozen officers. Police Sergeant Albert Salinas called the number listed for Bobby Coyle in the phone book and told the man who answered that the place was surrounded. He ordered Brian McNary and Robert Knorr to back out of the trailer with their hands up.

The next day, the district attorney filed robbery and first-degree murder charges against the pair. Investigators tracked down a third suspect, William Wesenberg, to Kansas. Unlike McNary and Knorr, Wesenberg had worked for Ward and had been fired by him a week before the murder. According to prosecutors, Wesenberg was the most likely person to have instigated the robbery.

But the district attorney never had enough evidence to charge Wesenberg. In addition, the eyewitness who had supplied police with the descriptions of Knorr and McNary checked into a mental hospital in Colorado a few months after the murder. Before the case of *People* v. *McNary and Knorr* even went to preliminary hearing, it was in trouble.

Both men were held without bail and did not go to trial until nearly eighteen months later. The prosecution believed it had a strong circumstantial case, but not so strong that it would not accept a plea bargain.

On May 25, 1993, the day before the jury was to hear opening arguments, Robert and McNary cut a deal. They agreed to testify against Wesenberg in the event that he was charged. In exchange, the district attorney allowed the pair to enter a nolo contendere plea to second-degree murder. They would not face Nevada's death penalty.

The following day, another inmate at the Clark County jail chased Robert down and beat him to a pulp after calling him a dirty snitch.

On July 1, 1993, Robert Knorr, twenty-four, and Brian McNary, twenty-five, were sentenced to fifteen years in the maximum-security Nevada State Prison outside of Ely, in the desolate eastern Nevada desert. They were told that if they cooperated during their incarceration, they would be eligible for parole by the end of the century.

Wesenberg, whom Knorr and McNary belatedly claimed to have been the triggerman that night at Redd's Place, was never charged.

XVII

The calendar that hung on Mrs. Michael Groves's kitchen wall read October 25, 1993. She sighed a hopeless, bourbon-flavored sigh, wiped a tear from her face, and switched on the television set.

Halloween was near again and another year was winding to a close for the twenty-three-year-old woman whose maiden name had been Terry Marie Knorr. Five years had passed since the wisecracking blue-eyed blond bombshell in Lena Jackson's modeling lineup had left Sacramento for Salt Lake City.

During those years Terry had packed in a lifetime's worth of hedonism as well as her share of explosive violence and excruciating poverty.

She'd slept in dirt and eaten at the best restaurants; drunk from champagne flutes and jelly jars; charged expensive frocks at the finest department stores and worn the same fourth-hand thrift-store rags for weeks at a time because she couldn't afford anything better. She had driven across five states at ninety miles an hour in gleaming high-test street chariots with a hard-body stud at the wheel, and had limped desperately through desert towns all by herself, piloting ratty vehicles with expired registrations and body rot.

She'd posed topless for a biker magazine, slept with God-know's-who while she was stoned out of her mind, and spent a disappointing night with a porn star who claimed to have been John Holmes's roommate, but still had trouble getting his substantial codpiece to stand at attention. She'd gotten pregnant, only to discover that it was a tubal pregnancy and that the likelihood of her ever being able to have children was slim at best.

She'd been married three times, two of those times to the same man: a Salt Lake City Mormon named Michael Groves who still lived with his parents even though he was the same age, size, and temperament as Terry's brother Howard Sanders.

The third marriage, sandwiched in between the two to Groves, was a 1992 union with an auto mechanic named Dennis Roper, also the same age, size, and temperament as her oldest brother. She'd met Roper before Groves, back in Sacramento. In fact, it was Roper who whisked her off her feet and drove her to Salt Lake City in the first place, way back in 1987. Never mind that he belted her so hard on the way that he broke her nose. She loved him.

After she'd polished off a fifth of Jim Beam one night, she even let Roper tattoo PROPERTY OF DKR (for Dennis K. Roper) across her ass. He spent money on her. Bought her the things she'd always dreamed of having: designer-label clothes, perfume, even a little jewelry now and then. When he decided to leave Utah in a hurry, he took her with him. They stayed at nice motels and ate at great restaurants all the way from Ogden to Seattle.

Even after they found a place to stay in Vancouver, Washington, right across the Columbia River Gorge from Oregon, and even after Terry became a management trainee at Wendy's in order to help pay the rent, Dennis continued to spend lavishly. He also belted her lavishly.

Once they got in a row over who got to use the shower first, and Dennis busted her up pretty badly. "I clocked him over the head with a cast-iron skillet, and the son of a bitch still came at me," said Terry. "Did not stop. He had a head from hell. Six-foot-four, 250 pounds."

She remembered that event because it occurred on the day she went to a battered women's shelter and filed a police report against Dennis for battery. When the cops showed up, they found they had more than an abusive boyfriend on their hands. A computer check showed that Roper was wanted in Utah for passing thousands of dollars' worth of bad checks all over the western United States.

Roper wound up spending three years in prison, and once more, Terry was alone, until Michael came along to rescue her.

It was 1990. Dennis Roper had just started his sentence in Utah State Prison in Bluffdale, and Terry was living in the basement of a friend's house in the Salt Lake suburb of Sandy. To pay the rent, she ran the front counter at a McDonald's. One night a tall, swarthy-looking dude came sauntering to the front of the line with his eyes glued right to Terry's baby blues.

"He leans over and says, 'I want a Big Mac, french fries, and your phone number.' Hell of an opening line. I actually thought it was so cute I gave him my number," said Terry.

He didn't care that Terry wore a tattoo on her ankle that said CLASSIC BITCH and another on her butt that proclaimed her to be the property of some other man. He was interested in the third one, on her shoulder blade, which depicted a heart with a banner across it that read THERESA.

"The purpose of that is to show that I will *always* love me," Terry told him. "If there's nobody else out there to love me, I will."

After three dates Michael decided he loved her, too. He asked her to marry him. "I had nowhere else to go, so I did," she said.

After Dennis, Terry wanted nothing more than to be

normal. Throughout her odyssey with Roper, there was not a drug, pill, mushroom, doobie, or white powdery substance that Terry hadn't consumed. Drugs helped ease her nightmares, she believed.

But Michael's love was not enough. When her memories of burning corpses and skeletal remains became severe, she turned to drugs again. A couple of times, when her secret pain overwhelmed her, she attempted to overdose. Once it was a handful of two-hundred-milligram aspirin tablets and a bottle of vodka. Another time it was a cocktail made of Haldol, Prozac, aspirin, and Seagram's 7. In each instance, Michael got her to a hospital and a stomach pump in time. But he was afraid he might not be there for her a third time.

"I'm not afraid to die," Terry explained to her husband. "I'm just afraid to die in pain. See, I don't wanna die like my sisters did. I don't wanna die. But on the other hand, I wanna be with my sisters. And I don't wanna survive anymore. I enjoy life. Everything spills out of me. . . ."

Everything did spill out of her. She told him the whole awful truth about her mother, her brothers, her sisters, her tragedy.

Michael was stunned. If these murders were all true, why hadn't anyone done anything about them?

Encouraged by Michael's angry incredulity, Terry began telling her story to others. Eventually she told Heidi Sorenson, the ex-wife of Michael's best friend and, as it turned out, a woman with a very sympathetic ear.

Heidi told her to quit carrying the burden around and unload it on the police. Let them track down her murdering mother. Heidi's sister once dated a cop in Woods Cross, a tiny settlement about ten miles north of Salt Lake City. Maybe he'd listen.

Woods Cross had a population of six thousand, and since the city's founding in 1960, exactly one murder had been committed there. Nevertheless, when Police Chief Paul Howard got a briefing on Terry's story from one of his patrolmen, he insisted on taking a formal statement.

Chief Howard called her story "pretty bizarre," but sent a one-and-a-half-page certified letter to the Sacramento police summarizing Terry's statement anyway. He specifically pointed out that she had said that one of the victims' bodies had been dumped near Truckee. He addressed the letter to Lieutenant Ken Walker, then head of the Sacramento Police Homicide Division. It was postmarked September 5, 1990.

Lieutenant Walker assigned a detective to check Terry's story out. The detective phoned Chief Howard a few weeks later. After checking on unidentified female bodies in Sacramento and even phoning Nevada County authorities up in Truckee, the detective claimed that he had found no matches. The information was apparently bogus.

Chief Howard accepted the detective's findings, set the report aside, and went about his business.

"Basically, nothing happened," said Terry.

The Woods Cross incident only fueled Michael's concern over his wife's apparently overactive imagination. When she got crazy drunk and began throwing things at him, he fought back. The police were called on domestic disturbances at the Groves house with disagreeable regularity.

Michael and Terry were together nearly one and a half years before Terry decided to leave him. "He wouldn't move out of his parents' house, he was drinking up all of our money, we never did anything except sit around, and it just got to be a bore," she said.

After Dennis Roper completed his three-year sentence, he reappeared in Terry's life in 1992 just as dramatically as he had left it. When she broke off with Michael and he filed for divorce, Dennis asked her if she wanted to get hitched. He sent her a bus ticket and asked her to come stay with him in the Los Angeles suburb of Ontario.

Terry caught the next Greyhound, and they were married immediately in nearby Cucamonga. That union turned out to be null and void because her divorce from Groves had never become final. Still, Dennis and Terry were together for about a year the second time around. Unfortunately, he was as heavy-handed with her as he had been the first time. When she was pregnant, he hit her and she wound up in the hospital. She lost the fetus.

"Dennis was the only man I ever got close to, and he beat the shit out of me," said Terry.

In fact, all of Terry's boyfriends and husbands beat her at some point in their relationship, but she was gradually coming to accept her half of the blame. After her breakup with Dennis, she admitted that she, too, could be obnoxious and violent; that she, too, was manipulative, alternately playing the roles of poor little abused girl and shrieking banshee from hell.

"I acted the way my mom acted: 'When I tell you to sit down and shit, you better shit, 'cause I'm your wife and I'm telling you to!' " said Terry. "I don't like to act that way, but I tend to see myself doing it." She might not have deserved to be hit, but she certainly did everything possible to provoke it.

After her aborted pregnancy, she filed for divorce and called Michael to see if he would take her back. "Michael still loved me very much, which he still does," said Terry. "I'm not saying the love wasn't there on his part. It just wasn't there on my part. I didn't know what I wanted."

Michael sent her a bus ticket. Terry arrived back in Sandy, Utah, on July 5, 1993, and married him all over again.

She started work again, this time at a grocery store where she had a good shot at advancement. Michael worked steadily, too, and though they continued to live with Michael's parents, it looked like they would soon have a place of their own.

Michael still didn't believe her tale of midnight murder and the sacrifice of her sisters in the High Sierras after the embarrassing fiasco with the Sandy police, but who could blame him? No one believed her. Terry sometimes questioned her own sanity. Perhaps it was all just a bad dream and she never really had sisters at all. Perhaps it was all just one big mistake. Like all the other mistakes she'd made in her life, it was just something she had to learn to live with. For whatever else people might say about Terry Groves, they could not say that she hadn't lived. She had lived, by God. She had *definitely* lived.

And her sisters had not.

That was why, as she sat in front of the television watching *America's Most Wanted* during the final week of October 1993, she was once more slowly getting plastered and sobbing softly to herself. The tears rolled from her pale blue eyes and splashed on the floor. She poured herself another drink.

Terry had finally settled down to a safe, comfortable life of TV, monogamy, and steady work in a grocery store. But it still was not enough.

"Mike and I had gotten into a big argument over my family that day," she recalled. "He told me basically that I was a liar. He said my story about how my sisters got murdered was bullshit. So I got all drunk, and I was watching *America's Most Wanted*, and I decided to get on the phone and do something about it."

She reached a woman named Sherry who told her that *America's Most Wanted* really could not help her because the crime had not been investigated. *America's Most Wanted* only took tips from viewers who had information about people charged with a crime.

Terry broke down in sobs.

"Well, what am I going to *do* about this?" she cried.

"Ma'am, the only thing I can tell you to do is call the county where this happened," Sherry said.

It happened near Donner Summit, said Terry.

That should be Nevada County, responded Sherry.

Terry wiped away the tears, got out the map, broke out the phone book, and started calling directory information for Northern California. She got the number for the Nevada County sheriff.

"I called, got a desk sergeant, and he said Sergeant Ron Perea was the only homicide detective and he wasn't there at that hour," said Terry. "He said he'd have to call me tomorrow.

"The very next day, Ron Perea called and I told him what I knew. And he said he thought it would be a Placer County case, but he'd check it out and get back to me the following week."

Two days later Perea called the Placer County Sheriff's Substation in Tahoe City and got Sergeant John FitzGerald. Perea had checked his files and found a Jane Doe that had been dumped near Martis Creek Campground back in 1985, but the case had been inactive for many years because Nevada County investigators had fixed the blame on a Texas truck driver. Could the other Jane Doe Mrs. Groves described be an open Placer County case?

While Terry was at work that same day, the phone rang off the hook at her home. Terry's father-in-law finally called her at midday to tell her that some cop from California had been calling her over and over for the past several hours.

"I got off an hour early that night, went home, found out the cop's name was John FitzGerald," said Terry. "I said, 'That's not the same guy.' I knew he wasn't from Nevada County because they had only one homicide detective there and that was Ron Perea. So I figured John FitzGerald's got to be from Placer County."

When she called the Placer County Sheriff's Substation in Tahoe City, she was told Sergeant FitzGerald had left for the night. "I said, 'I don't think so. Look around. I guarantee you he's there, and he's waiting for my call,' " said Terry.

Moments later a brusque but friendly voice came on

the line. FitzGerald began by telling her that he was fairly certain that hers was the call he had been waiting for, for many years. Terry gushed.

"She started talking as fast as she could," said Fitz-Gerald. "She was very emotional, very upset. I could tell by her tone. I felt this person had good information, 'cause she just kept talking nonstop.

"So I let her talk, and the more she talked the more I felt she knew what she was talking about."

When she told him how many times she had tried to find someone who believed her, her hands shook so badly she nearly dropped the receiver. Nobody believed her. No one. Not even her own husband.

FitzGerald let her pause for a few seconds to collect herself and then he said, "Young lady, if it's any consolation to you, you can tell your husband this: I found a seventeen-year-old female burning near Squaw Creek on July 17, 1984. I believe she was your sister."

The conversation lasted about two hours, FitzGerald recalled. When he asked for specifics, Terry described an antique wedding ring Suesan was wearing the last time she had seen her. FitzGerald made a note. It was the same kind of ring Jane Doe had been wearing.

The following day, Sergeant John FitzGerald and Inspector Johnnie Smith flew to Salt Lake City. For most of the afternoon they sat at Terry Groves's dining-room table, taping her statement.

When it was over, she was asked what she felt.

Relief, of course. Vindication for sure. And something else: the emptiness that follows the betrayal of someone you've loved when that someone has committed an unpardonable sin. "My mom raised us kids like in a coven almost," Terry said. "It's kind of a trip. That's why I feel so bad because I've broken something about the family that would never have been broken had she done to me what she did to my sisters. She never would've been caught, I have a feeling.

"You know something my mother always told me?

Still waters run very deep. That's why I'm not a still water. I'm very outspoken. I don't run very deep. I'm very shallow, as a matter of fact. "If somebody says something to me that I don't like, screw that person. I'll cut that person out of my life. Even if that person has meant something to me and screwed me over, I'll cut that person out of my life. Just like I'd cut this arm off if it was rotten. Just like my mother."

Sergeant FitzGerald and Inspector Smith felt they had more than enough information to seek a warrant. They were on the next flight back to California. The following week they asked the Placer County district attorney to begin preparing a case against Theresa Jimmie Cross, William Robert Knorr, and Robert Wallace Knorr Jr. for two counts of first-degree murder and two counts of conspiracy to commit murder.

Robert Knorr Jr., who, at this time, was doing fifteen years for second-degree murder in a Nevada prison, was easy enough to find. William turned out not to be difficult to locate either.

Within four days Placer County Sheriff's Lieutenant Chal DeCecco was knocking on the front door of the Sacramento area apartment that Terry's older brother shared with his wife of two years, DeLois Ann Knorr. He was told Bill was at work, at the Target warehouse in Woodland, and that's where DeCecco found him. He asked Bill to accompany him to the sheriff's department up in Placer County, and he taped their conversation on the way.

"Is it Bill or is it William?" DeCecco asked.

"It's William," said Bill.

"You like to be called William?" asked DeCecco.

"Yeah," said Bill.

"Okay. William, basically we have a warrant here for your arrest," said DeCecco.

Bill Knorr was flabbergasted. He'd been questioned

before about a murder, back in 1983 when his aunt Rosemary had been killed, and figured this must somehow be connected to that. But after he waived his rights to an attorney and DeCecco got more and more detailed about just what it was Bill was being charged with, the horror of realization began to descend on him like a slow-motion avalanche.

Bill had worked hard to overcome his roots, he explained. He married a vivacious, ambitious young blonde who worked as an office manager for a franchising company. Bill himself had worked up to the position of warehouseman at a Sacramento distribution center for the Target department-store chain. Despite his lack of a high-school diploma, William Knorr had done something constructive and positive with his life.

He told DeCecco how he left his loser of a family and struck out on his own, even before he quit high school. "I never tried to get in contact with any of them," he said. "I never want to see any of them ever again. When I left, I was like: 'I'm out.' I know what the real world's like. I'm leaving, forgetting this whole seedy affair. With the abuse and the putting-the-kids-against-each-other crap. I just . . . I was out and I was staying out."

He started drinking heavily when he was seventeen, but only experimented a few times with cocaine, methamphetamines, and marijuana. The drinking, along with recurrent bad dreams about his childhood, contributed to the end of his first long-term relationship with Emily Lewis in 1987.

But he kept working and building friendships. He continued to play music with his band. At one time he wanted to be a disc jockey, but he didn't have the right voice.

In 1988, he reunited with his father. "My dad got in touch with me when I was twenty-one years old," said Bill. "I hadn't seen him in seventeen years."

Bill didn't want to meet his father at Bob's house. He

recalled all that his mother had told him about the evil that his father had done, and he was wary. They would meet, Bill told his father, but at a public place.

Bob Knorr was overjoyed. He gathered his wife, Jeanette, and their children and drove out to a Carl's Jr. that Bill had picked out. With tears in his eyes, Bob shook hands with, and then embraced, the son he'd never known.

With his sandy-blond hair, quick grin, and lean six-foot frame, Bill Knorr was the spitting image of Bob Knorr. When father and son finally became reacquainted, Bob marveled at how very much he and his son resembled one another. A casual observer comparing Bill's 1991 wedding photos with Bob's 1966 Marine-Corps portrait would barely detect a difference.

One of the first things Bob wanted to know was what had become of his other children. "He asked me about Suesan, and I told him what I knew," Bill told DeCecco.

What he knew, he told his father, was that Suesan had run off to Alaska. He'd heard somewhere that Robert was in jail in Nevada. But he had no idea where Terry was. What was more, he didn't care. She had called him once from Los Angeles, and he pretended as though he didn't know who she was. "I told her that I wasn't who she thought I was and hung up the phone," Bill told DeCecco. "My wife was there when I got the call.

"Terry turned out to be a loser. The only thing I know about her is that when my father assumed custody over her a couple years ago, she was doing nothing but getting into trouble."

Bill wasn't alone in his feelings about his family. He'd recently heard from his half brother, Howard, who was finalizing his divorce from Connie and trying to get his life back in order after years of trouble with the law. Like Bill, Howard was reluctant to reconnect with most of his family.

"Howard was the same way," said Bill. "He never

contacted any of us for the longest time, and then he finally got ahold of me, like I said, earlier this year, probably like three or four months ago. Maybe a little bit
longer than that."

When they finally did get together, the brothers' conversation centered on a common enemy. The woman
who damaged both of their lives, their mother, seemed
to have disappeared. Neither brother had heard from or
about her in several years. One point they agreed on:
where she was or what she was doing didn't matter as
long as they didn't have to have anything to do with
her.

Howard also asked Bill if he knew what had happened to their sisters. Bill said he didn't know. Howard
had his own suspicions, he told his younger brother.
"He thinks that Sheila and Suesan may have been killed
by my mom because Suesan kept trying to run away,
and Sheila was working her way out of the house," Bill
told DeCecco.

By the time they had arrived at sheriff's headquarters,
it was time for DeCecco to end the cat-and-mouse
game. He took Bill into an interrogation room and sat
down with John FitzGerald to take the rest of Bill's
statement. They revealed exactly what the arrest warrant
was for, and like an eight-year-old house of cards, Bill's
excuses and guesses about what had really become of
his sisters Suesan and Sheila began collapsing.

In a halting voice that quickly became a torrent of explanations and rationales, the truths that he'd kept
locked away in memory for most of his adult life spilled
out into DeCecco's tape recorder. How he had accompanied his mother and brother on the ride up I-80 that
night in 1984 and set a comatose Suesan out by the
roadside with all of her worldly possessions. How they
baptized the place with gasoline. And how Bill was ordered to light the fatal match.

He told about Sheila and how he and Robert had
been instructed to load her decomposing remains in a

cardboard box. He told about the long ride back up I-80 almost exactly one year after the burning of Suesan. "I still have nightmares," said Bill. "My wife knows about them."

FitzGerald glanced at DeCecco. They just about had their case sewn up. There was just one more thing. Where was Mother Theresa? "Do you have any gut feeling from back at that time as to where you think she might be going?" asked FitzGerald.

"I have no idea where she was going," said Bill.

All the horrors Terry had related to John FitzGerald and Johnnie Smith on the day before Halloween were true. In addition to Bill Knorr's incriminating statement, they also got interviews with Howard Sanders and his ex-wife, Connie, all corroborating the worst aspects of Terry's tragic tale.

It was too sensational a story to keep from the media. Two days after FitzGerald and DeCecco booked Bill Knorr for murder, the story broke on the national news wires. In the November 6, 1993, Saturday-morning edition of the *Sacramento Bee*, the headline screamed: MOTHER SOUGHT IN GRISLY SLAYINGS; 2 DAUGHTERS BURNED, STARVED.

Law enforcement knew who their target was, according to the news stories. *The search for Theresa Jimmie Knorr, 47, was extended nationwide yesterday,* said the Associated Press. *She was described as a 5-foot-4-inch, 250-pound convalescent home worker.*

But the truth was, investigators hadn't a clue as to where she might be.

FitzGerald and Smith were searching for a woman with a dozen different aliases who knew how to create a totally new identity for herself, with no bureaucrat being any the wiser. The detectives' usual sources of information—the National Criminal Information Center, the department of motor vehicles, courts, property records—turned up nothing. No warrants, no arrests—not so much as a parking ticket.

The best picture they had of Theresa was a scratched and outdated mug shot that she had taken for her California driver's license several years earlier, when she was still using the name Theresa Knorr. But it was doubtful that she still used this last name, or first name, for that matter. A search of the personnel rosters of Sacramento-area convalescent homes and hospitals turned up nothing. The best that FitzGerald was able to do was track her last known whereabouts to Reno in 1988. From there, the trail grew cold.

FitzGerald was beginning to worry. If Theresa was as clever as she seemed, would all the publicity tip her off and send her even deeper underground than she already was? Or had she died long ago and all this effort was just an exercise in futility? No matter which turn the case might take, the police had to undertake the tedious process of systematically eliminating all of her potential aliases. This effort was dealt a severe blow when Terry decided to take matters into her own hands. "She contacted the local TV station, told them who she was, and they put her on TV," said FitzGerald.

Up to that point, all the police had been telling reporters was that an unidentified female informant had reopened the double-murder investigation. On Saturday night, the audience of KUTV News in Salt Lake City learned firsthand just who that informant was.

"My mother is very sick," said a grim-faced young woman identified only as "Theresa" for the TV cameras. "What the heck gave her the right to take my sisters from me?"

A few miles away from the KUTV studios, in the Liberty Park section of Salt Lake City, a rounded block of a middle-aged nurse who liked to wear wigs and eat home-delivered pizza sat in the front room of her patient's home.

The name the woman had given her employer, Bud Sullivan, was Theresa Cross. In Sullivan's estimation, she was just about the best damned live-in nurse he'd been able to find for his eighty-six-year-old invalid mother, Alice Sullivan. For more than two years Theresa dressed her, fed her, took her to the doctor, gave her her medicine, and generally took full responsibility for the woman. Thanks to Theresa, the Sullivans didn't have to put their mother in a convalescent home. "She did an absolute super job," Sullivan said.

On the other hand, Theresa could be difficult to deal with at times. She had always been an "odd duck," according to the Sullivans and every other family who had hired her. "It's hard to explain Theresa," said Debbie Cheney, whose own mother, Alice Powell, had been under Theresa's care two years earlier. "She took incredible care of my mother. Just really good care. She'd take her places. Pack up the wheelchair, pack up Mom. We had family reunions that were an hour's drive away, and she'd bring her on up to spend the day."

At the time of the KUTV newscast, neither Debbie nor Bud had any inkling as to who Theresa Cross might be. She had good credentials as far as the Sullivans could tell and had earned their absolute trust after just a few months on the job.

So when Theresa asked Bud for a $4,600 cash advance the day after Terry went on TV, he didn't hesitate. Theresa told him she needed the money in order to pay back taxes to the IRS. Her taxes were her business, and if she needed a little help paying them, she was certainly worth it. Sullivan had no reason to believe that she would bolt, even though she'd left for brief periods before—usually with little or no advance notice. She was evasive and mysterious, but she was essential to his mother's well-being and she always came back. She was exactly the same way with Alice Powell.

"I mean, you knew when the woman was lying," said

Debbie Cheney. "She'd make up these stories and you'd think: 'Why are you lying?'

"There were a couple of times when she just took off. Once she said she was going to have surgery on her toes and that she was going to stay with her son in California. And we knew damn well when she came back she hadn't had any surgery. But she maintained that she went to have this surgery done, and we just went along with it.

"Another time she took off and said she had pneumonia or the flu or something. She couldn't stay here with my mom. And Mother had to have round-the-clock care. You couldn't just leave her.

"I ended up having to come down with my kids and spend a couple of days. I mean, it was no big deal, but it didn't make sense. This last-minute type of thing. She said she was going to a motel room to sweat her pneumonia out and the motel didn't have a phone. Now, what motel room doesn't have a phone?

"She told us another time that she had stayed in the Comfort Inn and couldn't be reached. Well, I know for *sure* that the Comfort Inn has a phone in every room. It was just things that she would say that didn't quite make any sense. We'd call her on it, and she'd just lie her way right out of it. In fact, my niece Paula said to her once: 'Theresa, what are you hiding? Why are you lying?' "

FitzGerald and the other investigators didn't know it, but they were running out of time. Theresa could vanish into thin air with the ease of a bona fide witch.

Since she had abandoned her son Robert in a seedy Reno hotel room nearly five years earlier, Theresa had learned how to turn her skills as a nurse's aide into a very comfortable and anonymous livelihood. Because Salt Lake City was the headquarters for the Church of Latter-Day Saints and the Mormons were known to be big on caring for their elderly family members, she gravitated there.

All she had to do was answer newspaper ads for skilled live-in nursing care, and she generally got the job on the spot. She looked the part of a stern but kind caregiver. She spoke the part. She did the job, usually above her employers' expectations.

In addition to a salary, Theresa found that she could get free room and board and, sometimes, free access to a car as well.

She also got to travel.

While she was living and working for another family in Salt Lake City, a man in New York by the name of Robert Kirsch had heard the same thing Theresa had heard: that the Mormons needed good caretakers and that advertising for a live-in type in the Salt Lake newspapers was a great way to land a dependable nurse. He placed an ad.

Theresa responded to the ad. Kirsch liked what he heard and wired her the money to drive to New York. There, Theresa started taking care of Kirsch's aging mother.

"I'm sure we weren't the first house she'd been to," said Kirsch. "She used to wear wigs, you know? Maybe her purpose was to just not be found. She was certainly nice to my mother. Very bright and friendly, nice smile, but very strange in a lot of ways. Thank goodness she didn't get that close to us."

Theresa lived in the house with Kirsch, his mother, wife, and children. She had her own room that she kept locked, and she didn't use the family's mailbox or their phone. She'd always leave the house to make phone calls and apparently had her own post office box, too. She lived with the Kirsches for about four months, and everything seemed to be working out spectacularly. What did it matter that she was a little evasive about some things? Everyone was entitled to their privacy.

One day Theresa told Kirsch that she was going to the corner to make a phone call. She never returned.

When she hadn't come back for several days, the

Kirsches became worried and broke into her room. It was empty. She had apparently been sneaking her belongings out of the house for the better part of a week and piling them in her car so that, when the time came, she could make a smooth, clean getaway.

The family searched the rest of the house, but nothing seemed to be missing. Theresa was deceitful and a pathological liar, but she was apparently not a thief—at least, not this time.

After her New York sojourn, she headed back to Salt Lake City. It was then that she went to work caring for Alice Sullivan, finding that job the same way she had found the job of caring for Alice Powell shortly after she first came to Salt Lake City.

"She answered a newspaper ad," said Debbie Cheney. "One thing she told us was that she had two sons and one of them was killed in a motorcycle accident. She never mentioned having daughters."

In fact, Theresa often treated Debbie's two girls almost as if they were her own. "She bought my girls each a pair of fifty-dollar L.A. Gear shoes, just out of the blue, for no reason," said Debbie. "And for Christmas, she bought fourteen-carat-gold emerald-stud earrings for them. She said, 'You know I love to spoil your girls. I never had any girls to spoil.'

"Naturally, my girls thought she was great and so did I. She was a free baby-sitter. Who's going to turn that down? I'd get ready to go out shopping or something and she'd say, 'Oh, leave the girls. We'll watch movies and order a pizza.' "

Theresa seemed quirky, but harmless. The Cheneys could only recall a handful of instances when her obsessions and compulsions took on a menacing sheen.

"My nephews came down to stay once," said Debbie. "They're from Montana and usually there's no problem staying at Grandma's. Well, Theresa threw an absolute fit. She said that her bishop said she was a single female and that these two boys could not stay. If they stayed under the same roof as Theresa, she would have to go to a motel."

Theresa got so agitated about it that Debbie gave in and sent her nephews to stay with other relatives during their visit, but she never understood what had set Theresa off.

In another instance, Debbie's sister Sheila and her daughter came to visit. From the moment Theresa laid eyes on Sheila's daughter, sparks flew. There was no explaining it. Theresa simply did not like the little girl. The feeling seemed to be mutual. The girl was afraid of Theresa. During her stay, Sheila kept her daughter close to her and even let her sleep in her room.

"Twice, Sheila woke up real early, like maybe five A.M., and Theresa was standing in her room, staring at her and at her daughter," said Debbie. "It was startling. Sheila would sit up and Theresa would say, 'Oh, I thought you'd like to know what your mother's blood sugar reading is this morning.' Right. Who cares what a blood sugar reading is at five o'clock in the morning?"

There were hints of Theresa's secret life, but never any revelations. She had no friends, and her only recreation seemed to be going to the movies. As Robert Kirsch discovered, she also had a predilection for wigs—so much so that she did not seem to know where her own hair ended and the wig began.

"She wore a poufy blond wig all the time," said Debbie. "It was kind of an ash-blond wig, very full. My kids called it the football-helmet look.

"But it was very, very obvious that it was a wig. Well, I walked into the house one day and Theresa comes into the kitchen wearing a short, straight jet-black wig. I about fell over backward.

"I guess she must have seen the look on my face, and she said, 'Oh, I thought I'd dye my hair back to its natural color for a change.' And I stood there and thought to myself: Theresa, *you* know it's a wig, *I* know it's a wig. Who are you kidding with natural hair color?"

"Three days later she had the poufy blond wig back on, claiming it was her real hair."

In November of 1993, while Theresa was packing her bags at the Sullivan house and preparing to get out of town, FitzGerald was running all of her known aliases through every computer database he could think of. One of them was the Utah Department of Motor Vehicles. In 1992, a Theresa Jimmie Cross obtained a driver's license with an address in Bountiful. After a few quick phone calls, FitzGerald's contact at the Salt Lake City Police Department zeroed in on the Sullivans' house.

"Theresa and Terry were living about twenty-five miles apart and never knew it," said FitzGerald.

FitzGerald and Johnnie Smith returned to Utah, got off the plane, flagged down a uniformed Salt Lake City police officer, and asked him to take them to the Sullivans' house. By five P.M., just ten days after taking Terry's initial statement, the two lawmen were standing outside Theresa's front door with a warrant for her arrest.

When they knocked, a chunky woman with sallow cheeks and an indelible frown answered the door. There was no one home, she told them. Just herself and the invalid woman she took care of. When FitzGerald introduced himself and told her who they were looking for, she showed not the slightest anxiety. She just blinked at them and repeated that there was no one home except for herself and the old lady.

"She at first was evasive," said FitzGerald. "I felt based on the way she looked, and the pictures I had of her, that she was Theresa Knorr."

Gradually, they coaxed morsels of truth out of her. "She told me she didn't like using the name Knorr," said FitzGerald. "She was using the name Cross. That was her maiden name, and it was one of her AKAs."

Theresa remained cool, even when the two detectives

displayed the warrant. She said that she hadn't known she was going to jail right at that time and asked if she could get somebody to take care of the old lady.

They nodded, but FitzGerald ducked around to the back of the house as soon as Theresa left the front door. Just as he had figured, Theresa was chugging out the back way when she looked up and saw the silver-haired detective waiting for her with a pair of handcuffs, not unlike the pair she had once used on her children.

"Theresa Jimmie Cross, I am placing you under arrest . . ." FitzGerald began, clicking her wrists together behind her back.

Later that evening, after booking Theresa Cross into the Salt Lake City Jail, John FitzGerald called her daughter Terry Groves with the news. She cried.

She was a survivor, she said, and she was proud to be a survivor. But surviving didn't necessarily feel good.

"Why did I get away?" asked Terry. "Was it because I was her namesake? I don't *want* to be her namesake. I'm Terry, not Theresa."

It had nothing to do with names, said her brother Robert, whom she came to know and love once again in the days that followed her mother's arrest.

From his prison cell in Ely where he awaited judgment on his own complicity in the deaths of Suesan and Sheila, Robert traced his surviving sister's emotional turmoil to the paradox of a child's natural love for her mother coupled with the fact that her mother was a cruel, self-serving monster. Like himself, Terry did what she had to do to survive, he said. She saved herself first, and when she wasn't able to save her sisters as well, she condemned herself.

"The way we grew up, it was like being a Jew at Auschwitz: it was better them than you," said Robert. "Human nobility doesn't enter into the equation. You're a child. You can't say, 'Well, I did my best to prevent this or this.' It's more like, 'Well, I'm glad it wasn't me this time. I could be next.' "

The mind says save yourself. The heart says save everyone around you.

"I live with a certain numbness," Terry said. "When you're a child you really don't pay all that much attention to what family means. It's just there. But when you become an adult, family becomes the most important thing of all. I had sisters. They were family. And they were taken away from me by my mother, who was also family. I lived with that all those years and it ate away at me. Now I'm having to search for the answers that I never got before."

Epilogue

Theresa Jimmie Cross wasted no time proclaiming her innocence. She refused to return to California with John FitzGerald and Johnnie Smith, choosing instead to remain in the Salt Lake City Jail until Placer County authorities formally extradited her.

On November 15, 1993, she was charged in the torture slayings of two of her daughters and arraigned in the Third Circuit Court in Salt Lake City. Then she was returned to her cell without bail until the courts could rule on her demand to remain in Utah.

Theresa was not the only defendant fighting extradition. Robert Knorr Jr.'s court-appointed attorney back in Placer County also questioned whether his client could legally be brought back from Nevada State Prison at Ely to stand trial along with his mother and brother.

"Whether the district attorney can proceed in this case is open to question," Mark Berg told reporters immediately following a November 29 court appearance on behalf of Robert in Placer County Superior Court in Auburn, California.

Both Berg and the attorneys representing William Knorr raised two other troubling questions about the brothers' prosecution.

First, neither Robert, twenty-four, nor William, twenty-six, were legal adults when their sisters died. It remained unclear, therefore, whether the two could even be tried as adults. Juvenile court invariably deals with offenders far more leniently than adult court, and that was precisely what defense lawyers were angling for.

Second, the bodies of the two girls were found in two different counties. It was clear that Placer County had jurisdiction in the case of Suesan Knorr, but what about Sheila Sanders, whose remains were found just on the other side of the Nevada county line? From the defense point of view, these were two separate deaths in two different jurisdictions, which meant two separate murder trials—one in the Placer County seat at Auburn, and the other twenty miles to the northeast, in the Nevada County seat at Nevada City.

While Placer County's prosecutor Dan Gong wrestled with all of those knotty legal issues, Theresa was finally refused sanctuary in the Salt Lake City Jail. On December 18, 1993, John FitzGerald flew back to Utah to bring Theresa home to stand trial for murdering her daughters. Theresa's only request was that she be escorted back to California by train or car because she had a sinus infection and didn't want to fly in an airplane.

FitzGerald cuffed her and flew her back.

The following Monday Theresa and Bill were arraigned together in Placer County Superior Court. Dressed in a jail-issue orange jumpsuit, Bill entered the courtroom shackled to about a half dozen other male inmates. A few moments later his mother entered, wearing the red jumpsuit issued to female prisoners. Bill cowered, looked at the floor, and would not make eye contact with Theresa. His attorney, Michael K. Brady, said later that his client became distraught and afraid the moment that his mother walked in the courtroom.

Bill's father, who sat in the second row of the gallery, was not so intimidated by the sight of his ex-wife. As deputies escorted Theresa to a seat against the back wall of the court, Bob Knorr sneered and shouted at the mother of his children: "I hope you burn in hell for what you did to my kids, woman!"

The bailiff warned Bob that any further outburst would make him subject to arrest, so the burly ex-marine sat quietly through the remainder of the brief hearing, tears streaming past his glasses and down his cheeks.

Theresa demanded that the court address her by her maiden name. She would be known as Theresa Cross and not by Knorr or any of her other married names. As Theresa Jimmie Cross she was formally charged with two counts of murder, two counts of conspiracy to commit murder, and two special circumstances—multiple murder and murder by torture—that could, if proved, result in the death penalty.

Because both of her sons were juveniles when the crimes were committed, neither of them had to face the death penalty under California law.

Theresa postponed entering her plea until January 31, 1994. When she finally did answer the charges, she spoke a barely audible "not guilty" to each of the counts against her.

Bill's attorney, Kevin Clymo, asked that the trial be moved to Sacramento. Both girls had been murdered there, after all, so that there would be no dispute over jurisdiction.

Clymo also demanded that Bill be tried as a juvenile and that the court rule out the possibility of life imprisonment. He had no prior criminal history and had been raised "by a mother who was extremely physically and emotionally abusive," he told the court.

But Placer County Superior Court Judge J. Richard Couzens ruled against Clymo's motions. At twenty-six, Bill was too old to be rehabilitated in a juvenile facility. If found guilty, he'd have to do his time in an adult prison.

Couzens did set bail, however. Bill scored a "ten" on

his probation report, meaning that he was deemed to be a minimal flight risk. In addition, five friends and former employers testified at a bail hearing that Bill was a young man of exemplary character and that he led a stable life.

The prosecution asked for $1 million bail, while Clymo asked that Couzens require only $50,000 for his client. The judge agreed to set Bill Knorr free once he posted $150,000.

Even after his family and friends had scraped up $15,000 for Bill's bail bond later that spring, his brother Robert remained in Nevada State Prison. Using both the jurisdictional and the juvenile arguments, Mark Berg managed to hold off Robert's extradition until the end of June. John FitzGerald finally brought the last of the three defendants in *People* v. *Knorr, Knorr & Cross* back to California to stand trial on June 29, 1994.

But the jurisdictional battle between Nevada and Placer Counties continued through most of the summer. Under state law, a county can claim a murder victim as its own if the body is no more than 1,500 feet beyond the county line. When Placer County finally hired a surveying team to measure the distance from the county line to the spot where Sheila Sanders's corpse was dumped, the official distance was 1,555 feet inside Nevada County—55 feet over the legal limit. Unless the case was moved to Sacramento, there would have to be two trials: one for Suesan's murder in Placer County and another for Sheila's in Nevada County.

On August 12, four days before the long-delayed preliminary hearing was to have taken place, Judge Couzens gave in and ordered the trial of Theresa Jimmie Cross and her two sons moved to Sacramento County.

While the lawyers wrestled in court, the shattered remnants of Theresa's family bound their wounds and went on living.

Bob Knorr found Suesan's unmarked grave in the county cemetery in Auburn and bought a small headstone for his daughter.

Howard Sanders found a new fiancée after his divorce from Connie was final. He studied to become a chef, reestablished ties with his sister, Terry, and worked hard at mending relations with his two young sons. Connie continued to protest his visits with the boys unless a court-approved counselor was there to supervise. When Howard sought custody, she moved and left no forwarding address, taking the boys with her. Through his attorney, Carl Swain, he declined to comment about the accusations of abuse and drug use leveled against him by his ex-wife and his siblings. Swain said his client did not want to discuss his family because he hoped to sell his story to TV or motion picture producers.

Bill's marriage could not withstand the threat of his trial or the possibility of his imprisonment. DeLois left him less than a year after his arrest. He still has the support of Bob Knorr and his family, along with a large circle of friends. Bill remains out on bail, working and waiting for his day in court.

Robert lives on the protective-custody tier at the Sacramento County Jail. He reads and writes and looks forward to a time when he can start his life over the right way. Once he's back in Ely, serving out the rest of his murder sentence at Nevada State Prison, he hopes to enroll in college courses and earn a degree in psychological counseling.

Robert struck a deal with the Sacramento County District Attorney in the autumn of 1994, volunteering his testimony in exchange for reduced charges. A week before Christmas the DA dropped all the charges against him involving Suesan's murder. By February the DA had dropped all the remaining charges except the single count of conspiracy to aid his mother in the murder of his sister Sheila.

As for Theresa, she spends much of her time isolated in her protective-custody room in the women's wing of the Sacramento County Jail. She writes or calls friends and former employers in Utah, but she has no visitors except her lawyers.

Once, during a brief court appearance in November, a slimmed-down Theresa became briefly hysterical and fell to the floor in a faint. Usually she appears stoic and silent in court, her deep, deep frown hanging from her sadly defiant face like the permanent scowls etched across the faces of the damned souls in Dante's *Inferno*. If she ever knew joy, it perished long ago along with any sparkle in her eyes.

At the beginning of 1995, as another spring approached, Theresa agreed with her attorney that she ought to seek a sanity hearing to determine whether she could, or should, stand trial. She shaved her head and underwent examination by two psychiatrists who arrived at opposing conclusions: One declared her sane and the other did not.

In a March 7 article in the *Sacramento Bee*, staff writer Wayne Wilson quoted some of those who regularly saw Theresa as witnessing a woman suffering from the illusion that jail was "just a hotel with really bad room service." A formal sanity hearing was scheduled for June.

As for her one surviving daughter and namesake, Terry Groves tried repeatedly to turn her life around— with mixed results—once she had turned her mother in. Before the first anniversary of her mother's arrest, Terry had divorced, remarried, and filed for divorce again.

She moved from Utah to California, working off and on as a butcher's assistant, fast-food clerk, manicurist, baby-sitter, and maid. In June 1994, she married an acquaintance she'd met through a friend with whom she'd lived briefly. By Labor Day she and her new husband, Bill Gilbert, had broken up and been thrown out of their apartment. Two months later Terry was broke, strung out, and paying fifty dollars a month to sleep alone in a lean-to next to a ramshackle trailer in the run-down southwest sector of Sacramento.

One morning at three A.M., she called me collect from the Sacramento Airport. She was crying. She wanted to fly to Kansas, to be with her estranged husband, Bill, who had traveled back east to live with his aging parents.

Could I loan her the airfare?

I did. Her reunion with Bill didn't last long. Terry left to live with a girlfriend named Lydia—a single mother with two small children. Within a month or two, Terry and Lydia had quarreled; Terry moved on, and got back together with Bill. At this writing, the two of them rent a trailer near Junction City, Kansas. Terry suffered her second tubal pregnancy in April. Following surgery, she was told by her doctor that she would never have children.

She cried for a week. When the tears dried, she did what she has always done best: she got on with her life.

When she gets back on her feet, which should be anytime now, she said she wants to start a day-care center or maybe a home for abused children and name it for her two sisters. She wants to finance it with whatever money she can get for selling her life story to a TV or movie producer. The Suesan Marline Knorr and Sheila Gay Sanders Home for Abused Children will be a haven, she said. It will be a good and safe place for babies to grow, Terry promised.

With or without their mothers' love.

Dennis McDougal, May 1995